Psychosocial Wellness of Refugees

March 12, 2001

To Dorothy and Ausan,

Here's a small token
of our friendship. When you
see and read it, I hope
that you recall our times
together in Washington. All
the best,

Fred Ahearn

STUDIES IN FORCED MIGRATION

General Editors: Dawn Chatty, Refugee Studies Programme,
International Development Centre, University of Oxford, and
Chaloka Beyani, Law Department, London School of Economics

Psychosocial Wellness of Refugees

ISSUES IN QUALITATIVE AND QUANTITATIVE RESEARCH

Frederick L. Ahearn, Jr., Editor

Berghahn Books
NEW YORK · OXFORD

First published in 2000 by

Berghahn Books
www.berghahnbooks.com

© 2000 Frederick L. Ahearn, Jr.

Library of Congress Cataloging-in-Publication Data

Psychosocial wellness of refugees : issues in qualitative and
quantitative research / edited by Frederick L. Ahearn, Jr.
    p.   cm. – (Studies in forced migration ; v. 7)
  Includes bibliographical references and index.
  ISBN 1-57181-204-0 (alk. paper). – ISBN 1-57181-205-9 (alk.
paper)
    1. Refugees–Mental health Cross-cultural studies. 2. Refugees–Mental
health–Research. I. Ahearn, Frederick L. II. Series.
RC451.4.R43P77   1999   99-15628
362.2'086'91–dc21   CIP

British Library Cataloguing in Publication Data

A catalogue record for this book is available from the British Library

Printed in the United States on acid-free paper

Contents

Part III: Case Studies of Refugee Psychosocial Wellness: Quantitative Approaches

Part IV: Case Studies of Refugee Psychosocial Wellness: Mixed Approaches

List of Tables and Figures

Tables

Figures

For the Lights of My Life ...

Laura, Peggy, Kerry, and Especially Eileen

Acknowledgments

In 1996 after eleven years of academic administration, I had the opportunity to take a sabbatical leave in order to refresh and revitalize my interest in research, especially the study of refugees. This desire led me to the Refugee Studies Programme (RSP) at the University of Oxford where I was able to immerse myself in the nature of global displacement, human rights and refugee law, the social and psychological consequences of leaving one's home and country, and conflict resolution and the issues of peace-making. It was here where I met Alastair Ager and Derek Summerfield in a course of the psychological aspects of being a refugee. They encouraged me to revisit an area that had so intrigued me for years. At the same time, I met Barbara Harrell-Bond who immediately asked that I take on a dozen or so projects. She always had that many "balls in the air" at one time and, as I found out later, she was the sort of person who welcomed collaboration, assistance, and pure toil.

I accepted several memorable assignments from Dr. Harrell-Bond that I found exciting and rewarding. First, she asked if I would design a training program for the many volunteer visitors of Campsfield Prison, the local detention center of asylees and illegal immigrants. Another project involved facilitating a research design for a psychosocial evaluation in refugee camps in Uganda and Kenya. However, the most propitious offer from Dr. Harrell-Bond was to plan and moderate the weekly RSP lecture series. I agreed on one condition: that I could put together a series about the psychosocial wellness of refugees and that I could develop it into a book. She readily agreed and was of great support. For the opportunity and her assistance, I am most grateful.

I am thankful to the authors who contributed to the original lecture series and later to the book. They offered many suggestions on how to organize the task, and I leaned much from them. All are well-known researchers in the area of the psychological and social aspects of displacement. I asked each of them to discuss the topic of refugee "psychosocial wellness," how he/she approached the study of the topic, and what were the strengths and limitations of his/her research methodology. As you read this volume, you will surely see the richness of their contribution to the field of refugee studies.

While in Oxford, I had the opportunity to reside at Campion Hall, a residence for Jesuit scholars and a few others like me. I tried out many of my ideas at meal table with my Campion colleagues, some of whom were quite expert in refugee studies. They were helpful and encouraging. Also at the RSP, I met numerous staff, visitors, and students who probably became bored with my talking about this project. The result, however, was considerable interest, comments, and critique. Among those who always listened were: Belinda Allen, Maryanne Loughry, the new Director David Turton, Sean Loughna, Adalaida Reyes, and Matt Gibney. Balgit Soroya of Ruskin College escorted me to a number of Oxford's famous pubs while we shared our common interest in the psychosocial aspects of refugees.

The faculty at the Catholic University of America, especially Dean Ann Patrick Conrad and my colleague, John Noble, were of immense help. The Dean encouraged and approved the original sabbatical request and Dr. Noble became a sounding board for ideas, interpretations, and approaches dealing with refugee displacement.

Finally, special thanks is due my family who permitted me to absorb myself for the past months while I worked on this project. They provided me with the strength, encouragement, and love, the ingredients for reaching my goal of orchestrating the completion of this book.

Frederick L. Ahearn, Jr.
Washington, DC
July 3, 1999

Foreword

This book represents a *benchmark* in academic publication on the psychological consequences for people who have been uprooted against their will. The editor, Frederick Ahearn, has brought together some of the most well-known researchers in refugee studies from a number of disciplinary backgrounds to discuss how they have met the challenges of researching in this cross-cultural, comparative field. This book will soon be required reading for mental health practitioners and all who conduct research on refugees, for one reason especially–its emphasis on *wellness* rather than *pathology*. As such, it will act as a profoundly important corrective to much of the contemporary literature in the field.[1]

The study of populations that have been forcibly uprooted, whether they have crossed a border or remain "internally displaced," is necessarily multidisciplinary. Were we, however, to create a "hierarchy" of disciplines in terms of relevance to refugee studies, psychology should be among the first.

From research conducted after the Second World War, it has been known that those who have been forcibly uprooted are at greater risk of mental ill-health than are those who voluntarily migrate, but it is only since the 1990s that non-governmental organizations (NGOs) have focused on providing "therapy" for refugees.[2]

In the early 1980s, when I was conducting my own research among Ugandan refugees in southern Sudan, it was not possible to convince NGOs working there that special attention should be paid to the mental health of African refugees, much less to designing interventions to mitigate the stresses associated with their experiences–violence, death and bereavement, uprooting, flight or the challenges of survival and adaptation in exile.[3] Indeed, up to the late 1980s, calls for basic socio-psychological research to be conducted–beginning with refugee children, encountered stiff resistance. An emphasis on research was interpreted by humanitarians as implying they were neglecting their duties.

For NGOs and refugees, the war in Yugoslavia was a watershed. By this time the diagnostic criteria, "PTSD"[4] had become part of the agency jargon. Millions of dollars became available for humanitarian agency-sponsored "psychosocial" interventions and a myriad of foreign organizations migrated there to establish programs on behalf of the victims of war. These interventions were underpinned by the assumption that *all* former Yugoslavians, including their mental health professionals, were too traumatized to help themselves or their fellows.[5]

This "fashion" for mounting psychosocial interventions has now spread throughout Africa, with the reins of control still firmly in the hands of foreigners who have access to donor funds. We now even have "barefoot" psychologists even though the concept of barefoot doctors was long ago found to be inappropriate. For example, in northern Uganda, there are several agencies working with abducted children who have been released by–or who have escaped from–the Lord's Resistance Army. The "therapies" offered are diverse. For example, some insist on the religious conversion of these children.[6]

Unfortunately, the principal driving force behind so many of these psychosocial interventions in these refugee situations is and remains, as Alistair Ager notes in this book, "concern rather than reasoned extrapolation from rigorous empirical study."[7] This book will reverse that trend by not only promoting the dignity and agency of refugees, but also by providing the methodological tools for gathering data that will assist NGOs who aim to meet the specific mental health needs of the uprooted.

Barbara Harrell-Bond

Notes

1. See Summerfield, D. (1995). Assisting surivors of war and atrocity: notes on "psychosocial" issues for NGO workers. *Development in Practice,* 5:352-356.
2. Ager, A. (1994). *Mental health issues in refugee populations: a review,* Working Paper of the Harvard Center for the Study of Culture and Medicine, Harvard Medical School, Department of Social Medicine.
3. Harrell-Bond, B.E. (1986). *Imposing aid: Emergency assistance to refugees,* Oxford University Press, Oxford.
4. Post-Traumatic Stress Disorder. See Summerfield, D. op. cit. But see also Worden, Jessica Lind "Tossing the baby with the bath water: Controversy over cross-

cultural Use of DSM diagnostic categories in situations of armed conflict," unpublished, RSP Documentation Centre.

5. See Agger, I. (1994) *The Blue Room: Trauma and testimony among refugee women: A psychosocial exploration,* Zed Books, London and Agger, I. *Theory and practice of psycho-social projects under war conditions in Bosnia-Herzegovina and Croatia,* ECHO, Brussels, and Ajdukovic, Dean (Ed.) (1997). *Trauma recovering training: Lessons learned,* Society for Psychological Assistance, Zabreb.

6. The agency that is perhaps the best funded in Gulu District takes the latter approach and regards it as more important than reuniting children with their parents. According to a member of staff of another agency that bitterly objects to such practices, in one case at least the parents were not informed for more than a year that their child was safe.

7. Chapter Two and also see Ager, A. (1994) op. cit.

Introduction

The idea for this book came about in 1996 as a result of a discussion with several associates of the Refugee Studies Programme (RSP) at Queen Elizabeth House, University of Oxford, about the increased awareness of and interest in providing psychological assistance to refugees. So, when I was asked to plan and direct the weekly RSP Seminar Series that treated current topics of interest to the university community about refugees and forced migrants, I accepted the offer with the idea that a full exploration and discussion of the subject of refugee mental health would clarify a number of issues, especially the issues of trauma, stress, anxiety, depression, and psychological adaptation and how these are defined and studied. The result was a lecture series entitled "Psychosocial Wellness of Refugees" held during Hilary Term at Oxford University, which presented many approaches to the study of the psychological aspects of the refugee experience. Most of the chapters of this book came from that series.

While there have been practitioners and researchers who regularly discussed the emotional toll of migration trauma, refugee programs with a psychosocial emphasis remained scarce until the war in the former Yugoslavia. There was a time in the field of refugee studies and services when the psychological aspect of refugee life was not considered, or if considered, not felt to be important. However, given the concern and generous financing of the international community and the readiness of the mental health establishment in Croatia, Bosnia, and Serbia as well as the organization of many nongovernmental organizations (NGOs), more than one hundred psychosocial projects were established to provide psychological services, including emotional support, individual and group therapy, psychiatric attention, and, in some cases, social services.

This new emphasis on psychological services to refugees and displaced persons sparked a lively debate about the efficacy of such programs.[1] The concern for refugee mental health in the international response to a crisis such as Bosnia, Serbia, and Croatia has been based upon the assumption that the stresses and traumas of war, migration, and resettlement have a negative effect upon the physical and mental health of refugees and displaced persons, affecting their daily functioning and long-term adjustment. However, the challenge for practitioners and researchers alike has been to identify these psychological consequences, understand their relationships with the events themselves and the process of adaptation, and explain how any therapeutic intervention assists individuals, families, and communities in this process. Others have been more skeptical, noting that the literature concerning trauma, stress, and refugee adjustment does not answer these questions, and besides, they argue, increased funding for these efforts have actually diverted funds that normally would have financed other activities and services for this population.

Most agree that researchers and practitioners alike, need to defend the assumptions of their psychosocial programs and demonstrate the efficacy and appropriateness of their interventions. It is through a careful application of research that definitions and program outcomes may be clarified, which, in turn, will fuel the discussion of policy, planning, and funding of psychosocial programs.

The nature of research today is often framed by one's professional orientation. Many social scientists, especially sociologists and psychologists, have attempted to study the relationship of stress, trauma, and forced migration by emphasizing operational definitions of the elements under study, controlling the research process, and employing quantitative analysis to discover "truth." Anthropologists and others, on the other hand, disagree, noting that a qualitative approach would be a better way of understanding refugee stress and trauma. A "bottom-up" process would allow refugees' "voices" to define and clarify their emotional struggles and psychological reality.

Most of the literature in this field focuses upon the study of stress, trauma, and emotional symptoms as indicators of psychological maladjustment. We prefer to emphasize the term "wellness" in our review of ways to study the relationship between the refugee experience and psychological consequences and adaptation because it highlights the perspective of strengths, resilience, and independence. It avoids, hopefully, the portrayal of refugees and displaced persons as "psychiatric patients," "victims," "emotional cripples," or as always dependent and helpless.

It is our goal to present students, practitioners, and researchers who are interested in understanding and investigating refugee psychosocial wellness with examples and suggestions, as well as the strengths and limitations of quantitative and qualitative approaches in this field. Hopefully, readers will gain an appreciation of the difficulties of doing this type of research and draw concrete recommendations for conducting quantitative, qualitative, and mixed-method studies of psychological wellness of refugees.

As decision-makers in the international scene of refugee assistance, the NGOs, United Nations, and governmental agencies and ministries design, fund, and implement psychological assistance projects for displaced populations, they must be mindful of their responsibility for sound, appropriate, comprehensive, and effective services that result from a clear and carefully crafted policy. Decision-makers, program administrators, and service providers also should be cognizant of their accountability not only to their boards of directors, constituents, and funders, but also to the individuals and families who need and use their services. Crucial in the process of accountability is the monitoring and evaluation of psychological assistance programs that are provided for refugees. Finally, this book may be of assistance also to policy-makers, governmental ministers and planners, mental health consultants and promoters, and executives and service providers of psychosocial programs as they address the effectiveness of their policies, programs, services, and interventions in meeting the mental health needs of refugees and forced migrants.

Frederick L. Ahearn, Jr.

Note

1. Stubbs, P. and Soroya, B. (1996). War trauma, psychosocial projects and social development in Croatia. *Medicine, Conflict and Survival, 12*:303-314.

Part I

THEORETICAL ISSUES IN QUALITATIVE AND QUANTITATIVE RESEARCH

The purpose of this section is to review the broad issues in the use of qualitative and quantitative methodologies that are used to study the question of refugee psychosocial wellness. In the first chapter, Frederick Ahearn explores through searches of various psychological databases the meaning of psychosocial well-being as currently used by researchers. Given the currency of the psychodynamic approach in these publications, he addresses the dimensions of stress, loss, social supports, separation, trauma, and coping and discusses difficulties in doing cross-cultural investigations using Western concepts and instruments. In addition, he identifies the strengths and weaknesses that are inherent in qualitative and quantitative research designs and, finally, argues that a researcher studying refugee behavior in the aftermath of displacement should: 1) focus on a person's strengths rather than a person's deficits (well-being instead of pathology); 2) utilize both quantitative and qualitative strategies; and 3) make every effort to replicate, validate, and standardize their instruments and measurements. Recommendations are offered to students, practitioners, researchers, policy-makers, administrators, and educators for the study of the psychosocial well-being of refugees and displaced persons.

In the second chapter, Alastair Ager speaks of the need for research and evaluation in the field of psychosocial intervention as crucial elements in the process of policy-setting, planning, and implementing sound and appropriate programs and services for refugees. In his theoretical discussion of quantitative methodologies, he illustrates through case examples the key questions of measurements, the definition and operationalization of concepts, reliability, validity, bias, and sampling. He notes the importance of connecting one's interpretation and the significance of one's findings with the ability to generalize these to other groups. In like manner, Ager also explores theoretical concerns in the use of qualitative approaches, especially the points of measurement, interpretation, triangulation, comprehensiveness, and transferability of findings. Again he employs case examples to highlight these points. Finally, there is a discussion of the use of multimethod approaches in the study of refugee psychosocial wellness.

The purpose of this section then is to give the reader an orientation to the broad theoretical issues involved in doing research with refugees and in evaluating psychosocial programs. Competent research will provide answers to questions regarding a program's effectiveness, explore and further deepen our understanding of the psychological reactions of refugees, and provide a basis for accountability for program managers and practitioners. Finally, these two chapters, in their description of the underpinnings of quantitative and qualitative methods, set the stage for the case illustrations that are presented in subsequent chapters.

1

Psychosocial Wellness

METHODOLOGICAL APPROACHES TO THE STUDY OF REFUGEES

Frederick L. Ahearn, Jr.

There has been considerable interest in the plight of refugees, especially how they cope with the effects of forced migration. Researchers have been keen to answer the question, "How does an ordinary person experience an extraordinary event?" This increased interest in mental health concerns of displaced persons is evidenced by the large number of publications in professional journals about emotional and physical behavior within their home countries, in flight, in camps, and in countries where they resettle. With this increased interest has come the question about how best to measure the psychological and somatic consequences of displacement, and what the research findings of refugees' psychosocial well-being actually mean.

This chapter explores the meaning of pychosocial well-being and examines how the terms have been defined and operationalized by investigators. First, there is the consideration of how to define, and then study, well-being. Second, the discussion focuses on key concepts regularly employed by researchers to investigate refugee mental health. These concepts are: loss, separation, stress, coping, social supports, and trauma. Third, the analysis focuses upon methodological issues in doing both quantitative and qualitative investigations, such as the difficulties in doing cross-cultural studies using Western concepts and instruments. As there is considerable debate about the use of qualitative and quantitative methods in cross-cultural investigations, the strengths and weakness of each are reviewed, giving examples drawn from the professional literature. The conclusion drawn is that it is advisable to integrate both methodologies into one's research design. Finally, as it is absolutely essential to be aware of (and be sensitive to) cultural differences, recommendations are offered for those conducting studies of refugees and those training refugee workers as a means of developing a future research agenda for the study of the psychosocial well-being of refugees and displaced persons and their communities.

Psychosocial Well-Being

Definition

The Oxford English Dictionary (Simpson and Weiner 1991) defines psychosocial as "pertaining to the influence of social factors on an individual's mind or behavior, and to the interrelation of behavioral and social factors." Well-being, a term that is frequently used interchangeably with wellness, is defined as "the state of being or doing well in life; happy, healthy, or prosperous condition; moral or physical welfare (of a person or community)." An immediate problem is the meaning of behavioral and social factors, good health, and physical welfare. What are the particular dimensions that constitute each of these? Clarity of definition is important since many mental health investigators utilize the terms "psychosocial well-being" as it was popularized by the World Heath Organization (1996). That organization considers mental health well-being to be part of the general definition of health, and they define it as "a state of complete physical, mental, and social well-being and not merely the absence of disease or infirmity."

Still, there is a need for a more exact statement of what is meant by well-being. One definition that is helpful explores well-being in terms of a person's "ability to do valuable acts or reach valuable states of being" (Sen, 1993). In order to act, one needs to have agency, independence, and self-determination, and, in order to reach a positive state of being, one requires the necessities of life to be satisfied and happy (Dasgupta, 1993). In other words, refugee psychosocial well-being would consist of the ability, independence, and freedom to act and the possession of the requisite goods and services to be psychologically content.[1]

Surprisingly, few scholars incorporate the concept of psychosocial well-being into their research scheme, and those who do usually address the risks to a refugee's well-being. In her study of refugee children, McCallin studied the negative consequences of trauma, stressful events, and lack of social supports as contributors to poor well-being (McCallin, n.d.). Furthermore, she cited the burden of poverty, isolation, and separation from parents as placing refugee children's well-being at risk. Other research approaches to the study of psychosocial well-being of refugees have analyzed: income levels, household size, and wealth holdings (Armstrong, 1988); pre- and postmigration traumas (Hermansson et al., 1996); self-sufficiency, employment, schooling, and social networks (McSpadden, 1987); education, social supports, length of time in the country, age, and marital status (Tran et al., 1987); a refugee's self-definition as to how they feel (Tran, 1994); cultural identity (Kassabian, 1996); and, personality traits, family environment, extra-familial support, and openness to a new society, all of which promoted psychosocial well-being (Edwards and Beiser, 1994).

It is interesting to observe that there is little agreement as to what constitutes psychosocial well-being. It is much easier to describe factors associated with well-being, especially negative factors that connote a lack of well-being. This approach has limitations for it highlights weakness and pathology rather than strength and health. It focuses on the negative rather than the positive, oftentimes "medicalizing" the problem, and, as described below, the vast majority of researchers in this field prefer to study trauma, stress, and the like rather than investigate psychosocial well-being.

Refugee Mental Health

The study of refugee mental health has been dominated by an orientation toward psychology and psychiatry. One cannot read the literature about the psychosocial well-being of refugees today without being impressed with the number of investigations that are based upon concepts drawn largely from psychodynamic theory and, to a lesser degree, from social learning and cognitive theories. It is useful to examine the key concepts that are most often utilized in the analysis of refugee mental health in order to understand current approaches to the measurement of the psychological and social consequences of forced migration. These are the concepts of loss, separation, stress, coping, social supports, and trauma.

Generally, as pointed out in Figure 1.1, wellness, that is health, is influenced and affected by loss, separation, stress, and trauma (among other things) that are mediated by one's coping ability and social and emotional supports. This is the common explanatory model that one finds in the literature which attempts to integrate these concepts of refugee behavior. Below follows a discussion of each of these concepts and some of the findings in the literature that pertain to refugees.

Concept of Loss

Eric Lindemann (1944), a Harvard psychiatrist, studied the effects of a major fire at Coconut Grove, a popular Boston nightclub, where over a hundred persons lost their lives. He postulated that loss was an important variable in explaining how survivors and families coped with the tragedy. It was Kubler-Ross (1989) who later popularized the stages of grief after the death or loss of a loved one as denial, rejection, anger, negotiation, and acceptance. For refugees and immigrants, loss is a defining characteristic of their experience for their homes and possessions are destroyed, members of their families die, and their support systems disappear.

Studies have demonstrated that a variety of emotional and physical expressions are associated with bereavement (Raphael, 1983). In her study of Haitian, Southeast Asian, and Soviet refugees, Drachman (1992) noted that refugees accumulate numerous losses before they leave their homes, during flight and first asylum, and during the process of resettlement. Another study found a similar pattern of severe loss among Cambodian refugees, including death of family members and friends, destruction of home and community, and complete separation, leading to long-lasting emotional problems (Bernier, 1992). Another researcher has reported that individuals and families who have been displaced from their homes due to economic development programs "grieve for their lost homes," a process of mourning for the destruction of emotional and social supports that are inherent in the fabric of most neighborhoods and communities (Fried, 1968).

Loss is associated with depression, anxiety, and somatic complaints. Croatians who lost their homes and social and cultural environment demonstrated high levels of anxiety and depression (Kondic and Marvar, 1992). Among Southeast Asian refugees in Canada, loss of employment led to depression, loss of self-esteem, and loss of social contact. Finally, there is a case study of an Ethiopian woman who lost her baby while fleeing her home and later was unable to undergo the traditional rites of purification. Somatic complaints and continual grief characterized her behavior until the ritual was arranged and performed (Schreiber, 1995). Therefore, investigators have concluded with considerable confidence that, as displaced persons sustain loss in flight, in seeking asylum, or in resettlement, they likewise will experience stages of bereavement and be susceptible to serious physical and emotional symptoms. However, little work has been done to apply the concept of loss and grief to the levels of family, neighborhood, and community.

Figure 1.1 A Common Psychosocial Approach to the Study of Refugee Wellness

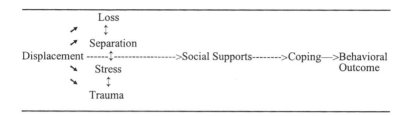

Separation

A type of loss that may be temporary or permanent, especially among children, is separation. The work of Freud and Bellingham (1943) revealed that English children removed from cities to the safety of the countryside during the blitz of the Second World War fared worse that those children who stayed in the war area with their parents. Separation from parents resulted in significant negative psychological reactions. Bowlby (1984) also stressed pernicious consequences of separation and loss for preschool-age children. It has been shown that separation from one's homeland or place of identification represents a major life event (Ager, et al., 1991) and often leads to anger and "cultural bereavement" (Eisenbruch, 1992). Furthermore, Brown (1982) discovered that Indochinese who resettled in the United States responded to separation with guilt, a sense of obligation, and misapprehension, while Masser (1992) reported that Central American youth who were separated from their primary caretaker exhibited poor psychosocial functioning.

Stress

During both World Wars, the United States military conducted psychological studies of troops in action and found that a common reaction under the duress of battle was "shell shock" and "battle fatigue." Mental health professionals came to believe that war experiences cause both short- and long-term emotional problems. By the 1970s, considerable theoretical work dealing with the topic of stress was carried out, notably by Selye (1974), Lazarus and Launier (1978). Stress, conceptualized as a multifaceted element in mental health, creates a burden for the individual that may be expressed by physical and/or psychological symptoms. On one hand, stress may be caused by outside agents (events or life situations), while in other cases, stress may be produced by an internal process through the actions or thinking of an individual. Garmezy and Rutter (1983) speak of stress manifesting itself as: 1) a stimulus, an event, or class of events; 2) a human response that is accompanied by physical and/or emotional changes, such as sweating, anxiety, or fear; or, 3) a blending of the two through interaction. Stresses may be acute or endemic and are usually cumulative.

In refugee work, the external events of displacement and resettlement are frequently viewed as "stressors," while internal reactions of individuals to these events are seen as "stresses." For example, investigators found that Vietnamese adults and youth who suffered from premigration and acculturation stressors were prone to depression, nightmares, and physical illness (Duingtraan, 1996; Tran, 1993). For refugees and immigrants, stresses are caused by change, acculturation, and bereavement (Bernier, 1992). More specifically, Hirayama, Hirayama, and Cetingok (1993) cite family and intergenerational conflict, occupational and economic uncertainty, and cultural adjustment as sources of resettlement stress. According to Orley (1994), refugee stresses in resettlement come from cultural differences, loss of status, possessions, and employment, lack of family supports, discrimination, and poor physical health.

Coping

Paralleling the theoretical work of stress theorists is the work of researchers who have presented fundamental ways by which persons cope with loss and stress. These analyses of coping strategies, such as control, toleration, and minimization (Pearlin and Schooler, 1978), have been applied, in general, to the study of victims (Perloff, 1983), and in particular to rape victims (Burgess and Holmstrom, 1984), refugee children (Eth and Pynoss, 1985), and disaster survivors (Cohen and Ahearn, 1980).

Investigations of refugee coping has revealed a number of styles and outcomes. Among Vietnamese boat people who survived attacks by pirates, positive coping was related to religious faith and mastery of a previous trauma (Kleinman, 1990). Citing the importance of appropriate developmental tasks for children and adolescents, Bromley (1988) established that inadequate coping skills hindered identity formation during adolescence among Southeast Asian youth. Furthermore, Timberlake and Cook (1984) noted the importance of coping strategies among resettled Vietnamese who mainly utilized denial and somatic responses as coping mechanisms.

Social Supports

An additional body of literature represents a number of investigations of social supports as mediating factors, that facilitate and ease adjustment or readjustment. Internal characteristics, such as intelligence, personality, age and experience, resilience and fortitude, and belief systems including ideology, serve as supportive guides to daily life. External supports that are most important to the individual in this regard are family, relatives, friends, neighbors, the school, church, and civic or mutual-aid associations. In addition, the availability of, and accessibility to, community resources, services, financial assistance,and networks are important supports in confronting and coping with stressful life events.

For example, Glassman and Skonik (1984) emphasize the importance of support and community for Indochinese refugees who recently arrived in the United States. The lack of social support and social interaction has been linked with alienation (Tran et al., 1987) and poor mental health status in refugees (Nishimoto et. al., 1989). Similarly, Mui (1996) found that depression among immigrant Chinese elderly was associated with living alone, dissatisfaction with family, and perceived poor health. Finally, Fox and her colleagues (1994) discovered that social support and presence of family were correlated positively with the adaptation of refugee children from Southeast Asia.

Trauma

Another interrelated concept frequently used to understand the experiences of refugees and immigrants is the concept of trauma. In the aftermath of the Vietnam War, a movement grew calling attention to the emotional problems of veterans and advocating for the creation of local service centers to provide counseling to this group. It was widely believed that the experience of the war, a traumatic event, produced a range of long-lasting emotional and physical consequences. The United States Congress passed legislation establishing centers and clinics to deal with the problems of the Vietnam veterans. Soon after, the American Psychiatric Association (1980) accepted a new diagnosis of Post-Traumatic Stress Disorder (PTSD) as part of the *Diagnostic and Statistical Manual of Mental Disorders.*[2]

The literature of mental health practice with refugees and immigrants frequently refers to trauma and PTSD as outcomes of displacement. For example, investigators have reported that displaced individuals suffer long-term vulnerability to the effects of trauma from separation (Zima, 1987), flight and uprooting (Timberlake and Cook, 1984), persecution, oppression, torture (Hjern et al., 1991), and stressful life events (Duingtraan, 1996). In addition, the literature is replete with reports of traumatized refugees–Salvadorean (Bowen et al., 1992), African (Peltzer, 1989), Cambodian (Sack et al., 1996), Vietnamese (Snodgrass et al., 1993), Afghani (Lipson et al., 1995), and Bosnian (Weine et al., 1995). Trauma and, in particular PTSD, is perhaps the most popular descriptor of refugee health or lack of health today.

Researchers consider displacement as an event, often violent and horrible, that produces loss, separation, stress, and trauma that is, in turn, mediated by support systems and coping ability. The outcome is behavior that may be expressed in terms of adaptation/maladaptation, wellness/illness, or acculturation/non-acculturation. The reader may again view this approach in Figure 1.1. Admittedly this figure portrays an explanatory model that is unilinear with minimum interactive effects. In fairness, most researchers employ a more dynamic paradigm for study. However, for understanding at this point, one can comprehend this popular strategy for the study of refugee well-being, including the various dimensions in the process that one observes and measures.

Methodological Approaches and Measurement

This section contains a summation of the most frequently used measures in quantitative studies of refugee mental health, a discussion of the issues and difficulties in doing cross-cultural investigations, and a definition and description of qualitative and quantitative methodologies with their strengths and limitations in assessing the psychosocial wellness of refugees.

Measures from the Literature

A selective review[3] of the literature demonstrates that researchers studying psychosocial well-being of refugees draw upon numerous scales, inventories, profiles, indices, and surveys as listed in Table 1.1. They adopt measures of refugee well-being which have been standardized elsewhere, most often from the United States and Western Europe. An example is the Diagnostic Interview Schedule (DIS), an instrument measuring mental symptoms and disorders, which has been standardized through an epidemiologic study in the United States. Norms for this assessment tool have established prevalence rates for various mental conditions. Other measures, such as the Hopkins Symptoms Checklist, SCL-90, and Vietnamese Depression Scale, have been standardized for some refugee populations. While most of the measures in Table 1.1 deal with psychiatric symptoms (stress, depression, mood) and health status, one observes the absence of a scale for psychosocial well-being. The most frequently used tool in this selected group of studies was the *Diagnostic and Statistical Manual for Mental Disorders* from which the measure of PTSD comes. While this diagnostic and research tool has been approved by the American Psychiatric Association, there are few acceptable norms for refugee groups.

Table 1.1 Measurements in Selective Studies of Refugee Mental Health

Study	Population	Measures Utilized	Variables
Birman and Tyler (1994)	Soviet women	Behavioral Acculturation Scale Alienation Scale	Acculturation Adjustment Alienation
Cheung (1994)	Cambodians	General Health Questionnaire	PTSD Coping
Ebata and Miyake (1989)	Vietnamese	Cornell Medical Index	Health status Trauma and stress
Hauff and Vaglum (1995)	Vietnamese	SCL-90	PTSD Stress
Hirayama et al. (1993)	Southeast Asians	Bloom's Life Events Scale Albee's Prevention Model	Prevention Trauma and stress
Kroll et al. (1989)	Southeast Asians	19-Item Symptom Checklist	PTSD Depression Loss
Liebkind (1996)	Vietnamese	Vietnamese Depression Scale Hopkins Symptom Checklist Identity Scale Berry's Acculturation Model	Depression Acculturation Identity Acculturation
Peltzer (1989)	Zambians	35-Item Lusaka Assessment Scale	PTSD
Rosseau et al. (1989)	Latin American children	Achenbach's Traumatic Events Child Behavioral Profile Clinical Evaluation Scale	Trauma and stress Anxiety Depression
Sack et al. (1995)	Khmer adolescents	Diagnostic Interview Schedule (DIS)	PTSD Depression Adjustment
Strober (1994)	Cambodians	Derogatis Symptom Inventory Acculturation Scale Social support Network	Acculturation Social Support Distress
Westermeyer et al. (1990)	Hmong	90-Item Symptom Checklist Zung Depression Scale Global Assessment Scale	Adjustment Depression

Issues in Cross-Cultural Research

Marsella and Kameoka (1989) posit that culture is learned behavior that is shared and transmitted from one generation to another for purposes of human adjustment, adaptation, and growth. Culture has both external referents (artifacts, institutions, roles) and internal referents (values and beliefs), each of which influences psychosocial well-being. While many peoples have similar values and behaviors, these may be uniquely embedded in culture. In other words, one cannot assume that a definition or expression of well-being from one culture to another is the same or largely similar. While all cultures have standards for what is normal and abnormal, for what is well-being and what is illness, it is important for researchers to understand what cultures have in common and what values, structures, or expectations are idiosyncratic.

As discussed earlier, there are many ways in which investigators have interpreted psychosocial well-being. Indeed, there are hundreds of variables, scales, inventories, profiles, and interview schedules that attempt to appraise well-being, but most have one thing in common—they have been developed by Westerners for Westerners based upon Western values, assumptions, and norms. How then can these assessment tools be utilized for other cultures and peoples? Researchers in the refugee field have to ponder the appropriateness of adopting these criteria for assessing non-Western groups and use them only when they are sure that the measurers are appropriate. As emphasized by Marsella and his colleagues (1996), Western measures may indeed be useful in studying mental health phenomena in other cultures, but such tools must be validated before embarking on a study.

When asking if measures are equivalent from one culture to another, it becomes apparent that there are a number of problems in cross-cultural investigations. First, there is language. Do translated words mean or connote the same thing? Investigators use back translation, that is the translation of the translation by a native speaker, to control for this issue. Second, there is the question of whether the item, scale, or measure is conceptually equivalent. For instance, does the concept of independence, work, honesty, or love have the same meaning across cultures? Thus, Bracken, Giller, and Summerfield (1995) question the universality of PTSD as a measure of trauma. While they do not oppose the utilization of this measure, they opine that in many instances it is employed inappropriately. Third, when investigators ask subjects to respond to true and false questions, rate items from high to low, or select points on a thermometer, the responses may not be interpreted by respondents the way the research expects. Researchers must worry about the cultural relevance of their instruments (Marsella and Kameoka, 1989).

As noted earlier, there is the question of equivalency of values or norms that set the standards for morality and behavioral expectations. For example, among the Hmong, to take a neighbor's tool is not stealing, as there is a strong value that all things belong to the community, that is, belong to everyone. Andean indigenous groups chew coca leaves since the use of stimulants is not prohibited. The point is that Western values and definitions cannot be applied automatically to behavior, events, or things as these are oftentimes inappropriate and irrelevant in other cultures.

Overall, there are two serious issues associated with equivalency that influence the implementation of cross-cultural studies. First, Western researchers, particularly American investigators, conceive of the person as a self-contained unit, an individual, an isolate completely independent of others. In Western societies, the person is placed at the center of the cosmos and all else revolves around him or her. This is a peculiar notion that is not shared by many other societies that conceive of the individual as part of a family, special group, or community. The other problem in doing cross-cultural work is the assumption that Western forms of therapy work equally as well for non-Western populations. In many cultures, the use of talk therapy does not work because of an individual's sense of shyness or shame. Then again, the assumption that Western technologies for treatment are universally appropriate negates the application of indigenous interventions that may be more effective. Therefore, researchers are cautioned to face each of these concerns before automatically applying Western instruments when studying refugees.

Research Methodologies

A study's design will impact not only assumptions, research aims, and approaches, but also the types of questions asked and how they are asked. For a hundred years, social scientists have debated the efficacy of qualitative versus quantitative methods to study the world. In a sense, it is the difference between inductive and deductive, or top-down versus bottom-up, reasoning. The quantitative analyst usually has a road map in hand, knows where he or she is going, and has specific plans for the journey. On the other hand, the qualitative scholar investigates the world as an explorer who is excited with discovery and meaning. Let us take a closer look at these two methods.

Quantitative Approach

Quantitative investigators set out to describe and categorize information, test assumptions, and prove theories. Guided by the "scientific method," they carefully plan the study with rigorous and precise groundwork including the selection of hypotheses, study design, sample, instruments, statistical devices, and manner of data analysis. They know the way and map the terrain as they proceed. Little deviation occurs once the study gets under way.

Several important decisions are made at the onset of the study. The nature of the problem is clearly articulated in order to determine the type of study design and to formulate instruments to collect information. The design may be experimental, requiring a randomization of subjects, comparative measures, measurements at different time intervals, and sophisticated statistical analysis. The design may be quasi-experimental, relying on one-shot, *ex post facto*, time-series studies, or descriptive, using case studies or simple comparisons of groups. Instrumentation, therefore, is the logical result from the definition of the study problem or question and the type of research design that is employed.

With quantitative methods, the reliability and validity of measures selected for use are very important. Measures are standardized in order to improve reliability, that is, to enhance dependability and reproducibility of the instrument. Will it achieve the same results time after time with the same population? Validity, on the other hand, refers to accuracy and truth. Does the instrument measure what it purports to measure? There are a number of ways to insure reliability and validity of measures, most of which involve complicated statistical procedures. The imperative here is that before one can quantify, one must be able to qualify, i.e., specify the features of the object or phenomenon to be represented by means of observational procedures.

A case example illustrates this approach to measurement. Using Berry's model of acculturation (1992) and drawing on the work of Beiser (1991), Karmela Liebkind (1996) studied the acculturative stress of Vietnamese refugees who resettled in Finland. She hypothesized that the degree of acculturation (defined as anxiety/depression, psychosomatic symptoms, and lower self-esteem) would predict stress in a refugee family. The author employed Kinzie's Vietnamese Depression Scale to measure anxiety and depression, Mollica's adaptation of the Hopkins Symptom Checklist-25 to ascertain psychosomatic symptoms, and an Identity Scale constructed by the investigator to tap into the level of self-esteem. The first two measures had been previously translated into Vietnamese and had produced acceptable reliability scores. However, no reliability scores were offered for the Identity Scale.

In her study, Liebkind assumed that predictors of acculturative stress would be the socio-demographic characteristics of the person, their pre- and postmigration experiences, the social context of the host country, and these would be mediated by one's acculturation attitudes and degree of acculturation. The results of her regression analysis revealed that the best predictors of acculturative stress were gender and age.

The strength of this approach is its careful, conceptual design. It builds upon the previous work of Berry and Beiser, clearly tests a proposition, has a sample size of 159 young refugees and 121 of the children's parents or caretakers, employs several standardized measures, and probably is generalizable to other groups of Vietnamese settlers in Finland. If one were to replicate this study in Finland, it is likely that the investigator would encounter similar results. This study adopts measures that had established reliability scores with Vietnamese populations. Finally, another strength of Liebkind's research is its potential usefulness for policy and programs in countries that receive Vietnamese refugees.

Quantitative design, as has already been suggested, has potential weaknesses. Can it be assumed that Western measures can be applied to this population of Vietnamese? It would be necessary first to understand their struggle in Finland and other cultural issues before drawing final conclusions. On the other hand, it certainly may be appropriate to use a Western scale, index, or checklist with Vietnamese refugees if the meaning of the items and their validity and reliability have been established in use with this group. One final problem in Liebkind's study is the sample: while large enough to allow analysis, it was not random for though the author collected names from many sources, some of these sources were judged to be inaccurate.

Qualitative Approach

It has been said, rather facetiously, that qualitative research is what you do when you don't have enough data or don't understand statistics. Investigators who use qualitative methods endeavor to look at and interpret a slice of life. They are not concerned primarily with proof or verification, but rather with the discovery of meaning through observation, description, decoding, and translation. This journey or adventure depends upon the reflexive, thoughtful interpretation of people, their places, and their activities. Qualitative researchers do not claim objectivity. In fact, their's is a subjective testimonial to other people's voices. The work calls for careful planning and much flexibility to change course as one goes. Their approach draws upon interviews, life histories, focus groups, and observation.

Very few of the studies reviewed in this chapter relied upon qualitative methods. One study that utilized participant observation, focus groups, key informants, and interviews at three different stages is the work of Canda and Phaobtong (1992). They analyzed the role of Buddhism in the provision of human services to Southeast Asian refugees through Buddhist mutual assistance associations in the United States. The authors established that Buddhism is linked to both traditional lifestyle as well as current efforts to overcome the effects of war and trauma that have forced the migration of these refugees. In particular, Canda and Phaobtong examined the physical, psychological, social, and spiritual services provided in the Lao and Khmer temples. These findings have an obvious relevance for strengthening indigenous support systems and delivering the needed social services that Buddhist mutual assistance associations provide to these refugee communities.

Another example of qualitative measures comes from Gilad's investigation (1990) of the impact of separation on refugees' concepts of family after flight compared with the views of non-refugees. The researcher conducted intensive interviews, held informal discussions, and observed nine families in depth. These case studies dealt with the ordeal of clandestine departure, the guilt that some refugees felt and the lack of guilt experienced by others, the issue of separation and then reunion, the question of dependency, and lastly, the scarcity of family and group resources.

The strengths of qualitative studies are their richness, humanism, and timeliness. As the story unfolds, an understanding of people's lives increases, illuminating their relationships and interactions, and giving meaning to processes, patterns, and purposes. The study of the human situation or condition is the story, the text, and the narrative as these are placed within a cultural context. The investigator, through this method, can make instruments and measures sensitive and appropriate to the situation. Finally, this method often leads to serendipitous discovery that adds to theoretical understanding and generates new areas of inquiry.

The weaknesses of this methodology are rather obvious. First, the approach requires discipline and considerable skill. Some researchers do not have the technical ability, experience, or personal adaptability to assimilate the data as the study progresses and make the necessary mid-course changes that may be required. Second, since the participants in the study are not drawn at random and sample sizes are very small, it is impossible to apply the findings to other groups. Study results often describe and explain one particular group, and one group only. Some critics have questioned the usefulness of many of these qualitative studies as they seldom have an impact on policy and program decisions. Third, the implementation of good ethnographic work is costly in both time and money. Much time must be spent in preparation, in the field, and in analysis of notes, journals, interviews, and observations. The net result is that such projects are invariably expensive.[4]

Recommendations

This review has described serious limitations in the use of Western definitions and measures of well-being, and the respective strengths and weaknesses of quantitative and qualitative methodologies in studying and assessing a refugee's reaction to forced migration. All empirical research, both quantitative and qualitative, must satisfy the reliability principle, i.e., another observer should be able to replicate a researcher's explicit procedures and come up with the same findings.[5] It is easier to criticize this fact than to offer suggestions of how best to proceed. The remainder of this chapter offers some recommendations to both quantitative and qualitative researchers as well as to teachers and professors who are in charge of training students who work with and study refugees in order to stimulate a debate that may arrive at a consensus on an agenda for future research in this field.

First, quantitative investigators should make use of indigenous definitions and interpretations in order to broaden their understanding of local definitions and meanings of well-being as a way of selecting the most appropriate measures for a study. Before quantifying, the researcher must be able to qualify; before measuring, it is necessary to define. Second, utilize both quantitative and qualitative measures in a study in order to increase understanding, explain context, and check, recheck, validate, and confirm measures and findings. Third, employ standardized measures across groups so as to discern intra- and inter-group differences and to develop group norms for a variety of measures for assessing psychological well-being. Replicate, contrast, and compare each other's instruments. Fourth, work to develop a new research approach, inclusive of qualitative and quantitative methods, that strengthens and deepens the study of refugee health and well-being.

The following recommendations are addressed to the qualitative investigator. First, broaden the usefulness of research findings through the selection of larger, more representative samples, replicate studies with similar groups, and include some standardized measures that would allow greater generalization of the findings. Second, work to develop a new research approach that utilizes both qualitative and quantitative methodologies that will strengthen and deepen the study of refugee health and well-being. Third, remember that a good story is only that, a good story. The question, "*qui bono*," must be asked—what good is my research? In what way will the findings advance our understanding of refugee behavior and in what way will the findings impact program and policy?

The following advice applies to both quantifiers and qualifiers. Insure that the measures used are based on local, culturally appropriate definitions. Ask if other researchers would be able to use the same measures and find similar results with like groups. Then, whatever is measured must have some useful purpose. Will the psychosocial indicators of well-being prevent the mental collapse of another human being or will the findings provide the impetus to change policy or add funding for a project, or point to new ways to relieve suffering? In addition, accentuate the positive by focusing on health and well-being instead of illness and pathology. Employ a strengths and not a deficit model of behavior.

Finally, reconsider the target of the research. It is important to move away from focusing on the individual as the unit of analysis and incorporate a well-being perspective of family, group, neighborhood, and community. Research findings, then, could point to ways to improve the psychosocial functioning of groups as well as individuals.

It is essential that those in charge of training programs for psychiatrists, psychologists, social workers, and refugee workers develop curricula that emphasize an awareness and understanding of cultural differences, especially in the performance of cross-cultural studies. Students must be trained in both quantitative and qualitative tools for the study of refugees. Lastly, students need to learn how to focus upon a strengths perspective and avoid an emphasis on pathology that invariably "medicalizes" the problems of refugees.

It has been the purpose of this chapter to call attention to the extensive emphasis on the mental health of refugees that one encounters today in most professional journals, the dependency on the use of the psychodynamic concepts to explain refugee behavior, the predominance of Western measures employed in cross-cultural studies, and the dominance of quantitative methodologies in the design of refugee studies. Some have begun to question the validity of these things, and I join them in calling for awareness, sensitivity, and a change of strategy in studying the psychosocial well-being of refugees.

Notes

1. There is and has been considerable debate about this emphasis on agency, freedom to act, and independence as critics have charged that this notion is essentially Eurocentric and does not reflect the fact that most non-Western societies are based upon inter-dependence, mutuality, and cooperation. How much agency and freedom is possessed at any point in time is a controversial matter open to discussion. Obviously, claims about the degree of agency and freedom need to be substantiated and explored in greater depth.
2. This is often referred to as the DSM-IV, IV being the fourth and most recent revision of this diagnostic system. See American Psychiatric Association (1994).
3. The basis for this selective review was drawn from a search of *Psych Abstracts* from 1989 through 1996 and then an identification of studies that focused on measuring mental health outcomes of refugees.
4. One anthropologist with whom I spoke disagreed with this point. She thought that qualitative studies might be costlier in time, but not money. She argued that quantitative research is often more expensive because it usually requires more research assistants, supplies (such as thousands of surveys), and then fancy computers to analyze the data, whereas an ethnographic study often requires one hapless researcher willing to live out in the middle of nowhere for a year or two at virtually no cost. In her opinion, the main deterrent to qualitative work is not money but rather the amount of time and effort it takes to do it well. There is usually a foreign language (or two or three) to learn, a lot of groundwork to do to establish rapport, and a lot of ambiguity to deal with because the project is always changing shape–as it should be.
5. This is still a very controversial point. Some anthropologists have said that there is no such thing as a replicable study. It is like the Buddhist saying that you can not put your foot into the same river twice. They argue that quantitative research is not value-free since all stages of the process are influenced by interactions and decisions that are made relative to the endeavor.

References

Ager, A., Ager, W., and Long, L. (1991). *A case study of refugee women in Malawi: A Report for the United Nations High Commissioner for Refugees.* Zomba: Centre for Social Research.

American Psychiatric Association (1994). *Diagnostic and Statistical Manual of Mental Disorders: DSM-IV.* Washington, DC: Author.

Armstrong, A. (1988). Aspects of refugee well-being in settlement schemes: An examination of the Tanzanian case. *Journal of Refugee Studies,* 7:1:57-73.

Beiser, M. (1991). The mental health of refugees in resettlement countries. In Adelman, H., (Ed.), *Refugee policy.* Toronto: York Lanes Press, 427-442.

Bernier, D. (1992). The Indochinese refugee: A perspective from various stress theories. *Journal of Multicultural Social Work, 2*:1:15-30.

Berry, J. W. (1992). Acculturation and adaptation in a new society. *International Migration Review, 30*:69-85.

Birman, D. and Tyler, F. B. (1994). Acculturation and alienation of Soviet Jewish refugees in the United States. *Genetic, Social, and General Psychology Monographs, 120*:1:101-115.

Bowen, D. J., Carscadden, L., Beighle, K., and Fleming, I. (1992). Posttraumatic disorder among Salvadoran women. *Women and Therapy, 13*:3:267-289.

Bowlby, J. (1984). *Attachment and loss* (2nd ed.). Hamondsworth: Penguin Books.

Bracken, P. J., Giller, J. E., and Summerfield, D. (1995). Psychological responses to war and atrocity: The limitations of current concepts. *Social Science and Medicine, 40*:8:1073-1082.

Bromley, M. A. (1988). Identity as a central adjustment issue for the Southeast Asian unaccompanied refugee minor. *Child and Youth Care Quarterly, 12*:104-114.

Brown, G. (1982). Issues in the resettlement of Indochinese refugees. *Social Casework, 63*:3:155-159.

Burgess, A. W. and Holmstrom, L. L. (1984). Coping behavior and the rape victim. *American Journal of Psychiatry, 133*:302-305.

Canda, E. and Phaobtong, T. (1992). Buddhism as a social support for Southeast Asian refugees. *Social Work, 37*:1:61-67.

Cheung, P. (1994). Posttraumatic stress disorder among Cambodian refugees in New Zealand. *International Journal of Social Psychiatry, 40*:1:17-26.

Cohen, R. and Ahearn, F. L. (1980). *Handbook for mental health care of disaster victims*. Baltimore: Johns Hopkins University Press.

Dasgupta, P. (1993). *An inquiry into well-being and destitution*. Oxford: Clarendon Press.

Drachman, D. (1992). A stage-of-migration framework for social service to immigrant populations. *Social Work, 37*:1:68-72.

Duingtraan, Q. (1996). Psychological correlates of depression in Vietnamese adolescents. *Child and Adolescent Social Work, 13*:1:41-50.

Ebata, K. and Miyake, Y. (1989). A mental health study of the Vietnamese refugee in Japan. *Journal of Social Psychiatry, 35*:2:164-172.

Edwards, R. G. and Beiser, M. (1994). Southeast Asian youth in Canada: The determinants of competence and successful coping. *Canada's Mental Health, 42*:1:1-5.

Eisenbruch, M. (1992). Toward a culturally-sensitive DSM: Cultural bereavement in Cambodian refugees and the traditional healer as taxonomist. *Journal of Nervous and Mental Disease, 180*:8-10.

Eth, S. and Pynoss, R.S. (1985). Interaction of trauma and grief in childhood. In Eth, S. and Pynos, R. S., (Eds.), *Post-traumatic stress disorder in children*. Washington: American Psychiatric Association Press, 168-186.

Fox, P.G., Cowell, J. M., and Montgomery, A.C. (1994). The effects of violence on health and adjustment of Southeast Asian refugee children: An integrative review. *Public Health Nursing, 11*:3:195-201.

Freud, A. and Bellingham, D. T. (1943). *War and children.* New York: Ernst Willard.

Fried, M. (1968). Grieving for a lost home. In Duhl, L. J. (Ed.), *The urban condition.* New York: Basic Books.

Garmezy, N. and Rutter, M., (Eds.). (1983). *Stress, coping, and development in children.* New York: McGraw-Hill.

Gilad, L. (1990). Refugees in Newfoundland: Families after flight. *Journal of Comparative Family Studies, 4*:3:379-396.

Glassman, U. and Skolnik, L. (1984). The role of social group work in refugee resettlement. *Social Work with Groups, 7*:1:45-62.

Hauff, E. and Vaglum, P. (1995). Organised violence and the stress of exile: Predictors of mental health in a community cohort of Vietnamese refugees three years after resettlement. *British Journal of Psychiatry, 166*:3:360-367.

Hermansson, A., Hornquist, J. O., and Timka, T. (1996). The well-being of war-wounded asylum applicants and quota refugees following arrival in Sweden. *Journal of Refugees Studies, 9*:2:166-181.

Hirayama, K. K., Hirayama, H, and Cetingok, M. (1993), Mental health promotion for Southeast Asian refugees in the USA. *International Social Work, 36*:2:119-129.

Hjern, A., Angel, B., and Hoejer, B. (1991). Persecution and behavior: A report of refugee children from Chile. *Child Abuse and Neglect, 15*:3:239-248.

Kassabian, L. (1996). Displacement and bicultural integration: Factors contributing to the psychological well-being of Armenian-Americans. In Rynearson, A.M. and Phillips, J., (Eds.), *Selected papers on refugee issues: IV.* Alexandria, VA: American Anthropological Association, 73-104.

Kleinman, S. B. (1990). Terror at sea: Vietnamese victims of piracy. *American Journal of Psychoanalysis, 50*:4:351-362.

Kondic, L. and Marvar, M. (1992). Anxiety and depressive reactions in refugees. *Psychologische Beitrage, 34*:3-4:157-164.

Kroll, J., Habeniecht, M., MacKensie, T., Yang, M., et al., (1989). Depression and posttraumatic stress disorder in Southeast Asian refugees. *American Journal of Psychiatry, 146*:12:1592-1597.

Kubler-Ross, E. (1989). *On death and dying.* London: Tavistock/Routledge.

Lazarus, R. S. and Launier, R. (1978). Stress-related transactions between person and environment. In Pervin, A. and Lewis, M., (Eds.), *Perspectives in international psychology.* New York: Plenum, 287-327.

Liebkind, K. (1996). Acculturation and stress: Refugees in Finland. *Journal of Cross-Cultural Psychology, 27*:2:161-180.

Lindemann, E. (1944). Symptomotology and management of acute grief. *American Journal of Psychiatry, 101*:141-148.

Lipson, J. G., Omidian, P. A., and Paul, S. M. (1995). Afghan health education project: A community survey. *Public Health Nursing, 12*:3:143-150.

Marsella, A. J., Freidman, M. J., Gerrity, E. T., and Scurfield, R. M. (1996), Introduction. In Marsella, A. J., Freidman, M. J., Gerrity, E. T., and Scurfield, R. M., (Eds.), *Ethnocultural aspects of posttraumatic stress disorder.* Washington: The American Psychological Association Press, 4.

Marsella, A. and Kameoka, V. A. (1989). Ethnographic approaches in the assessment of pathology. In Wetzler, S., (Ed.), *Measuring mental illness: psychometric assessment for clinicians.* Washington: The American Psychiatric Association Press, 229-256.

Masser, D. S. (1992). Psychosocial functioning of Central American refugee children. *Child Welfare, 71*:5:439-456.

McCallin, M. (n.d.). *The psychological well-being of refugee children: Research, practice and policy.* Geneva: International Catholic Child Bureau.

McSpadden, L. A. (1987). Ethiopian refugee resettlement in the Western United States: Social context and psychological well-being. *International Migration Review, xxi*:3:796-819.

Mui, A. C. (1996). Depression among elderly Chinese immigrants: An exploratory study. *Social Work, 41*:6:633-645.

Nishimoto, R. H., Chau, K. L., and Roberts, R. L. (1989). The psychological status of Vietnamese Chinese women in refugee camps. *Affilia: Journal of Women and Social Work, 4*:3:51-64.

Orley, J. (1994). Psychological disorders among refugees: Some clinical and epidemiological considerations. In Marsella, A., Bornemann, T., Ekblad, S., and Orley, J., (Eds.), *Amidst peril and pain.* Washington: American Psychological Association, 193-206.

Pearlin, L. I. and Schooler, C. (1978). The structure of coping. *Journal of Health and Social Behavior, 19*:1:2-21.

Perloff, H. (1983). Perceptions of vulnerability to victimization. *Journal of Social Issues, 39*:1:41-61.

Peltzer, K. (1989). Assessment and treatment of psychosocial problems of refugees in Zambia. *International Journal of Mental Health, 18*:2:113-121.

Raphael, B. (1983). *The anatomy of bereavement.* New York: Basic Books.

Rousseau, C. , Corin, E. and Renaud, C. (1989). Conflit arme et trauma: une etude clinique chez des enfants refugies latino-americains. (Armed conflict and trauma: A clinical study among Latin American refugee children). *Canadian Journal of Psychiatry, 34*:5:376-385.

Sack, W. H., Clarke, G. N., and Seeley, J. (1995). Posttraumatic stress disorder across two generations of Cambodian refugees. *Journal of the American Academy of Child and Adolescent Psychiatry, 34*:9:1160-1166.

Sack, W. H., Clarke, G. N., and Seeley, J. (1996). Multiple forms of stress in Cambodian adolescent refugees. *Child Development, 67*:107-116.

Schreiber, S. (1995). Migration, traumatic bereavement and transcultural aspects of psychological healing: Loss and grief of a refugee woman from Begameter County in Ethiopia. *British Journal of Medical Psychology, 68*:2:135-142.

Selye, H. (1974). *Stress without distress*. Philadelphia: Lippincott.
Sen, A. (1993). Capability and well-being. In Nussbaum, M. C. and Sen, A., (Eds.), *The quality of life*. Oxford: Clarendon Press.
Simpson, J. A. and Weiner, E. S. C., (Eds.). (1991). *The Oxford English Dictionary*. (Second edition). Oxford: Oxford University Press.
Snodgrass, L. L., Yamamoto, J., Frederick, C., Ton-That, N., et al., (1993). Vietnamese refugees with PTSD symptomotology: Intervention via a coping skills model. *Journal of Traumatic Stress, 6*:4:560-575.
Strober, S. (1994). Social work intervention to alleviate Cambodian refugee psychological stress. *International Social Work, 37*:1:23-35.
Timberlake, E. and Cook, K. O. (1984). Social work and the Vietnamese refugee. *Social Work, 29*:2:108-113.
Tran, T. V. (1993). Psychological traumas and depression in a sample of Vietnamese people in the United States. *Health and Social Work, 18*:3:184-194.
Tran, T. V. (1994). Bilingualism and subjective well-being in a sample of elderly Hispanics. *Journal of Social Service Research, 20*:1-2:1-19.
Tran, T. V., Wright, R., and Mindel, C. H. (1987). Alienation among Vietnamese refugees. *Journal of Social Service Research, 11*:1:59-75.
Weine, S., Becker, D. F., McGlashan, T. H., and Vojvoda, D. (1995). Adolescent survivors of "ethnic-cleansing:" Observations on the first year in America. *Journal of the American Academy of Child and Adolescent Psychiatry, 34*:9:1153-1159.
Westermeyer, J., Callies, A., and Neider, J. (1990). Welfare status and psychological adjustment of 100 Hmong refugees. *Journal of Nervous and Mental Disease, 178*:5:300-306.
World Health Organization (1996). *Fact sheet of the World Health Organization, August 1996*. Geneva: World Health Organization.
Zima, S. (1987). Forty-two Ethiopian boys: Observations of their first year in Israel. *Social Work, 32*:4:359-360.

2

Psychosocial Programs

PRINCIPLES AND PRACTICE FOR RESEARCH AND EVALUATION

Alastair Ager

The Need for Research and Evaluation

Research and evaluation is crucial in the field of psychosocial intervention if we are to move on from the situation where the principal driving force for program developments "remains concern rather than reasoned extrapolation from rigorous empirical study" (Ager, 1994). Recent years have seen a welcome increase in the documentation of projects in this field (e.g. Agger, 1995; Tolfree, 1995), but the rapid escalation of interest in the area renders a firm foundation for program planning and implementation vital.

It is clear that to facilitate the identification and replication of good practice there needs to be commitment to the open and effective evaluation of programs. Such evaluation involves the assessment of the impact of programs against predetermined criteria. Given the embryonic nature of the field, broader research is, however, also a vital prerequisite. Defining appropriate evaluation criteria, determining process issues of potential relevance to outcomes and elaborating conceptual frameworks for the analysis of factors influencing psychosocial status all require a broader commitment to research than may be captured by program evaluation alone.

The agenda for the development of our understanding of psychosocial issues, therefore, very much involves both research and evaluation. However, since many of the methodological principles underlying effective research are also applicable to rigorous evaluation, the current chapter focuses primarily on the former domain. Illustrative examples are, however, also drawn from the psychosocial evaluation literature. In addition, a final section addresses the particular concerns of program evaluation.

Quantitative Approaches

Appropriate principles and practices in research are topics of considerable debate within the social sciences, particularly in recent times with respect to the adoption of quantitative or qualitative approaches. Such debate is reflected in the field of psychosocial intervention. Psychometrics, an explicitly scientific approach to the measurement of human behavior and adjustment, provides an established starting point for the evaluation of actions seeking to impact human adjustment to difficult circumstances. This quantitative approach, however, has been widely critiqued with respect to its positivistic assumptions. The primary bases of this critique are twofold. First, it has been argued that such an approach commonly involves superimposition of assumptions derived from Western culture upon individuals from cultures not sharing the same construction and understanding of the world (Ager, 1997; Gibbs, 1994; Summerfield, 1995). This renders the interpretation of findings misleading or irrelevant. Second, in a related but distinct criticism, psychometric approaches—in seeking to understand generalities and commonalties in behavior—are seen as failing to address personal and subjective understandings of experience (Silverman, 1993).

Such critique has tended to shift emphasis onto more "qualitative" means of study, that is, study which explicitly seeks to view the world from the perspective of the individuals studied. As discussed later, such approaches do indeed offer powerful insight into the impact of psychosocial programs, but there is a danger in that the potential contribution of the psychometric approach (particularly with regard to the generality of an observation or finding within a studied population) is prematurely ignored. The critique of the psychometric approach is telling. It emphasizes the need to validate assumptions. It emphasizes the common "externality" of analysis (in contrast to the "internality" of actors' own accounts). With these cautions noted, however, in many circumstances much can be gained by structuring elements of a research or program evaluation upon a rigorous psychometric foundation. A complementary strategy—combining the strengths of quantitative and qualitative approaches—will commonly be of relevance. For this reason, this review begins by considering the key principles of the psychometric tradition and their application in the psychosocial field.

Key Concepts of Measurement

Psychometric theory is based upon the premise that human belief and behavior–and the influences upon these domains–can be understood with respect to defined variables. Variables such as level of education, extent of war experience, and psychological adjustment share the characteristic of some means of assigning a value for the individual or group under consideration. The way in which a variable is defined–that is, what counts as evidence in assigning a value to it–is termed *operationalization.* Operationalization of a variable (e.g., level of education) allows a categorical value (e.g., primary level education) or, more commonly, a numerical value (e.g., six years of schooling) to be assigned to it.

Three major concepts are used to appraise the adequacy of the proposed means of measurement or operationalization. First, *reliability* concerns the extent to which the chosen method provides a consistent means of ascribing value to a variable. For example, if level of schooling is operationalized by local records of school enrollment, do these provide a sound means for identifying the number of years attended? Are they more reliable in some districts than others? Would self-report from respondents be a more (or less) reliable method of operationalization?

Second, *validity* refers to the extent that the method to be used genuinely does measure the variable in question. A measure can be reliable (provide consistent values) and yet still invalid (if it doesn't measure what it is thought to be measuring). To be valid, self-reports of war experience need to allow for difficulties associated with recall over time and, potentially, situational characteristics which may encourage over–or under–reporting (e.g., availability of financial assistance might encourage the former, disinclination to share personal and painful information with a stranger the latter). In general, the validity of measures is supported by two forms of evidence. One is the face validity of a measure, i.e., the extent to which it self-evidently addresses issues relevant to the variable in question. The other, more rigorous approach, is the presentation of evidence that scores on the measure are related closely to other relevant and established measures or criteria. In the case of reported war experiences, for example, are average scores on the measure higher in areas known to have experienced significant conflict? The stronger the association between scores on the measure and such other sources of data, the greater confidence can be placed in the validity of the measure.

Third, measures that are reliable and valid may still prove inadequate, because of their *insensitivity*. Most quantitative research studies are based upon some form of comparison of two or more conditions, with measures being used to determine if there is any differential impact or effect across them. A study may, for example, compare two forms of psychological intervention using a measure of subjective well-being, seeking to establish if one intervention has a greater therapeutic impact than the other. Or a study may consider the impact of political involvement on the stress of military occupation by measuring stress in individuals active and passive with regard to political resistance. In such circumstances one might have a reliable and valid measure of subjective well-being (in the former case) or perceived stress (in the latter case), which is nonetheless not sensitive enough to pick up differences between the two conditions. Psychometric measures are often (correctly) criticized for imprecise capture of data: a respondent to a questionnaire, for example, may consider that they could give two or three slightly different answers to a question given the way it is phrased (Hudelson, 1994). Such imprecision is a clear source of insensitivity. It is quite possible for a real difference between two or more conditions to get lost within the "noise" of varied responses on an insensitive measure. However, insensitivity is principally a concern when a study fails to find differences between conditions. Where a study establishes clear differences despite concerns over the relative insensitivity of the measures used, this rather points to the substantive nature of the difference found (which has been determined despite the level of general "noise" in the data).

It is important, in this regard, to separate concerns that relate to the insensitivity of a measure and those that relate to potential bias (generally a challenge to the validity of a measure). All measures have a degree of insensitivity; the task of researchers is to find a measure that is sensitive enough to detect the changes or impacts with which they are concerned. If differences are found, critiques of a measure's insensitivity are generally unimportant. However, if a measure is biased—to the extent that it shapes responses in a manner which may falsely suggest an impact or effect across conditions—this is always a crucial concern. A questionnaire in which a clinician asks clients "Have you been helped by the intervention that I have provided?" is clearly liable to bias; expectations and power relations between clinician and client are likely to significantly shape response in a particular direction. There are many other, more subtle, sources of potential bias to which researchers need to attend.

Key Concepts of Interpretation

Operationalization, reliability, validity, and sensitivity are key concepts in approaches to measurement within quantitative work. Interpretation of data within this tradition is also governed by certain key concepts. Principal among these is the concept of generalizability, and related notions of significance and representativeness.

Generalizability concerns the extent to which findings from a study can be taken to more broadly inform the understanding of an issue. Other than in the most focused of project evaluations, generalizability is nearly always a major concern, addressing the extent to which what has been found in one particular situation can be seen as relevant to other, potentially similar, situations. Given the common misunderstandings in this domain—and the frequent misapplication of concerns regarding, for example, sample size—it can be helpful to distinguish between the two concepts of significance and representativeness.

Significance essentially relates to the trustworthiness of a finding. A difference may have been found in the levels of stress reported by those involved, and those not involved, in political opposition to occupying forces. If a difference has been found then there is a difference—but is it a trustworthy one? Are we confident that if the study were repeated that we would find the same result? Our decision on this will depend upon at least three factors: the method of sample selection, the size of the sample, and the magnitude of difference found. Were participants randomly selected from clearly defined groupings of "politically active" and "politically inactive" people? This will seldom be the case in applied fieldwork in the psychosocial field, but the closer the approximation to this the more confident we might be that differences found are not chance effects derived from biased recruitment (e.g. even if there is no real effect of political involvement on stress we might just happen to recruit more stressed individuals to one of our groups). Larger sample sizes can to some extent compensate for non-random sampling, but it is important to beware of becoming too fixated on the benefits of large samples. Statistical tests that can be applied to quantitative data allow for the size of a sample in advising whether a particular finding is significant (i.e., trustworthy). Mirroring the discussion of sensitivity earlier, a study which demonstrates a trustworthy difference between conditions with a relatively small sample size is evidence of the robustness of the phenomena under investigation. Over-large sample sizes are not only difficult to attain in much psychosocial fieldwork, they can allow us to detect differences that, while trustworthy, are so small that they are of little practical implication.

Significance thus addresses the extent to which the findings of a study are trustworthy as an analysis of that situation. It addresses the generalizability of the particular findings as a substantive, reliable account of that situation. Generalizability of findings to other situations (the more common usage of the term) is dependent upon notions of *representativeness*. To what extent is the situation or situations studied representative of other situations in which there is interest? A study may demonstrate a significant, trustworthy impact of political involvement in ameliorating stress in a sample of one hundred Palestinian youths from two refugee camps in Gaza. What of youths from those two camps who were not enrolled in the study? What of youths in other camps in Gaza? Or Palestinian youths not living in camps? Or those living in the West Bank? Or Kurdish youths in Northern Iraq? The composition of the sample will determine the confidence with which we might take findings to be of relevance to these other situations. In this case, if selection of camps and participants was by a method supporting representativeness of the sample (if not randomized, then perhaps structured by age, clan, and experience of conflict in a manner representative of Palestinian youths living in camps in Gaza), generalization of findings to other youths and other camps may be made with some confidence. Conceptual analysis of the phenomenon may suggest that a similar effect should be found outside camps and in other territories, but further empirical work is required before generalization of findings to such situations can be claimed.

Illustrative Studies

The concepts discussed above provide a basis for the analysis and critique of psychosocial studies which have attempted quantitative forms of analysis. Agger and Mimica (1996) report on an evaluation of psychosocial programs in Bosnia and Croatia. Questionnaires distributed to the beneficiaries of programs addressed questions of war-related experience, symptoms of distress, and factors considered helpful in the course of intervention. With data collected from over two thousand beneficiaries, this represents one of the largest evaluations to date of psychosocial intervention. Data was collected from beneficiaries across Bosnia-Herzegovina and Croatia, and thus provides a broadly representative sample of beneficiaries from programs in the region. The large sample size supports the trustworthiness of findings.

War-related experiences were operationalized by the presentation of statements regarding particular experiences (e.g., "life was in danger," "loss of home and property," "rape or sexual violence") which respondents checked if appropriate. Such statements have a clear face validity as a measure of war-related experience and, given the anonymity of respondents and their distribution postintervention, there are few grounds to suspect their unreliability. Distilling war-experience into a few statements is clearly a somewhat insensitive gauge of respondents war histories, but proved sensitive enough to identify systematic trends in exposure to warfare across sites within Bosnia-Herzegovina and Croatia (e.g., Tusla cf. Mostar and Adriatic Coast cf. Slavonia), which correspond with known military activity in the region.

Operationalization of symptoms of distress into such categories as "lonely," "frightened," "lost and disoriented," etc., allows for a potentially reliable coding of reported distress. The validity of such measures as a gauge of overall psychosocial functioning is a point of some controversy, however. Symptom checklists such as the Harvard Trauma Questionnaire (Mollica et al., 1992) may have demonstrable validity in terms of their relationship with psychological well-being determined by a construct such as Post-Traumatic Stress Disorder (PTSD). But the relevance of such diagnosis in the context of psychosocial programming is a point of considerable dispute. The validity of the symptom checklist in the Agger and Mimica (1996) study would be supported if the frequency of symptom report were shown to correlate with an individual's overall sense of well-being, though such data is not presented.

Such difficulties in adequate operationalization of psychosocial concepts are illustrated most clearly by the use in this study of beneficiaries' judgments of the value of different forms of intervention as the major basis for evaluation of inputs. Beneficiaries' subjective appraisal of differing forms of intervention may be an effective operationalization of therapeutic preference, but it is an inadequate proxy for therapeutic effectiveness. Reliable, valid, and sensitive measures of therapeutic impact are, however, especially difficult to define for psychosocial fieldwork. This is particularly so when work spans differing cultures, where behavioral signifiers of adjustment and adaptation may vary markedly.

There have been a number of sophisticated attempts to address such problems. The work of Punamäki (1990, 1996) demonstrates consistent rigor in its psychometric analysis of well-operationalized variables, with data supporting the validity and reliability of measures. Nonetheless, such work consistently faces two major criticisms regarding its utility in developing our understanding of psychosocial processes. First, in defining reliable categories of personal adjustment and experience, the validity of such categories as indicative of holistic psychosocial functioning may be questionable. Validity with respect to tightly defined concepts such as PTSD may be established, but does this capture the essence of the phenomena in question? Muecke (1992), Summerfield (1995), and others have argued that it seldom does. The "positivistic" constraints of a quantitative approach produce a partial, shallow, and fragmented measure of well-being, which is potentially poorly predictive of the "real thing."

Second, this fragmented analysis is particularly deficient in that it tends to emphasize the external "objective" analysis of well-being, rather than an internal "subjective" account. In terms of the examples considered above, the sense beneficiaries make of the intervention is more important than predetermined and preconceptualized gains envisioned by researchers. Such critique, as was noted earlier, has drawn considerable interest toward qualitative forms of analysis.

Qualitative Approaches

There are three fundamental characteristics of qualitative research: an emphasis on providing a comprehensive or "holistic" understanding of phenomena; an attempt to describe social phenomena from the perspective of those being studied; and a research strategy that is generally flexible and iterative (Bryman, 1992; Hudelson, 1994). The former two of these characteristics may be seen as responses to the above critique of quantitative work. The latter is a reflection of the inductive (as opposed to deductive) method which characterizes such work. Ideas are shaped by a cyclical process of identifying themes and concepts, developing theory to relate them together, and then seeking further data to elaborate conceptual development.

Key Concepts of Measurement

Qualitative research is clearly more concerned with the qualities or attributes that may be used to describe a phenomenon than the quantifiable degree that such a quality or attribute is present. Measurement, in qualitative terms, is about "what?" rather than "how much?".

A wide range of methods and principles guide work within the qualitative tradition, but these generally share a concern to identify *emergent concepts,* which arise from open consideration and discussion in a situation rather than imposing concepts and structures from the outside.

Grounded theory (Straus, 1987) defines an approach where the development of categories and concepts is explicitly *grounded* in interrogation of the ideas, concepts, and understandings in the situation being studied. A study examining the impact of a psychosocial intervention program on war-affected children does not begin with conceptualizations of socialization processes, adjustment, and trauma; rather it seeks to identify emergent concepts that account for children's experience and response to the program. Grounded concepts may not necessarily be expressed in terms that participants studies would recognize, though this will often be the case. In such circumstances, checking back accounts with participants may provide a valuable confirmation of the level of *respondent validity*.

Key Concepts of Interpretation

Within qualitative work, principles of interpretation are particularly key to the development of meaningful analysis. While some critics have suggested that the subjectivity involved in such work provides a basis for partial (i.e., predetermined or "biased") analysis, it is now generally acknowledged there are defendable criteria for the rigor of qualitative analysis in a fashion analogous to those that may be defined for quantitative work.

Triangulation is a concept which enhances the explanatory power of concepts by seeking multiple sources of support for any interpretation. An interpretation is bolstered if there is evidence from differing sources supporting it. A focus group discussion involving participants from a women's psychosocial project may identify the development of trust within the group as key to its effectiveness. The importance of trust will be supported if individual women, in open-ended interviews, are proactive in citing examples of this. Tangible evidence of the gains achieved by a group achieving high levels of trust compared with another group known to be riven by disputes would be a further source of confirmatory information.

Comprehensiveness is a concept which drives analysis toward the holistic goal of qualitative work. With focus group discussion, open-ended interview, and observation—the principal methodological tools of the qualitative approach—the data that is obtained is generally detailed and voluminous. The capacity of an analytical structure to take into account the broadest range of statements and observations is a measure of its comprehensiveness. The goal of qualitative work is not an analysis of the "typical" situation, which allows for the neglect of a few atypical responses from "outliers." *Negative case analysis* forces adjustment of initial concepts and understandings such that observations from all sources of data are accommodated by the explanatory account. The goal is to map the dimensions of potential response to, in this instance, the experience of war, conflict, and forced migration. In mapping the conceptual space in which people respond to such challenges, the comprehensiveness and inclusivity of such an analysis is crucial to its utility.

Finally, *transferability* has been argued to be a key concept in determining the utility of a qualitative analysis. With intensive data collection with relatively small samples, the qualitative researcher seldom has grounds to generalize findings to other settings on the grounds of clear representativeness. Insightful conceptual analysis, however, may be valuably transferred to facilitate consideration of other settings. Thus the observed pattern of behavioral response to war experiences in Rwanda may be ungeneralizable to populations in Afghanistan, but the conceptual framework accounting for such patterns of response may be usefully transferred.

Illustrative Studies

While critiques of quantitative approaches to analyses of psychosocial interventions are common, examples of substantive, rigorous work of a qualitative nature are, as yet, infrequent. Boyden and Gibbs' (1996) analysis of psychosocial distress in Cambodia notes the dangers of positivistic assumptions shaping accounts of well-being of those in non-Western cultures, and adopts a broad qualitative approach in drawing together data from over three hundred participants (villagers, teachers, government officials, etc.). Such work is within a social anthropological or ethnographic tradition, though it is based upon a considerably shorter period of study (six weeks) than is typical of such an approach.

The concepts addressing issues of vulnerability and resilience of this Cambodian population are clearly grounded in the words and experience of studied participants. Triangulation from differing data sources supports interpretation. Constraints on the depth of analysis, however, have limited the comprehensiveness of accounts of their perceptions and responses. While the study provides valuable insights into factors influencing psychosocial impact, it does not provide a level of conceptual coherence providing a potentially transferable analysis of responses to war and displacement.

Such coherence is achieved in Agger's (1994) analysis of forty narratives of refugee women from the Middle East and Latin America as, in the author's words, the different stories become "a single testimony to one sex's painful struggle." The conceptual framework of the analysis clearly reflects the understandings of the women interviewed, though it may be considered to feature implicit psychological theorization rather than fully grounded analysis (a criticism of such work in general by Summerfield, 1995). The therapeutic context of the interviews also prevented any form of triangulation of data from external sources.

Multimethod Approaches

While for some the epistemological basis of quantitative and qualitative research renders the study that combines features of both unacceptable, there are strong grounds for asserting the value of such an approach. In methodological terms, combining the hypothesis-generating function of qualitative work with the hypothesis-testing function of quantitative work has clear attractions. Alternatively, qualitative approaches may facilitate a deeper analysis of a phenomenon identified by quantitative study.

In the psychosocial field there is another, more pragmatic, justification for an approach which incorporates elements of the two approaches. In the competition for scarce funding, psychosocial programs need to justify themselves in clear terms—and for many agencies this will mean some form of quantitative analysis. Qualitative data—particularly in the form of case studies or narrative comments of program beneficiaries—can powerfully illustrate the points less eloquently made by statistical analysis.

Ager, Ager, and Long (1995) describe a study of the impact of displacement on refugee women in Malawi which illustrates this approach. Core social and activity data were collected from over four hundred households. Every seventh household within administrative blocks was interviewed, having been selected at random within the settlements. Settlements, in turn, were selected to represent the range of settlement patterns prevailing in refugee impacted areas. Both the trustworthiness and representativeness of findings were supported by these sampling procedures. Reviewing all procedures upon completion of questionnaires supported the validity and reliability of findings. The quantitative picture provided was supplemented by in-depth interviews of a focal sample of twenty refugees, selected to match the age and income profile of the full sample. In-depth interviews and participant observation over a full-day period provided means of both triangulation and elaboration of findings from the main survey. Qualitative analysis was, in this example, not pursued to the point of comprehensiveness. Emergent concepts from open-ended interviews were, however, used as a basis to structure and "ground" a subsequent quantitative analysis of quality of life across the studies camps (Ager, 1992; see Figure 2.1).

The use of qualitative interviews to "ground" concepts that are subsequently examined in a more quantitative manner is one of the most fruitful combinations of the two approaches. In a study of coping strategies adopted by Mozambican refugees, Ager (1993) elicited narrative descriptions of responses to a range of events. While subsequent analysis grouped coping responses in a manner that facilitated quantitative analysis of the prevalence of problem or emotion-focused coping, such categorizations were grounded in the accounts of refugees rather than imposed by some external theoretical structure.

Figure 2.1 Quality of Life Assessment Derived from Prior Qualitative Interviews*

Quality of Life Profile

Setting:
Details

	Generally unmet	Inadequately met	Generally met
PHYSIOLOGICAL NEEDS			
Adequate quantity of food			
Variety of food			
Close access to water/ fuelwood supplies			
Prompt access to health facilities			
SAFETY NEEDS			
Safety from assault, abduction, etc.			
Security of property and possessions			
Adequate clothing			
Adequate shelter (regarding rain, cold, etc.)			
BELONGING NEEDS			
Living with intact family			
Proximity of other kin			
Experience of friendship			
Absence of partiality/ discrimination			
ESTEEM NEEDS			
Personal source of income			
Involvement in productive activity			
Access to education or training			
Ownership of non-essential household assets			
TRANSCENDENCE NEEDS			
Affinity with home and/or land			
Sense of personal freedom			
Awareness of divine providence/ blessing			
Confidence in future			

*This figure is based on the work of Ager (1992).

Program evaluation can benefit from drawing upon the principles of both quantitative and qualitative research methodology. The core question addressed by an evaluation must be "have the goals of the program been achieved?" Drawing upon previous sections, Figure 2.2 tabulates the issues that may be considered in useful in addressing this question.

Figure 2.2   A Checklist for Program Evaluation

GOALS

> What are the explicit goals of the project?
> What are the targeted outcome variables?
> What is the targeted population (i.e. who are intended beneficiaries)?

MEASUREMENT

> What are the most appropriate measures for operationalizing targeted
>   outcome variables?
> What evidence exists–or could be gathered–to support the reliability of
>   these measures?
> What evidence exists–or could be gathered–to support the validity of
>   these measures?
> To what extent are chosen measures likely to be sensitive to the degree of
>   change targeted by the project?
> What can been done to minimize (social, cultural, or other) bias in the
>   chosen measures?
> To what extent are the outcome variables considered grounded in the
>   experience of potential beneficiaries and/or having clear respondent
>   validity?

INTERPRETATION

> What means can be adopted for selection of participants in the evaluation
>   to maximize the trustworthiness of findings with respect to the full
>   targeted population?
> What comparisons are available to allow outcomes be meaningfully
>   related to program activity (e.g., pre- to postscores, outcomes for non-
>   program participants, etc.)?
> What bases are there for triangulating findings with other sources of data?
> Does the analysis provide a comprehensive account of the experience of
>   participants in the program?
> To what extent are participants representative of other groups/situations
>   of potential interest?
> Is theoretical analysis potentially transferable to other settings?

References

Ager, A. (1992). *The quality of life of Mozambican refugees in Malawi.* Report to the WHO Division of Mental Health. Zomba: University of Malawi.

Ager, A. (1993). *Coping strategies in Mozambican refugees.* Paper presented to the 3rd European Congress of Psychology, Tampere, Finland, July 1993.

Ager, A. (1994). *Mental health issues in refugee populations: a review.* Working Paper of the Harvard Center for the Study of Culture and Medicine. Harvard Medical School, Department of Social Medicine.

Ager, A. (1997). Tensions in the psychosocial discourse: implications for the planning of interventions with war-affected populations. *Development in Practice,* 7:4:402-407.

Ager, A., Ager, W. and Long, L. (1995). The differential experience of Mozambican refugee women and men. *Journal of Refugee Studies,* 8:3:1- 23.

Agger, I. (1994). *The blue room: Trauma and testimony among refugee women – A psychosocial exploration.* London: Zed Books.

Agger, I. (1995). *Theory and practice of psycho-social projects under war conditions in Bosnia-Herzegovina and Croatia.* Brussels: ECHO.

Agger, I. and Mimica, J. (1996). *Psycho-social assistance to victims of war in Bosnia-Herzegovina and Croatia: An Evaluation.* Brussels: ECHO.

Boyden, J. and Gibbs, S. (1996). *Vulnerability and resilience: perceptions and responses to psycho-social distress in Cambodia.* Oxford: INTRAC.

Bryman, A. (1992). *Quantity and quality in social research.* London: Routledge.

Gibbs, S. (1994). Post-war social reconstruction in Mozambique: Re-framing children's experience of trauma and healing. *Disasters,* 18:3:268-276.

Hudelson, P. M. (1994). *Qualitative research for health programs.* Geneva: WHO.

Mollica, R., Caspi-Yavin, Y., Bollini, P., Truong, T., Tor, S., and Lavelle, J. (1992). The Harvard Trauma Questionnaire: Validating a cross-cultural instrument for measuring torture, trauma and post-traumatic stress disorder in Indochinese refugees. *The Journal of Nervous and Mental Disease,* 180; 111-116.

Muecke, M.. (1992). New paradigms for refugee mental health problems. *Social Science and Medicine,* 35:515-523.

Punamäki, R.-L. (1990). Relationships between political violence and psychological responses among Palestinian women. *Journal of Peace Research,* 27:75-85.

Punamäki, R.-L. (1996). Can ideological commitment protect children's psychosocial well-being in situations of political violence? *Child Development,* 67:55-69.

Silverman, D. (1993). *Interpreting qualitative data: Methods for analysing talk, text and interaction.* London: Sage.

Straus, A. (1987). *Qualitative analysis for social scientists.* Cambridge: CUP.

Summerfield, D. (1995). Assisting survivors of war and atrocity: notes on "psychosocial" issues for NGO workers. *Development in Practice,* 5:352- 356.

Tolfree, D. (1995). *Restoring playfulness: Different approaches to assisting children who are psychologically affected by war or displacement.* Sweden: Swedish Save the Children.

Part II

CASE STUDIES OF
REFUGEE PSYCHOSOCIAL WELLNESS
Qualitative Approaches

In this part, we turn our attention to the key dimensions of qualitative research of refugee psychosocial wellness, which aims at exploring the world from the perspective of the person studied, "the insider's view." Qualitative investigations are inherently different from quantitative studies: different assumptions, different processes to construct and establish "the truth," and different ways to categorize information and make conclusions. The role of the qualitative researcher, as we will see from the following chapters, is to become immersed into a community in order to discover its values, norms, standards, rituals, relationships, and interactions, and ultimately the meanings of these.

In chapter 3, Patricia Omidian writes of her experiences as an anthropologist studying the lives and adjustment of Afghan refugees who resettled in the United States, offering a first-hand account of how she planned her research, approached the subjects of her study, and crafted and used the findings on behalf of her client group. She carefully defines the meaning of qualitative investigation, citing the issues of sampling, reliability, and validity. The array of methods that she employed in her work consisted of participant observation, questionnaires, life histories and case studies, and various types of group interviews, each centered in examples of her actual work with resettled Afghans. What one does with the data once it is collected is addressed, as are the personal issues that researchers discover when working with individuals and families who have experienced great loss.

In the next chapter, another anthropologist, Marita Eastmond, takes us by the hand through the qualitative research process, describing how she studied refugees from Chile, Bosnia, and Guatemala. As a medical anthropologist, her main concern has been the exploration of suffering and illness through an ethnographic perspective. In this approach, she locates the health and illness of refugees in the context of their local social worlds in an effort to investigate ways in which people, as part of their society and culture, interpret their experiences. Three examples of her work illustrate her assumptions, methods, and findings in assessing the psychosocial well-being of these refugee groups.

Also in this section, the reader will find an example of qualitative research that deals with Cambodians and Vietnamese in a refugee camp in Thailand. Didier Bertrand in chapter 5 presents the use of autobiography as an approach in investigating psychosocial well-being of refugees and demonstrates how the autobiographical interview touches the complexities of the refugee's life, his/her actions, and the meaning of these behaviors and the environment in which they take place. Empathy, neutrality, management of emotions, and their implications are essential parts of this process. Finally, Bertrand reviews the strategies that he has employed in his work to analyze biographical material and arrive at conclusions.

These three chapters, then, cover a range of approaches to qualitative studies in which the authors specify their assumptions, illustrate the techniques they used in the research process, and discuss the strategies they employed to collate, understand, and present their findings.

3

Qualitative Measures and Refugee Research

THE CASE OF AFGHAN REFUGEES

Patricia A. Omidian

There has been much debate, both in the literature and in the classroom, about the merits of quantitative versus qualitative research. Qualitative research methods are usually seen in opposition to or even as less rigorous than quantitative research, but the best research includes both. The hallmark of qualitative research is not the use of a single method for data collection and analysis, but the researcher's use of multiple methods of gathering data and on-going analysis. This process uncovers a different type of data from that of strictly statistical methodologies, which focus on broader, less contextual issues. The purpose of this chapter is to explore the range of qualitative methodological approaches in assessing refugee wellness with consideration of sample size, reliability, and validity in the process of data collection, and then to discuss methods of data analysis.

Qualitative Research

Qualitative research methods, including ethnographic research techniques such as observation, interviewing, and the use of open questions, are particularly suited to refugee research and draw from such fields as anthropology/ethnology and sociology. Although many disciplines use these techniques to gather data, most do so within a research context where qualitative data is used to generate larger studies which will use quantitative data-gathering techniques. In many of these studies there is an implicit assumption that qualitative research is the opposite of quantitative research, less reliable, and has few or no validity checks. In the realm of scientific knowledge, or rather the realm of "how do we know that what we know is the "truth," anthropological knowledge is seen as somehow less dependable and, therefore, less likely to be true. More "rigorous" methodologies are used to validate and verify the qualitative findings (Carlson et al., 1996; Collier, 1995).

In fact, quantitative research is no more truthful, valid or rigorous than ethnographic research. But, there are distinct value differences between quantitative and qualitative research that are embedded in the nature of the paradigmatic assumptions upon which data collection is based. The premise on which qualitative research is based is the value of the insiders' view: to understand their world from their perspective, rather than categorizing their experiences out of context or from the outsiders' view (Agar, 1986; Bernard, 1988; Spradley, 1979). Ethnographic research has three advantages: 1) it views behavior in its own setting; 2) it gains understanding from the native's point of view; and 3) it provides the researcher the flexibility and ability/opportunity to change the research design to fit new data. This "allows the researcher to be surprised" (Chadwick, 1984:211-12). The goal and value of this research is to get at "the 'meanings' people attach to their experiences", and note the discrepancies and interactions of people (Chadwick, 1984:222).

As anthropologist Michael Agar noted, "Without science, we lose our credibility. Without humanity, we lose our ability to understand others" (1980:13). Refugees, by definition, are people who have been forced to flee their homes to save themselves and their families, living outside of their home countries. In the field of refugee research, we cannot afford to lose our humanity, and the data we gather must be credible, since the people with whom we work are often so incredibly at risk.

My work with the Afghan refugee community in California began in 1985. Because of my long-term contacts in the community, close friends and adopted family members, my research has never stopped. But neither have the community's needs. Over the last eleven years, I have participated in or headed a number of formal research projects, including early Health Opinion Surveys, my dissertation research (Omidian, 1996a), the Afghan Health Education Project (Lipson et al., 1995), and my current interest in Afghan gang affiliation and youth adjustment issues. Two projects combined qualitative and quantitative research, while the other two relied on qualitative data. These projects will be used to illustrate methodological concerns.

Sample Size

Ethnographic research is not as dependent on sample size as other kinds of research are but, as Bernard notes, "samples are used to estimate true values" (1988:79) and one must sample broadly enough to understand community variability (Collier, 1996; Miles and Huber man, 1994). But, how does one know what is enough? The overriding premise of this research model is that members of a community understand "meanings of expressive behavior or simply how things work" (Bernard, 1988:80). The ethnologist assesses this by using several data-gathering techniques (called triangulation), as will be discussed below.

Truly random sampling in refugee communities nearly impossible, even in fairly bounded territories of refugee camps and villages. In countries where refugees are resettled, populations tend to be more scattered and formal sampling methods are unworkable. For instance in the U.S., census figures do breakdown numbers by "ethnicity" but those categories are politically determined and respondents may opt for one of several categories. Afghans may record their ethnicity as Asian (being from the Asian continent but not realizing that this term in the United States stands for East Asians), White (a category to which they are legally entitled as "Indo-Europeans"), or Other (a catch-all category that means "none of the above"). Descendants of immigrants and refugees, often called the second generation, are usually more politically aware of the ramifications of these categories and tend to manipulate the categories to their advantage. In addition, many refugees are reluctant to even respond to census questionnaires owing to a distrust for authority and the purposes of government record. This leads to estimates of community size like that of the Afghan population in the San Francisco area, where reported numbers range from 5,000-50,000. Without a clear sense of population size and distribution, random sampling is difficult at best.

Reliability

Reliability, an issue for the quantitative researcher, also concerns researchers such as myself. Yet, small sample size in phenomenological research does not invalidate the results. Again, because we look at internally constructed meanings through observation and interaction, reliability of the data is enhanced through the methods used. The issue of selection bias is not the problem that quantitative researchers think it is (Collier, 1995:461-67). "In surveys ... good questions are reliable, providing consistent measures in comparable situations" (Fowler, 1984:74).

In my research, an example of unreliable and invalid questions came in the Afghan Health Education Project (AHEM) health survey of 196 community members. The AHEM illustrates how the sample size and reliability of a refugee community study can be cross-checked. In a survey of 196 families a convenience, or snowball, sample was used. The means and frequencies of such variables as education, age, time in the U.S., and household size were calculated three times during data collection and found to be nearly the same. This suggested that, except for geographic location and gender, the interview sample was probably representative and the data reliable.

Validity

The term validity does not mean that there is some kind of "truth" to compare your results to, but it means the credibility of the description and conclusions (Maxwell, 1996:87). An internally valid small sample can be better than a survey of a whole population, partly due to history threat (Bernard, 1988:79-81). Validity means cross-checking data results for internal consistency to ensure that the answers one receives actually relate to the research question. It is not uncommon for surveys to be analyzed in terms of what the researcher thinks the answer means, not by what the answer really means to those being questioned (Fowler, 1984:75; Maxwell, 1996).

In spite of rigorous cross-checks and the development of the survey through consensus with the AHEM Steering Committee, one question in the AHEM health survey escaped review and revision. Respondents were asked to scale their "satisfaction" with life in the U.S. Such questions about life satisfaction are commonly asked in surveys assessing psychosocial health. The Afghans interviewed stated that they are either mostly satisfied (32 percent) or partly satisfied (49 percent) with life in the United States, even though all other data-collection methods noted high levels of discomfort and dissatisfaction, including depression due to the loss of social roles, or the disruption of family roles and statuses. When the results of quantitative data analysis came in, the Steering Committee returned to the original questionnaire and compared the results of the level of satisfaction to the number and kinds of difficulties identified. They decided that the word "satisfaction" does not translate well into a meaningful Afghan cultural category and that the word "acceptance" should have been used in this question instead. In Afghan culture, based on Islamic traditions, it would have been inappropriate to be too dissatisfied with life in the United States, after all, they are alive "Thanks to God."

Because these studies are attempting to grasp the insiders' view and/or meaning during the data gathering process, it is important to validate one's understanding of cultural patterns and issues by continually communicating with key informants. By taking a observational stance, in contrast to that of interviewer, one quickly sees common themes which resonate and have meaning to a community, but which change focus as one stays in the community and learns cultural patterns at successively deeper levels. The research question guides the choice of method, which in turn directs the sample size. In a community, such as the Afghan refugee community with its distrust of outsiders, it is more important to gain the trust and openness of a few reliable informants than to interview many people, and often receive incorrect answers.

Methodology: Data Collection

The objective of qualitative research is to describe "social realities from the perspective of the subject, not the observers" (Chadwick, 1984:207). The research strategies, therefore, will be different from those of quantitative methods. Anthropologists and others have relied heavily on participant observation, life-history and case-study construction, unstructured or open-ended interviewing with questionnaires, and other methods that fit the situation (Denain, 1982:18; Estroff, 1981:20). This flexibility of methods reflects the open nature of the approach.

Qualitative methods, and ethnographic field techniques, are based on the need to ask different questions from that of quantitative research. Instead of asking "how many" or "range of variation" regarding a particular pattern, disease, or problem, one asks "what kind of ..." and "what is the meaning of ..." questions. For a researcher working with a refugee population, both kinds of questions must be asked. In trying to understand mental health issues and the processes of coping and accommodation that occur in refugee communities, questions of meaning clarify the community's own notions of this process.

Approaches for Data Collection

There are a number of methods of collecting data while doing qualitative work. These are discussed below.

Participant Observation

Participant observation is the key to ethnographic research and simply involves spending enough time with a community to see what they routinely do and how they routinely interact. The participant observation process is one of social negotiation. Its purposes include 1) understanding meaning, 2) understanding context, 3) identifying unanticipated phenomena, 4) understanding the process by which events take place, and 5) developing explanations of causes (Maxwell, 1996:17-21). One does this by "hanging out" in the community one is researching. One spends a great deal of time viewing very little of interest, followed by moments of intense activity that can be overwhelming. Participant observation affords the researcher an understanding of the culture so that moments of activity can be more fully understood. According to Miles and Huberman (1994:6) participant observation is "conducted through an intense and/or prolonged contact with a 'field' or life situation" and these "situations are typically 'banal' or normal ones...." The difficulty in refugee research is that many of our subject are, in fact, living in "abnormal" situations and often speak of their losses and the sense of disorientation they feel. In the process of living in such a community, one tries to understand what is normal, yet in refugee research one is often told by community members that their lives are not normal. A common phrase I hear is "we do this here, but in Afghanistan it was different."

One of the major problems with participant observation comes from the researchers' propensity to record everything possible, creating mountains of data that is not pertinent to the research at hand. In fact, this very overload of data maybe useful in the end. I am constantly referring back to notes I gathered but did not use for my dissertation. These are invaluable to me since they illustrate changes in the Afghan community over time.

For instance, in 1985 at a local wedding, women sat on one side of the room away from the men. They did not dance or interact with the men. The people present were struggling to put on this wedding with very few resources at their disposal. Women in the community contributed to the event by cooking and bringing large quantities of food. The music was a combination of Pakistani and Afghan and was played by amateurs. The clothing styles of many of the women reflected the transition between home and the new country, with few signs of wealth. The wedding ceremony was completely "Afghan," and more traditional than many of the weddings held in Kabul before the war.

Ten years later the weddings became catered events that require a great deal of money, often borrowed from extended family members or saved over the course of several years by the bride and groom. Marriages are still often arranged, but the ceremonies contain elements of American influence intertwined with the Afghan traditions. Families sit together and listen to live Afghan music that is played by professionals; husbands dance with wives; and the unmarried boys and girls dance the night away. The bride wears a white bridal gown, and the couple usually dances together at least once.

In my most recent study, I relied heavily on old notes. In 1985 Afghans were new to the community. Youth were struggling to learn English and to fit into American society. There was little note of interethnic violence. In 1991, I observed that young males were starting to counter existing gangs for the purposes of protection, but they were still seen by local police as nonviolent and cooperative. By 1995, this had completely changed and the local authorities were trying to prevent violent conflicts between Afghan youth gangs and between Afghan gangs and other ethnic gangs. These changes are reflected in my field notes and show the value of meticulous note taking over the years. Participant observation gives the researcher some understanding of the insiders' view so that other kinds of research methods can be meaningfully used. Without the insiders' view one might impose inappropriate research strategies or questionnaires that ask questions based on erroneous assumptions. For example, Afghans are more open to questionnaires that ask open-ended questions and allow for lengthy explanations, and indirect questions work much better than direct questions.

In the process of participant observation, one ultimately is working with individuals. Refugee research presents special difficulties for the researcher because of the trauma and losses that refugees have faced. We are interviewing and working with people who may have been tortured or had family members tortured; who have lost many family members, some of whom disappeared in the night, never to be seen again; whose struggle to escape the political dangers of the city placed them in physical danger from planes strafing the escape route, or robbers, thieves, and rapists attacking their group. Within the Afghan community where I did my work, everyone I interviewed had some emotional or physical scars. The interviewing anthropologist may be the closest many of these people come to therapy (yet we are untrained and unskilled for the task). Almost everyone who agreed to be interviewed during the course of my research answered my questions in an open manner. At the end of the interview, many thanked me for just listening to their stories and being sympathetic to their situation (Omidian, 1996b).

As one proceeds in qualitative work, one needs to consider a range of techniques. In the course of my research my interpreter, Mrs. Hamid, and I reached a point when observation and recording were not enough. We felt that we had to act. But community action and volunteerism were not culturally valued by Mrs. Hamid, and she struggled with the transition to activism. In the beginning of the research with elderly, isolated, and depressed women, she often commented that the families of these women should do something. After many interviews conducted through a veil of tears, though, she was transformed into a community activist. She now manages an elderly women's program, sponsored by the Afghan Women's Association International of which she is a part that has over 150 women enrolled. These women attend monthly gatherings, picnics or religious events, and ESL (English as a Second Language) classes. The purpose of the project, as stated by Mrs. Hamid, is to reduce their isolation and depression. One-on-one interviewing within the context of participant observation is always an open dialogue. For refugees, the link with a researcher can have far-reaching effects (Omidian, 1996b). Community action can come from the changing perspective one gains when working with and living in a community. As one sees their needs and begins to understand the cultural dimensions of possible solutions, action becomes part of the research process.

Structured Questions

Structured questions are the standard survey questions that limit the options a respondent has when answering questions and can be easily ticked off on an answer sheet. After awhile when working with the community, more formal interviewing styles may be called for, including structured and semi-structured questions, and collecting life histories and case studies. This is still an individualized process since survey is also an interaction between researcher and respondent (Fowler, 1984:76). These questions may be formalized into a questionnaire or based on the events of the moment. Regardless of style, the purpose is to elicit specific kinds of data on particular topics. This means that assumptions about the context of the situation have already been made. But, at another level, these kinds of questions help verify and validate observations across a range of situations or people.

With the possible exception of epidemiological studies, structured questionnaires should not stand alone as the only data collected (Miles and Huberman, 1994; Scrimshaw and Hurtado, 1987). Even years in the field with the same population cannot prevent one from asking the wrong questions though without the participant observation experience, one may not understand the meaning of the data collected. One of my favorite stories comes from a study that was conducted in conjunction with the Afghan Health Education Project's Health Fair. A student from a local college, who also was a dental hygienist, wanted to quantify Afghan dental hygiene practices. To do this she developed a questionnaire and had Afghan assistants administer the survey during the Fair.

Positive responses were very high on two questions in particular. One was how often people brush their teeth and the other was to determine if they flossed their teeth. These questions are important since most Afghans in the area where this study took place utilize social service programs and have their health-care needs paid for by the state through the Medicare system. Dental care is very hard to get and most refugees have only minimal access to a dentist. At the same time, it quickly becomes obvious that many are in need of dental care, as adults have "long teeth" from receding gum lines and missing or broken teeth. Yet, to our surprise almost everyone answered that they brush their teeth after every meal and frequently floss. The student was thrilled that the community has rapidly learned "proper" dental care habits, but was suspicious.

A few months later, I had the opportunity to stay with a family for extended periods of time and realized that the questions asked were not the questions being answered. In Islamic tradition, most people will rinse their mouths after each meal, rubbing the right index finger over the teeth. This is the process of "brushing" that many had described. I did not see dental floss used unless a person was trying to remove food particles from around the teeth and if floss is not available a strand of a woman's long hair will do the trick. This illustrates Fowler's point: "good questions are reliable, providing consistent measures of compatible situations, and valid: answers correspond to what they are intended to measure" (1984:74). Participation observation allows one to know if and when the question is being answered and what that answer means.

Semi-structured Questions

Fowler (1984:87) also describes the use of open ended, semi-structured questions as allowing the researcher to obtain unanticipated answers and describe more closely the views of the respondent. Semi-structured, open questions are more general than structured questions and allow the interviewee to answer in their own style and with their own words. This kind of question is difficult to quantify and is often avoided for this reason, but in refugee research on psychosocial health, it is irreplaceable. In 1991, I was trying to understand accommodation processes and the mental health impact on individuals and families. Knowing that polygyny existed in Afghanistan I wanted to know how United States policy affected families and what kinds of disruptions occurred.

One of the problems I came across was how to ask people if they are part of polygynous families. In an early questionnaire I originally asked "how many wives or co-wives were in the family. I always got the same answer: one. This occurred even when I talked to people that I knew were in polygynous marriages, because they all knew that polygamy in the United States is illegal. I changed the question and asked how many mothers a person has or had and got important information. Almost 65 percent of the people I interviewed reported more than one mother. The question did not have the political ramifications of the former question and recognized an important aspect of Afghan culture. In addition, I learned that people who saw themselves as part of a close family would be denied family reunification status if they admitted to having a polygynous family. This was particularly true for elderly widows. Some families had to leave members behind or decide not to emigrate. Other families coped with the situation by bringing one wife as a "wife" and the other wife as a "sister" or "cousin."

Life Histories

Trying to understand the psychosocial status of a refugee requires an understanding of what has happened and what has been left behind. A life history is similar to a biography in that it contains the story of a person's life, but is used to understand cultural events and, particularly, culture change and the context of individual adaptation. Life histories provide a rich context through which the refugee process can be described. Mandlebaum, in his life history of Mahatma Gandhi, notes that adaptation is important to understand as it is "… a built-in process, [and] because every person must, in the course of his life, alter some of his established patterns of behavior to cope with new conditions. Each person changes his ways in order to maintain continuity, whether of group participation or social expectation or self-image or simply survival" (1973:181). His use of the life history approach to understand the process of adaptation lets one see the individual in the context of historic events and interpersonal interactions.

Case Studies

More common than life histories, due to their length, are case studies. The case-studies approach is a useful tool for analyzing qualitative information. Case studies, like life histories, illustrate the rapid changes in social identity and role shifts that refugees undergo from a personal perspective and with contextual information, but are shorter. Adaptation, accommodation, and the adjustments individuals and families make to war, flight, and resettlement can also be viewed through the case study. These events impact the refugee's ability to cope with their new setting and are, therefore, important (Omidian, 1996a).

Case studies are not exclusively narrative nor contextually pure. Elements may be added or deleted to protect the people being described. In addition, the interviewee may be unwilling to disclose some kinds of information for a variety of reasons, making them reconstructions of selected, recalled events as told to an researcher, who records the interview. The case studies are, therefore, reconstructions of observations, conversations, and activities of others, interpreted through a lens of time and space (Omidian, 1996a).

Groups

Within qualitative research methods are a number of possibilities for data collection among groups of varying sizes. Group settings can be advantageous due to their dynamic nature. Each group will have a particular flavor that can be used to the data collector's advantage. In field research with refugees, three processes are very helpful in data gathering: discussion groups, focus groups, and town meetings. They vary in formality and levels of structure, but their importance should not be overlooked.

A. Discussion Groups

Discussion groups offer a wonderful opportunity for the researcher to get a sense of the range of "acceptable" opinions. In my research, I have found them to be the most natural of the data collection situations and often the most fruitful. They can be a place for primary community consultants to analyze their own culture, as well as issues of accommodation and adjustment. Discussion groups are not random conversations, but topic-based and the interviewer maintains some control over what is discussed. I use an interview sheet with a series of topics which I hope to cover and never use a tape recorder unless all participants agree.

Researchers are often trained to carry out one-on-one, uninterrupted interviews, and the field of mental health (with its possibilities of stigma and disclosure issues) seems the most appropriate place for adhering to this standard. Although this may seem ideal, for many cultural groups, it will rarely happen. At the beginning of my research, I had at least three people present at every interview: the person being interviewed, the interpreter, and myself. But, in fact, it was rarely just the three of us. Almost every interview, even when I was able to conduct my own in Dari or German, had family members who would come into the discussion and put in their opinion, correct a statement that the principal interviewee had made or take over if the interviewee had to leave the room for a moment. Most were curious about me, what I wanted to know, and why I wanted to know it. They were also worried that wrong information or impressions might be given. Even with these restraints on each other, discussions would often be lively.

After initially struggling against this routine, I gave in to what I realized was a cultural style based on family collectivity. Afghans do not see themselves as individuals, but as part of a family. It would be rare for them to invite someone into their home and exclude others in the family from joining in. Each member of the family had the right to be part of the discussion and curiosity usually insured their presence. I found in the end that family discussion groups acted as the family relaxed with me to facilitate memory recall. It also provided an opportunity for "asides." For example, after statements were made and someone left the room, another person might interject a correction or clarification. Allowing for others to be present, in the end, relaxes the person being interviewed. And it is when the person is relaxed that the best data is gathered. My colleague, Juliene Lipson, in her research with Middle Eastern groups, found that the real data comes not from the formal interview protocol, but from other points in the encounter, such as the initial warm up period before the interview and the close of discussion as one is leaving. In between these times, discussions that arise from an interview question can act as a catalyst for deeper description and understanding of psychosocial issues for the community (Lipson, 1991; Lipson and Meleis, 1989; Omidian, 1996a).

The problem with discussion groups is that it is difficult to control where the conversation will go and one may not return to the presented topic without reasserting a formal structure. Yet, this is offset by the greater likelihood of being accepted by the family, which leads to trust and greater depth of discussion in the future. For people who are group or collectivist focused, imposition of an individualistic model of privacy and personal interviewing may not let them be comfortable enough to make up for loss of the chance to hear "secrets." At the same time, the interviewer must be ready to move the conversation forward. In formal discussion groups, this is common but for the informal, relaxed, and impromptu group discussions that arise in the course of other interviewing systems such control can be an imposition. Taping such events is also difficult, depending on the population. I found that when the recorder was turned on before the discussion, it was not a problem and most forgot about it, but if I tried to introduce it in the midst of an interview, the disruption was overwhelming.

B. Focus Groups

Focus groups are stylistically more formal than discussion groups, but the dynamics are the same. For a successful session, participants need to have common interests and be a fairly homogenous group. This method of data collection came from marketing studies but is very effective in data collection on specific topics, such as community health-care needs or problems. Unlike discussion groups, the efforts are directed toward specific outcomes in a controlled setting. In a focus group one strives for total participation with no one person dominating the group. When a group comes together for the purpose of a focus group it is best to have a trained facilitator lead the group and to help maintain concentration on the topic at hand (Morgan, 1988). Focus groups, as a data collection method, work best when used in conjunction with other forms of qualitative research.

Focus groups work well within the context of a participant observation study. They offer an "opportunity to observe a large amount of interaction on a topic in a limited period of time. The key to this ability is the observer's control over the assembly...." (Morgan, 1988: 15). Because of the setting, these gathering are "un-natural" and may seem to be the antithesis of interactive research. They are only workable when there is community participation and an understanding of cultural constructs.

The Afghan Health Education Project used focus groups in a number of settings. In the steering committee's development of a working mission statement, the focus group model was used to begin the process of constructing a goal that every member of the committee would support. During data collection on pressing community health problems, focus groups were used in small settings that concentrated on women's health needs. In the process of give and take in the dialogue, relatively spontaneous remarks are made (Morgan, 1988). These remarks lead to new ideas and new possibilities of exploration and analysis by the participants.

C. Town Meetings

The largest and potentially the most out of control setting for data collection in a group setting is the "town meeting." This forum is designed to allow for community involvement in the development of programs to meet their own needs, as they perceive them. They are information gathering sessions on a large scale. The process, like that of a focus group, is to used to gather qualitative data about individuals' perspectives, including opinions, feelings, and meanings of phenomena, in a setting where a each person can be motivated by the ideas and contributions of others. And like the focus group, participants in a town meeting should be from a common ethnic group or community.

The Afghan Health Education Project conducted several town meetings with varying results. Our purpose was to gather information on the community health needs in order to develop health education programs that would be useful and of interest to the recipients. In program development and community empowerment models, town meetings can work to enhance a community's sense of ownership in the project. On the down side, many can come out of this kind of meeting feeling that promises are being made but no real solutions are offered.

AHEM had both types of reactions occur and sometimes at the same meeting. For instance, at one town meeting a man was so enthusiastic and motivated that he went to the library to learn more about self-care models hat would help his family's psychosocial well-being. At the same meeting a man from another organization stood up, took the floor, and berated us for not including his organization and for promising things that we were not intending to deliver. At yet another meeting an elderly woman stood up and told us that we could talk about health and illness prevention programs all we want, but as soon as she receives news from Afghanistan, her blood-pressure will go up, again.

Triangulation

In the process of qualitative data collection, it is important to use multiple methods in order to cross-check the results—a process called triangulation (Maxwell, 1996). Participant observation, an excellent field method, cannot stand alone. The more methods used in data collection, both formal and informal, the better the data. In addition, the process of triangulation allows the researcher to be alert to sudden surprises or experiences. In the early stages of my research, I was told by almost every informant that Afghans stopped having plural marriages several generations ago. One of the signs that you are on the right track is when you keep getting the same answer in each interview. Without the process of triangulation and cross-checking data, I could have assumed, because of consistency, that this was true. The discrepancy was not in the answers from the questionnaire, but from what I learned hanging out in the community. I knew several women who were still co-wives, and the youngest was twenty-two. I also knew that several families had been separated from traditional support systems because the United States did not recognize step-mothers as relatives if the "real" mother was still alive. Because of this one man had to stay behind in Pakistan when his wife and children left for the United States. He could have brought his mother to the U.S. with him and the rest of his "family," but he could not bring his "other mother."

What, then, was the meaning of the answers I got from direct questions? I learned several things. First, Afghans often give evasive answers to direct questions, not in an effort to lie, but in order to assess the meaning behind the question, particularly with regard to the question of polygynous marriages. They are in the United States because they sought refuge from a country where everything you said could be taken out of context and turned against you. Second, many did not trust me enough to say the "truth," while others, such as a primary informant and friend, in this case thought that few Afghans had polygynous marriages. Finally, others, mindful of American sentiments regarding plural marriages, said what they thought I wanted to hear. All said the same thing—no polygyny. It became clear, however, through multiple methods of data collection, and a shift in how I asked the question based on the cultural knowledge I had gained, how United States policy had impacted on refugee families and their well-being. After losing their country, they had to lie about their family structure (some becoming ashamed of it as it is not Western) or miss an opportunity to emigrate.

Problems

Qualitative ethnographic research, has a number of methodological and ethical problems that must be addressed by the researcher at the onset. These include: 1) violation of rights of human subjects; 2) legal, moral, and injury risks to researcher; 3) undirected data collection that can lead to unusable data because it is too diverse; 4) the loss of detachment on part of researcher; and 5) problems of reliability and replicability (Chadwick, 1984:212-15). Many of these methodological problems have already been addressed; therefore, I will focus here on problems of safety and ethics.

In part because of a series of studies carried out, primarily in medical settings, the human rights protection for all research subjects was enacted. Most universities today have committees to review research proposals in order to protect the identity of those participating in research (Chadwick, 1984:224). Usually written consent from the interviewee is needed by a researcher in order to proceed with the project. Research techniques in qualitative studies make this very difficult. Most problematic is that of participant observation. In the process of "hanging out" together, one gets to know people and to become friends. People forget why we are with them and disclose things to us, as friends, that they otherwise would not say. But the methodology itself creates this dilemma. And it is up to every researcher to put the needs and rights of the community first. Their protection comes before that of the ethnographer and their career. Refugees are populations at risk for many psychosocial problems. Thus, this requirement is of even greater importance.

There are several ways to mitigate this problem. The first is to answer honestly when people ask why you want to learn about them, their culture, and the research topic. I told the people I met at parties and other informal settings that I was writing a book about their community. Afghans, particularly those with college education, were told as much as they wanted to know about my research interests. Yet, many thought I was a spy for the CIA or the Iranian government (since I have an Iranian surname). To those I interviewed one-on-one, I gave a letter of intent which included my phone number and that of my university. It was important that they had something to keep regarding the interaction, showing that I was honest in my intent and that I met the needs of my institution regarding human subjects protection.

This leads to the second ethics difficulty, that of a signed consent form granting permission to ask the questions. Refugees, and others who have strong cultural notions of trust combined with a fear of governmental activities, can be put off by the request for a signature. If they trust enough to consent they are insulted by the demand for a signature to verify that trust. It says to them that they cannot be trusted. At a deeper level, refugees and many of the other Middle Eastern and Central Asian peoples I have interviewed have learned to survive dictatorships and other repressive forms of government and have a "reality-based paranoia." Requesting a signature can be construed as an attempt by the government to trick them into disclosing something that could be used against them. Some of my interviewees were imprisoned and tortured. The signed consent form reminds them of this experience.

Methodology: Analysis

Goetz and LeCompte noted that the "[a]nalytic processes used in ethnography differ from those used in many other research designs. Differences in timing of analysis and its integration into other research tasks are the characteristics that make ethnography feel most foreign to researchers from other traditions" (1984:165). Links exist between the theoretical framework, the selection strategies and the data-collection methodologies. The basic categories developed by the researcher in the early phase of data collection underpins what goes together and what does not and is the first step in analysis.

Data Management

Research in anthropology has generally been something learned in the field, and the rule was go and start doing it without formal training in data collection or analysis. To do good research, or fieldwork, explicit techniques of data management will improve the depth of information and help the researcher see gaps. In addition, qualitative research tends to be a process of simultaneous data collection and analysis. Therefore, systematic control of the data is important. In addition, the techniques are important because the implicit assumptions that the researcher has are reflected in this process (Agar, 1980:9).

Field notes, the descriptive narratives of the participant observation experience, must be kept on a daily basis, often handwritten in small notebooks and later transcribed into texts that include the data and the researchers reactions. These reflexive remarks are invaluable data in and of themselves:

> When doing a write-up, whether by typing or dictation, the temptation is to plod along, converting raw notes into a coherent account. But that misses an important resource: the fieldworker's reflections and commentary on issues that emerge during the process (Miles and Huberman, 1994:4).

Taped interviews should be transcribed as quickly as possible, with notes regarding impressions, reactions, and other comments. It is best to code the informants so that if someone who is not to see the data gains access to it, the participants are protected. In my research I am careful to record peoples' names and addresses separately from the field notes in an address book which is coded to disguise their connection with the research. In addition, this book is kept at home, whereas the research is stored at my office. Copies of everything (disks and addresses) are kept in a secure place.

There are several warnings regarding tape recorders. The most important is to make sure it works, check it after any change in tape or battery, and take notes while it is recording. In my work with refugees, I found that it was a tool of minimal use because many refugees I have worked with refused to be recorded (Omidian, 1996a, 1996b, and 1994; cf. Shorish-Shamley, 1991). Again, this has to do with distrust and a history of oppression. The only time I was able to record interviews was when I had an injury and could not write. Interviewees felt sorry for me and were too polite to refuse the device. In addition, a one hour recording can take as much as five hours to transcribe, and most of the transcription is of minimal use, unless you are doing content analysis. Finally, the best data seems to always come before the recorder is turned on, while the researcher and the informant are getting to know each other, and after it is turned off and the researcher is preparing to leave.

Note taking can also be a problem. The less intrusive the technique, the more relaxed the interviewees will be. I could not always take notes, even when I was formally interviewing someone. I remember one interview in particular. I was talking to several women (a discussion) and had a semi-structured interview tool I had developed to gather information on perceptions of intergenerational changes. The women in the room were all illiterate in their own language. The setting was rather formal and someone was always leaving the room for more tea or sweets to serve the guests, including me. Each time I would begin to write a response, someone would call out (in Dari): "She is writing again." Eventually I gave up writing in front of them and would excuse myself to go to the toilet. There, I would take a few minutes to jot down brief reminders of conversations and quotable comments. Later, while in my car I fleshed out the notes and that evening at my computer I spent hours transcribing and organizing what I had learned that day.

In the end, long texts are generated through qualitative data collection. The management of this material is part of the on-going research process of collection and analysis. Even the act of typing up field notes is analytical. Once the data are recorded, the researcher returns to it often to read and reread, question and suggest avenues of inquiry. Coding is embedded in this process.

Coding

There are many ways of coding data, and computer programs exist to facilitate this process. In early stages, in particular, it is important to search for the discrepant case, a case which is a variant of the rule, and the negative case, the exception to rule (Goetz and LeCompte, 1984:176). Coding is simply placing the qualitative data into meaningful categories. It is important to check the coding process for continuity by having several people code the same section and see if the categories match, striving for at least a 70 percent match, or, on projects with only one researcher, code the same section twice on separate days to see if there are consistent categories (Miles and Huberman, 1994).

I still use my old method, where data is cataloged by date and event, then printed out for further reading. I then put pages in chronological order and number them in sequence. These pages are read many times, and themes are noted in the margins. After the material is read and analyzed for common themes, a code sheet is developed. Then I list common themes in categories, with their page numbers. For example, themes that involve the elderly, such as their expectations, needs, and roles were noted by page in separate subcategories.

Analysis and Interpretation

The hallmark of ethnographic research is the process of continual analysis, which affects the direction of research and allows the researcher to be taken by surprise. It is a process of collecting data, doing analysis, returning to the site for more collection to see if what you concluded makes sense.

The analyst attempts to discover and give meaning to the embodied, embedded, and situated practices that participants in the world find themselves caught up in and committed to (Denain, 1982:18-19). The purposes of analysis is to: 1) understand meaning, 2) understand context, 3) identify unanticipated phenomena, 4) understand the process by which events take place, and 5) develop causative explanations (Maxwell,1996:17-21). In this process one refines the interpretation of the data within the context of a "dialectical experience" (Agar, 1980:9). It is this constant movement between data and analysis that enriches the research, and which brings criticism by quantitative researchers. It is an interpretive process which includes a layering of interpretations of events (Clifford, 1983; Geertz, 1973, 1988).

In this way, ethnographic data, embedded as it is in participant observation, cannot be reduced to a single voice since there are at least three active voices to be heard in the story: that of the storyteller, that of the anthropologist voice (an interpreting voice), and that of the theoretical lens holder or reader.

I try to learn what every Afghan already knows, the insider's view, and the analysis what I see from both the insider and the outsider's perspective, generating categories of analysis that may not necessarily make sense to members of the community. For example, my findings of the frequency of polygynous marriages surprised a number of key informants. As well, when I realized that I only saw Afghan elderly women laughing and joking when they were alone together and not when men were present, I asked my friend if old women were supposed to be unhappy. It took him a moment, and then he said "come to think of it I have never seen a happy old lady." This was an important realization that was further tested in the field. This realization held up to further checks and cross-checks. The ramifications of this information was related to a mental health clinic doctor with a large number of Afghan clients. We began trying to distinguish between culturally expected "depressive behavior" and clinical depression. One needs treatment, the other needs understanding.

Problems with Research of Refugee Groups

Refugee research has a number of problems that may be of less importance in research of other populations. These include context, trust, and content. These are not issues of reliability or validity, but of social relationships and what it means to be a refugee. These are problems and issues for the researcher.

Context

The largest problem with which I have had to cope has been the incredible needs of the refugee community in general. Because I live in the area where the refugees live, I am always "on call." Much research is needed to understand processes of accommodation and adjustment that refugees undergo and the effects of forced migration on the health and mental health status of the individuals in these communities. And many times they must have immediate advocacy on their behalf in health care, legal, or educational settings.

Many of these needs are immediate, and often lead to dilemmas for the researcher. Every anthropologist I know who works with United States populations ends up in the role of social worker, legal assistant, "peer counselor," and tutor. In this way, we are often overwhelmed and at risk of burnout. Most of this effort is carried out as time permits and in a sense of obligation. In the process of gathering data, it is very important to give something back to the community. My work focuses in the end on community needs and program development. I cannot take without giving; the exchange must be based on reciprocity.

Trust

Having conducted research with Afghans, Arabs, and Iranians, I realize the difficulties in studying social behavior in this region. Trust is particularly difficult to foster, but must be developed in order to complete the research in an ethical manner (Omidian, 1994, 1992; Laffrey et al., 1989; Lipson and Meleis, 1989). The issue of trust effects entree into the community and access to informants. Without trust, one hears only either what the interviewee wants the researcher to hear or what they think one wants to hear. Neither is satisfactory.

In one incident, an Afghan research assistant was conducting a survey with a member of the community; when the questionnaire was completed, the assistant was preparing to leave the subject's home.

Typically, the assistant and the interviewee would continue to chat and share information on family and the refugee experience. After some discussion, the participant revealed that her answers were not truthful and asked to redo the interview. Once she decided to trust the interviewer, she did not hesitate.

Emotional Content of the Data

As anthropologists and qualitative researchers, we are often not trained in how to actually do fieldwork. Many stories abound regarding the mystique of fieldwork. A story is told to anthropology graduate students of a famous anthropologist's remark to a student who asked him for advice regarding fieldwork. The advice was to buy a good frying pan and to loan it to no one. Few anthropology programs in the United States actually teach fieldwork methods; they expect students to learn these techniques in the midst of research. I was lucky and had the benefit of a year-long course that taught many of the techniques I have mentioned in this paper.

What I was not taught, though, was how to deal with traumatic information. Unlike a therapist who is trained in debriefing techniques, I had no skills to cope with the stories of personal tragedy including: the horrors of surviving torture or prison; watching a husband or child be killed and the helplessness that comes from not being able to stop it.

For the researcher involved with a community with such enormous losses, the process of data collection is also difficult because the informants have been through some of life's most harrowing experiences—contexts and experiences that the researcher has not shared (Omidian, 1994). I remember completing four or five interviews with people who told me their stories of the mayhem of war, and going home to cry as I put the "data" into the computer. I was wounded by their stories. One man told me that he felt so much better, as if he had given me his grief and could now start to heal. That was positive. Another man yelled at me, as if I was the cause of the death of his twenty-one year old daughter, who died in his arms when planes had strafed the refugee caravan as they fled towards Pakistan. He had never told anyone and my questions released in him a fury that he was afraid he could not contain. And there I was, the anthropologist, with no skills to act as therapist for them, or for myself. All I could do is listen, but that was, in the end, what many of the interviewees wanted and needed. I recorded their emotions, and then mine, as well.

I called several friends to help me. One woman, who had worked with Cambodians, told me that after interviewing she would have nightmares where she was the refugee being tortured to death. Other researchers had similar stories. We even had a panel at an American Anthropology Association annual meeting on the impact of refugee research on the researcher. There are ways to ease the discomforts one sees or hears, a process of debriefing. First, it is important for the researcher to keep a personal journal. This personal document can be an important reflexive experience and is useful later as well. I realized when I reread mine that the process of acceptance by certain members of the community are illustrated as I became more aware of the emotional impact that war, flight, and resettlement had on their lives.

Second, whenever possible it is important to limit the number of intense interviews in a week. This allows the researcher time to recover between exchanges. Interviews are not social events, they need time to be assessed and processed. Emotional recovery time is critical. "Empathy brings out good data, but it also takes time to put those feelings of empathy into a proper perspective" (Omidian, 1994:173). In the end I found that I also had to grieve with the community and share their rites of mourning (Omidian, 1994).

Conclusion

Qualitative research is an art form, as well as a rigorous methodology. Rigor is not found in numbers, or even sample size, but in the diligence of the researcher to use multiple methods of data collection and analysis, to constantly question assumptions as one moves between data collection and analysis, and back again. Built into the research design is the realization that theoretical constructs are not the end product. The goal of refugee research, I feel, is action. Refugees are needy people, coping with loss of family members and country, and deserve more than research for the sake of the researcher. In my work, community use of the data I produce is the goal I set for myself. This action approach uses theoretical models to further the goals of community needs assessment and program development.

Qualitative methods contribute to the development of theories relating to population movements, the impact of forced migration on psychosocial health and community mental health, and the nature of accommodation to new environments. Theoretical concepts of diaspora and transnational communities, such as the Afghan population with whom I work, are best understood through the articulation of micro/macro comparisons based on the use of qualitative and quantitative data.

Further research is needed to advance our knowledge of these processes. For example, our understanding of the long term effects of war on the psychosocial health of the 1.5 generation (children born in the war zone, but raised outside the area) is very limited. And, there have been few studies of war and flight as it relates to the elderly in a community. Qualitative research, with its lens narrowly focused, is particularly useful in collecting and analyzing data on these topics. There is still much to be done. Refugee research requires the rigor of both qualitative and quantitative methodologies. This in turn gives us the cross-cultural data needed to develop theories that can be used in program development, policy and planning, advocacy and action.

References

Agar, M. H. (1980). *The professional stranger: An informal introduction to ethnography.* New York: Academic Press.

Agar, M. (1986). *Speaking of ethnography.* University Papers series on Qualitative Research Methods No. 2. Beverly Hills: Sage Publications.

Bernard, H. R. (1988). *Research methods in cultural anthropology.* Newbury Park, CA: Sage Publications.

Carlson, R. G., Siegal, H. A., Wang, J., and Flack, R. S. (1996). Attitudes toward needle "sharing" among injection drug users: Combining qualitative and quantitative research methods. *Human Organization, 55*:3:361-396.

Chadwick, B. A. (1984). *Social science research methods.* Englewood Cliffs, NJ: Prentice-Hall.

Clifford, J. (1983). Power and dialogue in ethnography: Marcel Griaule's initiation. In Stocking, G. W. Jr. (Ed.), *Observers observed: Essays on ethnographic fieldwork.* Madison: University of Wisconsin Press.

Collier, D. (1995). Translating quantitative methods for qualitative researchers: The case of selection bias. *American Political Science Review, 89*:2:461-467.

Collier, D., and Mahoney, J. (1996). Insights and pitfalls: Selection bias in qualitative research. *World Politics, 49*:1:56-92.

Denain, N. (1982). Contributions of anthropology and sociology to qualitative research methods. In Kuhns, E. and Martorana, S. V. (Eds.), *Qualitative methods for institutional research* (Vol. 34). San Francisco: Jossey-Bass Publishers, 17-26.

Estroff, S. E. (1981). *Making it crazy: An ethnography of psychiatric clients in an American community.* Berkeley: University of California Press.

Fowler, F. J. Jr. (1984). *Survey research methods.* Applied Social Research Methods Series. Vol. 1. Beverly Hills: Sage Publications.

Geertz, C. (1973). Thick description: Toward an interpretive theory of culture. In Geertz, C. (Ed.), *Interpretation of cultures.* New York: Basic Books.

Geertz, C. (1988). *Works and lives: The anthropologist as author.* Palo Alto: Stanford University Press.

Goetz, J. P. and LeCompte, M. D. (1984). *Ethnography and qualitative design in educational research.* New York: Academic Press.

Laffrey, S. C., Meleis, A. I., Lipson, J. G., Solomon, M., and Omidian, P. A. (1989). Assessing Arab-American health care needs. *Social Science and Medicine, 29*:7:877-883.

Lipson, J. G. (1991).Afghan refugee health: Some findings and suggestions. *Qualitative Health Research, 1*:3:349-369.

Lipson, J. G., Edmonston, F., Hossieni, T., Kabir, S., and Omidian, P.A. (1995). Health issues among Afghan women in California. *Health Care For Women International, 16*:4:279- 286.

Lipson, J. G. and Meleis, A. I. (1989). Methodological issues in research with immigrants. *Medical Anthropology 12*:103-115.

Mandlebaum, D. (1973). The study of life history: Ghandi. *Current Anthropology, 14*:3:177-206.

Maxwell, J. A. (1996). *Qualitative research design: An interactive approach.* Thousand Oaks: Sage Publications.

Miles, M. B.and Huber man, A. M. (1994). *Qualitative data analysis: A source book of new methods* (2nd. ed.). Beverly Hills: Sage Publications.

Morgan, D. L. (1988). *Focus groups as qualitative research* (University Paper Series in Qualitative Research Methods No. 16). Newbury Park: Sage Publications.

Omidian, P.A. (1994). Afghan refugee males: Betwixt and between. In Rainey, P. (Ed.), *Endangered minority male,* Volume 1. Bakersfield, CA: Heritage of Aztlan.

Omidian, P. A. (1996a). *Aging and family in an Afghan refugee community: Traditions and Transitions.* New York: Garland.

Omidian, P. A. (1996b). From fly on the wall to community participant: The Afghan Women's Day Project. *Practicing Anthropology, 18*:1:19-21.

Scrimshaw, S. C. M. and Hurtado, E. (1987). *Rapid assessment procedures for nutrition and primary health care: Anthropological approaches to improving program effectiveness.* Los Angeles: UCLA Latin American Center Publications.

Shorish-Shamley, Z. (1991). *The self and other in Afghan cosmology: Concepts of health and illness among Afghan refugees.* Ph.D. dissertation. Madison: University of Wisconsin.

Spradley, J. P. (1979). *The ethnographic interview.* New York: Holt, Rinehart and Winston.

Bibliography

Adler, P. A., and Adler, P. (1987). *Membership roles in field research.* University Paper series on Qualitative Research Methods No. 6. Newbury Park, CA: Sage Publications.

Aguilar, J. L. (1981). Insider research: An ethnography of a debate. In Messerschmidt, D. A. (Ed.), *Anthropologists at home in North America: Methods and issues in the study of one's own society.* New York: Cambridge University Press, 15-26.

Emerson, R. (1983). *Contemporary field research.* Boston: Little, Brown and Company.

Felepa, R. (1989). Cultural kinds: Imposition and discovery in anthropology. In Glassner, B. and Moreno, J. D. (Eds.), *The qualitative-quantitative distinction in the social sciences.* Netherlands: Kluwer Academic Publishers, 119-153.

Fielding, N. G. and Fielding, J. L. (1986). *Linking data.* University Paper series on Qualitative Research Methods No. 4. Newbury Park, CA: Sage Publications.

Flinders, D. J. and Mills, G. E. (1993). *Theory and concepts in qualitative research: Perspectives from the field.* New York: Teachers College Press.

Halmi, A. (1996). Qualitative approach to social work: An epistemological basis. *International Social Work, 39*:4:363-376.

Hastrup, K., and Elsass, P. (1990). Anthropological advocacy: A contradiction in terms. *Current Anthropology, 31*:3:301-307.

Herndon, S. L., and Kreps, G. L. (1993). *Qualitative research: Applications in organizational communication.* Cresskill, NJ: Hampton Press, Inc.

Jarratt, D. G. (1996). A comparison of two alternative interviewing techniques used within an integrated research design. *Marketing Intelligence and Planning, 14*:6:6-10.

Johnson, A. W. (1978). *Quantification in cultural anthropology: An introduction to research design.* Stanford: Stanford University Press.

Krueger, R. A. (1988). *Focus groups: A practical guide for applied research.* Newbury Park, CA: Sage Publications.

Marshall, C. and Rossman, G. B. (1989). *Designing qualitative research.* Newbury Park: Sage Publications.

McCracken, G. (1988). *The long interview* (University Paper Series in Qualitative Research Methods No. 13). Newbury Park: Sage Publications.

Morse, J. M. (1994). *Critical issues in qualitative research methods.* Thousand Oaks: Sage Publications.

O'Connor, K. and Chamberlain, K. (1996). Dimensions of life meaning: A qualitative investigation at mid-life. *British Journal of Psychology, 87*:3:461-478.

Patton, M. Q. (1990). *Qualitative evaluation and research methods,* (2nd. ed.). Newbury Park, CA: Sage Publications.

Peattie, L. R. (1960). The failure of the means-ends scheme in action anthropology. In Gearing, F., Netting, R. M., and Peattie, L. R. (Eds.), *Documentary history of the Fox Project: 1948-1959*. Chicago: University of Chicago, 300-304.

Piddington, R. (1960). Action anthropology. *Journal of the Polynesian Society*, *69*:119-213.

Silverman, D. (1985). *Qualitative methodology and sociology*. Brookfield, VT: Gower.

Spradley, J. P. and McCurdy, D. W. (1972). *The cultural experience: Ethnography in complex society*. Chicago: Science Research Associates.

Strauss, A. L. (1987). *Qualitative analysis for social scientists*. New York: Cambridge University Press.

Sylvan, D. J. (1989). The qualitative-quantitative distinction in political science. In Glassner, B. and Moreno, J. (Eds.), *The qualitative-quantitative distinction in the social sciences*, Dordrecht, The Netherlands: Kluwer Academic Publishers, 79-98.

Tax, S. (1958). The Fox Project. *Human Organization, 17*:17-19.

Thorne, B. (1980). "You still takin' notes?" Fieldwork and problems of informed consent. *Social Problems, 27*:3:284-296.

Weller, S. C. and Romney, A. K. (1988). *Systematic data collection* (University Paper Series in Qualitative Research Methods No. 10). Newbury Park: Sage Publications.

4

Refugees and Health

ETHNOGRAPHIC APPROACHES

Marita Eastmond

Introduction

Refugee health, as a rapidly growing field of research and clinical practice, is predominantly a discourse of the medical and behavioral sciences, and one grounded in Western theories and methods. One methodological tradition is primarily empirical and quantitative, such as epidemiological surveys or psychometric instruments developed for the clinical interview or to screen for mental health problems. Others, in particular psychodynamic theory and therapeutic practice, have more of a qualitative and interpretative approach, focusing on the individual or the family in intensive and long-term interaction and dialogue to restore social functioning and health. As such, they are epistemologically more akin to anthropology in its interpretative tradition, with a focus on lived experience and the role of meaning in human lives.

The afflictions and suffering of many refugees call for our human engagement as well as for an interdisciplinary enquiry. Such an inquiry also needs to be critical and reflexive. The experiences in question challenge both social science and medicine, as the language of both poorly accommodates, even resists, the experience of suffering (Kleinman, 1995), and tends to naturalize the relationship between social and political disorders or maladies, such as violence and displacement, and the human experience of distress and bodily signs of disorder. We face several dilemmas in attempting to capture the complexity of this experience. One is the cross-cultural nature of much research and clinical work with refugees; another is that, in the case of refugees and displaced people, this is a question of capturing patterns of social relations, cultural meanings, and identities in the process of their disruption and transformation. I will suggest some possible openings for a composite approach, and provide three brief cases of ethnographic enquiry.

I begin by outlining the approach of an interpretative and meaning-centered medical anthropology and an ethnographic method of inquiry. These are useful tools in exploring health and illness as socially and culturally mediated human experience, examining the meanings people themselves ascribe to health and illness, change and disruption in the social, political, and cultural contexts in which they occur. With such a contextualized approach, I address some of the methodological problems of culture variation frequently expressed in cross-cultural research, arguing that part of the problem is in the conception of culture as a static and uniformly distributed property of a group. In contrast to the medical tradition, anthropology is not primarily concerned with individuals or statistical units of population, but examines the ways in which people are related to one another, the webs of relations that make up a local community or, increasingly today, that connect people in many parts of the world. Culture is the dynamic and ever-changing contents of those relations and interactions, webs of significance that are shaped and re-shaped in social life and in relation to structures of power.

Thus, my concern here will be less with the hermeneutics of clinical practice itself (see Good and Good, 1980 for an outline of such a model) than with the wider contexts in which health systems and illness experiences are shaped. Anthropology's ethnographic approach situates health and illness, as a system of knowledge and practice and as lived experience, in the contexts of the local social world of the people concerned. Such a contextualized approach may provide a vital contribution of knowledge in the clinical encounter, and in cross-cultural contexts of research in particular, this kind of qualitative enquiry may generate knowledge about indigenous understandings and management of ill health as a vital basis for subsequent epidemiological and other quantitative investigations.

Culture, Health, and Illness

The anthropology of health is about the culturally varying ways in which people experience, define, and explain health and illness. It is also about the ways in which they communicate illness and distress and the kinds of treatments they seek. The contribution of anthropology was summed up by one of its "ancestors," Bronislaw Malinowski. Making the point that there is no human activity which we could regard as purely physiological, that is, "natural" or "untutored", he remarked that:

> Not even the simplest need, nor yet the physiological function most independent of environmental influence can be regarded as completely unaffected by culture. (Malinowski, 1944)

In other words, "biology" and "nature" are always interpreted phenomena: they are conceptualized, experienced, improved, and otherwise acted upon by members of a society. Human reproduction, sex, growth, and aging are examples of physiological processes that can generate very different cultural constructions as kinship, gender, and life cycles which form the basis of socially organized roles and relations. The premise of anthropology generally is that human beings always seek to categorize, order, and create meanings of their world and their experiences. Disruptions of such social and conceptual orders, as in the case of forced displacement and extreme violence, may have profound consequences in terms of well-being. As with the human experience of illness generally, a disorder, whatever its origin, provokes the need for those affected to make sense of what is happening to them. These social and cultural dimensions interact with biological processes in ways we so far know very little about.

The anthropological inquiry into health and illness generally have the following dimensions or analytical components.

Conceptions of Health and Illness

What are the social definitions of *normality* and how do they relate to health (often the two overlap)? What are considered pathological responses or medical problems in the group or community studied? Going beyond Western bio-medical separation of domains of experience, with its focus on the individual body or mind, we find that other systems may not so clearly distinguish the biological realm from the mental and emotional, the social and the cultural. For instance, the notions of ill health in a biomedical model may elsewhere be classified in a wider category of human misfortune, along with other kinds of threats and undesired states, such as accidents or curses; they may be defined as a social rather than a medical problem or as part of everyday life processes (pregnancy, child-birth, malnourishment, etc.), i.e., exist in or overlap with realms of human experience other than those defined by more narrow biomedical models. Among the Mam-speaking population of Guatemala, the indigenous polysemous term *chun-klal* encompasses life, health, and existence (Eastmond, 1991).

Balance seems to be a metaphor for "health" in many systems but what is to balance may be culturally variable. Balance may be physiological (e.g., hot-cold, wet-dry qualities) or refer to relations to other people, to spirits or to cosmic energies. The focus of balance may be located within the individual or between the individual and a larger whole. Such internal or external referents often correlate with the ways in which "self" or a "social person" is defined. The focus on inner processes and control in Western somatic and psychiatric medicine thus reflect Western ideals of self as a bounded and autonomous unit, whereas other ethnopsychologies may locate agency or locus of control differently. Thus, a disrupted balance between the individual and his or her social and natural environment is often seen to result in ill health and forms the basis of explanations and treatment. As we shall see, it is also relevant when considering refugee models of responses to war and displacement, in particular the idea of health as restoring significant relationships, healing in the sense of "making whole" that which has been ruptured.

Expression

Idioms of distress are the learned, conventional forms of communicating illness to particular persons and situations for recognition of a sick role and for treatment. Expression may be verbal, somatic, or through other symbolic forms: such as moving one's bed on the outside of the hut, or, conversely, withdrawing completely from social interaction. Western psychology emphasizes verbal and self-reflexive accounts of inner states as the "natural" expression and most effective treatment of emotional distress. In most other parts of the world, the somatic idiom is the norm, in some groups even considered the more mature form of expression (e.g., Tung in Eyton and Neuwirth, 1984).

Classification of Disease

This refers to the interpretation of signs and symptoms and the classification of pathologies into discreet disease entities (i.e., diagnosis). As such, disease is distinguished from illness, the experience of ill health.

Explanatory Models

Such models concern the different theories of what has brought on distress and disease, e.g., Godly punishment, a virus attack, or the evil eye (Sachs, 1983; Kleinman, 1980). When alcoholism was viewed as a moral weakness in European culture, moral or religious reform was seen as the cure; today it tends to be defined as a disease, which requires another form of treatment. As this example implies, the medical system is neither a static nor a clearly bounded entity: diagnosis, explanation, treatment, and cures are intimately intertwined with a people's worldview and the conditions which produce and sustain it.

Healing and the Organization of Health Care

Diagnosis and explanations shape health seeking strategies and forms of treatment. (Doing fieldwork in a small indigenous community in Guatemala, I found that, depending on what people thought they suffered from, they sought a *curandera, an espiritista,* a priest, or someone at the local health post.) Health care involves both the healing practices and the persons and institutions involved. To use Kleinman's distinction of sectors of health care, one may ask what is taken care of in the home, by the folk sector, and by the official health care system. (Kleinman, 1980)

An anthropological interpretative approach to health and illness, brings attention to the meanings humans ascribe to experience, to suffering, and how to interpret and respond to them. In contrast to medical empiricist models in which facts are there to be "uncovered," and symptoms are signs or manifestations of an underlying disorder, existing in pure form beneath the "layers of cultural camouflage" (Kleinman, 1977:4), an interpretative framework recognizes that all illness realities are meaningfully constituted, that "[W]hatever the biological grounds or correlates of a disease, sickness becomes a human experience and an object of therapeutic attention as it is made meaningful" (Good and Good, 1980:67). Illness and suffering are everywhere threats to human existence and are therefore moral and cosmological concerns. These include conceptions about human nature, and humans' relations to one another and to the spiritual, conceptions of self, time, life and death, and the meanings of suffering. These local moral worlds are the ethnographic terrain of a good deal of medical anthropological enquiries. Such ethnographic methods of intensive fieldwork are often required to explore people's categories and actions related to health in these wider contexts of their social existence. The challenge is to capture the complex and often ambiguous texture of everyday life, in which understandings and practices related to health and illness are embedded in relations between people, as located practice. A perspective from within the local social context also helps to see the multifaceted ways in which health is interwoven with social, political, and existential dimensions in the lives of sufferers. How do power relations (also global in scope) shape local health systems? Morsy (1996) underlines the need to include political-economic considerations in the phenomenological studies of such systems.

Critical Perspectives

Addressing health issues in their wider contexts and of particular relevance to forced migration and health, a critical medical anthropology takes an interest not only in the cultural constructions of illness but also in "the social production of disease." This refers to the wider social and economic forces that structure or rupture social relationships, shape collective experience, and make certain groups particularly vulnerable. The social dramas of war, violence, displacement, the experience of disruption of social existence, and dislocation of individuals from networks of relations and patterns of meaning cannot be captured in a narrow medical framework of understanding—the renewed attention in recent years to psychological trauma and PTSD (Post-Traumatic Stress Disorder) as diagnoses easily "medicalizes" such experiences. Looking at the social meanings and idioms with which refugee groups themselves try to make sense of their suffering, we find that it is often defined more as a moral, spiritual, existential, or ideological problem rather than a medical one. The political-ideological idiom described by Eastmond (1989; 1996) for Latin American refugees, the spiritual and religious focus of Cambodians (Eisenbruch, 1991) and Tibetans in exile (Corlin, 1990), and the revivalist movement of the Hmong in Thai camps (Tapp, 1989) are examples of different models of providing explanation, meaning, and hope and, as such, constituting collective therapeutic strategies. In these, individual afflictions are embedded in the collective predicament and even when such social maladies are somatically expressed as individual distress (as in the case of "nerves", see further below) such idioms often retain, for the individual, a wider social meaning. In contrast, the medical or psychological idiom usually implies a focus on the afflicted individual, abstracted from social and cultural contexts.

The issue is not only one of cultural interpretation but also the politics of *representation*: In what way are our own institutions involved in the construction of illness, apart from the social production of disease? Do we pathologize responses to poverty and powerlessness (Scheper-Hughes, 1992), problems of social order (Kleinman, 1995), or grief reactions for politically induced displacement (Eisenbruch, 1991; Eastmond, 1998a and 1998b; and Skultans, 1997)?

A critical and reflexive approach also recognizes that Western medicine is not automatically the arbiter of what is "scientific" or considered to be "irrational beliefs." Rather, it assumes that all knowledge is culturally shaped, that it is constituted in relation to distinctive forms of life and social organization. The Cartesian dualism of psyche and soma, so characteristic of biomedical thought, is not universally valid, but reflect culturally variable notions about the constitution of the person. This notion of the person is a prime example of what Kleinman (1977) refers to as a "category fallacy," discussed in current transcultural psychiatry as the most basic and perhaps the most crucial error one can make in cross-cultural research, i.e., superimposing the researcher's own categories in psychopathological assessments at the expense of indigenous categories. Eisenbruch, a psychiatrist also trained as an anthropologist, showed from his fieldwork with Cambodian refugee communities how the notion of "guilt," so predominant in Western grief theory, corresponds to a continuum of meanings in Khmer related to different acts and semantic contexts, including the spiritual realm (Eisenbruch 1990).

Cross-Cultural Contexts of Refugee Health

In the field of refugee health, there is a growing concern with culture difference, expressed as a problem of cross-cultural validity of research data or with culture-sensitive techniques in clinical interventions. A recognition of ethnocentric instruments and assessments have led to the development of techniques of cultural translation, to create equivalence or comparability in measures and self-rating scales (for a critical review, see Eyton and Neuwirth, 1984; cf., Marsella and Kameoka, 1989) through eliciting the meanings of terms and concepts with the help of culturally knowledgeable informants.

The most common technique used and expanded upon seems to be that of linguistic equivalence through "back translation" of instruments (Brislin et al., 1973).[1] This is an important step towards a more reflexive understanding of medical knowledge and illness experiences as culturally mediated. However, a problem of such decontextualized, empiricist approaches that seek to correct for cultural variation is usually the implicit assumptions they make about culture: Culture is conceptualized as the layers that camouflage an underlying essence or objective reality (Kleinman, 1977:4) and, further, these layers are assumed to form a static and uniformly distributed property among the members of an ethnic group, so that any one member can represent the whole. Rather, culture is processual, it is the dynamic flows of meaning, with individuals' cultural repertoires differently shaped by their social experience (class, gender, etc.), but also constantly processed and reshaped in the interactional contexts of everyday life. Thus, cultural meanings cannot so easily be isolated from their interactional contexts, or made verbally explicit by an informant as such eliciting interviews demand. Meanings are rather the abstractions of the anthropologist's analysis of field data, drawn from and found internally consistent (i.e., valid) with a broad range of informants and contexts of interaction over time.

The dynamics of social and cultural frameworks are an obvious feature of migrants' lives. In such contexts, it may be even more important to capture the fuzzy areas: fluidity and ambiguity of lives and meanings are often part of the (sometimes painful) transformations that people and cultural systems are going through as a response to war and forced migration. Such transitional conditions underline the need for more of an open-ended research strategy, one that inquires into and observes the use of categories in everyday interaction, in the domains in which explanation and relief may be sought, rather than relying on verbal statements out of context.

In interviews, respondents have a tendency to reflect the normative rather than the actual. Participant observation would also help explore the conflicts between the normative, representing the "ideal" of a community, and "actual" pragmatic actions and strategies required in a new situation, which often constitute conflicting demands in groups involved in transformations in which they have relatively little control. In general, it is wise to heed Good's warning against

> ... deducing "beliefs" about illness from the statements people make about what they think is going on; [it] ignores what is obvious after a long time in the field: that all discourse is located in social relationships, that ... assertions about illness experience are located in linguistic practices and most typically embedded in narratives about life and suffering. (1994:23)

Such a contextualized approach even more applies to understanding that which is not said. Silences, which can be equally misleading and methodologically problematic, is a recurring feature in traumatized groups of people, often constituting a tacit understanding between people concerning what cannot be expressed or talked about. While personal narratives may provide an entrance to the collectively unspeakable, they presuppose an in-depth understanding of the community involved, the political and moral conflicts that generate and maintain such "conspiracies of silence" (Eastmond, 1989).

Local Cultural Accounts: A Comparative Framework

Cultural accounts and practices in their local contexts may thus form the basis of cross-cultural and comparative understanding. Kleinman (1977), writing on depression, argues that the study of illness phenomena, the construction of questionnaires and other instruments used, should be preceded by and build on the systematic analysis and comparison of the relevant illness categories, explanations, and expressions through detailed phenomenological descriptions based in local cultural contexts. The study of heart distress in rural Iran by Good and Good (1982) is a classical example: They started with the local categories of distress and explored the full range of local meanings associated with these; only then they carried out an epidemiological study. Starting from the same premises, Eisenbruch in his work with Cambodian refugees designed an assessment instrument for the clinical interview, a semi-structured interview that moved through a sequence of complaints based on the terms and notions reflecting the Cambodian experience of distress which he had first identified through fieldwork with the Cambodian community (1990). With the same approach in a subsequent study (1991), he compared the Western categories (such as Post-Traumatic Stress Disorder, or PTSD) used in diagnosing distress in Cambodian refugees with their own interpretation of symptoms. He found that there were often instances of misdiagnosis on the basis of a "category fallacy." With an ethnographic, exploratory approach he then mapped the refugees' own interpretation of what was troubling them: visitations from ghosts or spirits from the homeland; yearning to complete obligations to the dead ancestors buried back home, i.e., cultural manifestations of grief rather than pathology. He also identified the comforting antidotes: religious belief and participation in religious gatherings, understood and performed in the tradition of Buddhist cosmology.

Similarly, the reactions to fear and helplessness of Guatemalan peasants in the face of extreme political terror are sometimes expressed as an affliction of *"susto"* (fear, often translated as "soul loss"), a common cultural category of illness in many parts of Latin America. *Susto* is seen as caused by inexplicable, unexpected, and atypical events, and as such may be translated into the PTSD diagnostic category. However, *susto* only makes sense within the indigenous cosmology and evokes a very different set of measures for recovery than the Western psychiatric diagnosis. It was thus adapted and applied by refugees from Guatemala to traumatized responses (Stepputat, 1992).

Lives in Transition: Refugees Narratives

These examples may help sum up my argument so far. Social disruptions and transformations of life by forced migration may cause suffering and distress, which may be expressed in different ways. Further, such responses may be easily medicalized or misdiagnosed by the institutions of the host society, and refugees' responses are best analyzed in their own terms and interpretation situated in the local cultural contexts of their experience. However, the changing contexts of refugees' lives present a challenge to conventional ethnographic methods, which have relied on the stable, local community, with its own history and culture, identified with a particular place. As for many other groups in today's globalized world, refugees may have their community of significant others dispersed in many parts of the world and their well-being may be intimately tied to events and relations in far-off places (such as the continuing war in their home country). Transnational lives and engagement with networks in other places may also affect the ways in which lives and communities are reconstituted in the host society. There may be very little of a community and supportive network, and for those that remain on the margins of the host society, such desocialization and social invisibility may be somatized and medicalized (Eastmond, 1996, 1998a).

Given the dynamics of refugee lives, narratives are a useful methodological strategy: They mirror the complex relation to time and place of refugees through their memories and storied experiences. Focusing on the individual and family or household, they provide a point of entry into the life-world of change and loss, where vital bases of social life, identity, and history located elsewhere are absent, inaccessible to both fieldworker and narrator. As stories about disruptions and (often dramatic) change, they invite the narrator's own reflections on the meanings and responses they generate.

The narrative approach in anthropology is based on the assumption that narratives form part of the meaning-making process, structuring personal meaning out of events and processes, constituted in the telling, and thus mediating between personal experience and cultural explanations. For people in transition, narratives may help capture the changing relationship between the individual and sociocultural system, capitalizing on the reflexivity inherent in the lived experience of change.[2] The kinds of stories that accompany illness experiences have received particular attention in medical anthropology in recent years, as well as in medicine and psychodynamic theory and practice. Researching refugees and distress, I have combined such illness narratives with a life story approach into *narratives of suffering,* analyzing peoples' storied experiences in the context of their biographies as well as in the wider, and changing, social and cultural contexts of refugees' lives.[3] "Suffering" here covers a wide range of domains beyond the medical that also encompass the existential and moral dimensions that accompany reactions to loss and bereavement, connecting the individual, the prime concern of bio-medicine, to a wider socio-cultural context.

Thus, I listen to the stories people tell me and each other of their lived experience, of life when it was "normal," of disruptions and dramatic changes, and of life in exile and the ways in which they make sense of these changes. They are stories addressing radical discontinuity but also attempts to recover a sense of continuity and well-being; the narratives usually have something to say about the cultural values and norms that may be threatened or otherwise reflected upon with the distance brought by changing social contexts of life. My experience with exile communities is that standards and norms are constantly negotiated, in the different clusters of community (such as families, political associations, friendship networks)–sometimes being frozen and idealized, sometimes in flux, but always of concern. This local context and its constant negotiation with the past and life "before" the war or exile is central to the analysis of the narratives, while taking into account the multiple linkages with people in other places that constitute the life-world of many refugees.

Thus, the stories and the wider contexts in which they are generated and gain their meaning form the basis of analysis. They also form a point of departure for a continuing dialogue and exchange with the professions involved with refugees and health. As a method, narratives may help bridge clinical and anthropological traditions, such as the individual focus of the clinical interview and the ethnographic or community focus of the anthropologist (e.g., Good, 1994). The ways in which narratives can be used as tools of therapeutic intervention are described by Herbst, 1992; Lifton, 1993; also Woodcock, 1997.

Suffering, Morality, and Meaning: Three Ethnographic Cases

A large number of medical anthropological studies have shown that sickness is universally experienced as a *moral* event (Good, 1994), a rupture of normality that invokes questions about cause and responsibility, and attempts to make sense of suffering and find hope to go forward. There are attempts to answer the questions of "why me/us?" in terms of a moral order. In the same way, organized violence and displacement are disruptions of a normal order and the moral dimension of change and loss are recurring themes in the refugees' narratives that I have collected over the years. They often explore the actions of self and others in terms of right and wrong, justifications as part of a meaningful constitution of personal experience (Eastmond, 1996) in terms of that order.

Seen through this anthropological lens, survival guilt, which is prominent in traumatization and grief theories as a common response of survivors of violence, may be understood as socially mediated by the moral order of the community. Lifton's approach (1993), from psychodynamic theory, and his concept of *failed enactment,* can be usefully adapted here. It refers to an individual's lingering self- condemnation for having failed to respond by "ordinary standards" because of extreme helplessness in a situation of overpowering threat. The psychological and existential dimensions of such responses are often recognized in theories focusing on the individual but we also need to be aware of the cultural mediation of such responses. On the level of social meaning, then, such perception of failure is framed by the moral order which defines an individual's social role and responsibilities (for instance, as a parent, a husband, an elder, a guerilla member, etc.). The individual focus of moral responsibility in Western conceptions of guilt often clouds our understanding that much of the glue in social relations is moral in nature. Especially in social communities, where the welfare of individuals is not the obligation of a state, individuals are connected in a dense fabric of multiple kinds of interdependencies. The normative structure of such a fabric, regulating rights and obligations between people, may be anchored in a divine or cosmological order or in other, more worldly power structures. The breakdown of such orders have implications for the individual defined by many social ties and responsibilities.

Moral commitments can also be tied to other non-localized social collectivities and based on ideological convictions, such as political movement. My study of refugees from the Chilean *Movimiento Popular* showed that their primary moral focus was solidarity within the movement, measured by one's ability to live up to the responsibilities as a *militante* (Eastmond, 1989). The Cambodian refugees in Australia and the United States described by Eisenbruch (1991) and their responses to grief focused on failures in relation to the structure of moral obligations to elders and to ancestors buried back home. Unable to fulfill these, they were disturbed by repeated visitations by ghosts from the homeland, hearing the voices of their ancestors. Their responses to this predicament, defined by them as culturally appropriate grief rather than as pathological reactions, were made meaningful within the moral framework of Buddhist cosmology. For instance, guilt was addressed and partly relieved through services administered by ritual specialists (Buddhist monks or traditional healers, *kruu kmae*) through merit-making rites for the ancestors.

Religion and rituals were thus important means of healing, making whole the relations ruptured by the failure to live up to moral obligations as understood in the Cambodian cosmology.

As the latter case suggests, this moral framework shapes the strategies people employ to reconstitute meaningful social worlds and well-being and may be important information for interventions that wish to enlist the resources of the refugee collective. For Chilean refugees, as indicated above, this moral code was primarily defined in terms of their political ideology and it clearly shaped their response to exile and to traumatization. Their ideology was the framework that provided both explanation of suffering and hope for the future, of defeating an unjust political order and eventual return to Chile. It also provided the basis of organization in exile and significant support networks.

My fieldwork in one community of Chilean refugees in northern California in the mid 1980s revealed the theme constantly debated and negotiated, i.e., the defeat of their government in 1973 by the military junta, who politically was to blame for their failure to defend the "movement" and hold on to power. Also debated were the central cultural values of the movement to be maintained in exile and protected from the influence of United States society. Personal traumas and losses tended to be subsumed by the collective political discourse, and the remedy was seen to be continued political commitment and collective action. Thus, the somatic complaints of many of these ex-prisoners and *militantes* as the embodied experience of persecution and torture provided the acceptable idiom of personal distress. They were also constant reminders of a commitment they were not allowed to forget. Equally important, I learned of that which could not be talked about within the community, the tacit understandings about personal suffering and about members' own failures, during torture and imprisonment, to defend their commitment and to protect the movement. This "conspiracy of silence," as it was examined, unfolded a complex relation described elsewhere between personal history, political ideology, and the refugee community (Eastmond, 1989). It also points to the importance of exploring the collective dimensions of silence and the cultural values they encode and may attempt to protect, in particular for interventions with traumatized refugees.

In contrast to the Cambodian and Chilean responses to disruption, the moral focus of the Bosnian Muslims in my current study (Eastmond, 1998a) is a different one: responsibility is to the family, as symbolized by the *kuca* or household, the center of a person's lifeworld as described by Bringa (1995) in her ethnography of a small village in central Bosnia. There the primary moral environment is traditionally that of the household, the family extended to kin (and at least in many villages, further extended to one's ethnoreligious group or *nacija*), and symbolized through the house. In the local moral world of the village, sociality and reciprocity were central values that connected households and families to each other through relations of mutual exchange of visits, labor, and other forms of assistance in social life. With the war and the ethnic cleansing operations, these local worlds have been disrupted, members of households and their social networks dead or dispersed, houses have been destroyed or are now occupied by strangers. Attempts are made to widen that moral focus, as postwar nationalist politics since the war promote the nation as a moral community; a new national identity of Muslims as *Bosnjaks* is being depicted as the morally exclusive category (Eastmond, 1998a). Nevertheless, in spite of the nation-building at macropolitical levels, the family welfare project is, for the Bosnians, still the primary moral obligation and the safest bet. The suffering from "failed enactments" in Lifton's sense would here apply first to the inability to protect the *kuca*, the members of the family as well as the house and property. It is also related to the inability to maintain the family welfare, a concern with work and economic security for its members. Failure to take on such roles in the present, to "normalize life" in the continuing economic marginal position of the host society, is a substantial part of the distress expressed by many Bosnians. The silence within families about war experiences (and possible failures to act as expected of a spouse or parent) may also be an attempt to protect close relations and to maintain the moral environment that the household represents.

These ethnographic examples indicate the need to understand reactions, here the moral concern that is so often present in grief reactions, within the particular web of social relations (past and present) that is most significant for an individual in a particular group. Thus, for the refugees from Bosnia, reconstituting life and health center on consolidating the household, family reunification and reconstituting the family welfare project. In contrast, in the first few years at least, the Chileans were reconstituting the political movement in exile and were absorbed by exile politics.

Health and Well-Being as Multidimensional

The Bosnian Muslim refugees in Sweden differ in some respects from the institutions of the receiving society in conceptualizing and managing distress and physical signs of bodily disorder related to war and exile. While "traumatization" (and sometimes the PTSD diagnosis) is widely applied in the refugee health services to Bosnians coming out of the recent war, the narrow focus on the physical and mental effects of the war contrasts, in many respects, with the broader perspective of the refugees themselves. In Swedish society, the term "Bosnian refugees" has become synonymous with traumatized refugees.

Focusing on the physical and mental effects on individuals, usually abstracted from their social and cultural contexts, such a medical label contrast with the refugees' own and more multifaceted definitions of their problems. Among themselves, Bosnian refugees rarely talk in terms of trauma and traumatization. Despite its increasing usage in Swedish popular discourse, it does not influence how Bosnians, irrespective of social background, conceptualize their distress. In everyday social interaction, people rather refer to problems with terms such as "disrupted normality" or "nerves." Normality refers to the individual as well as to normally-functioning family or society— the three levels are interwoven. Disrupted normality in the individual is usually expressed in the idiom of nerves and being nervous, *nervosa/nervozna.* Nerves are a widespread and well- documented phenomenon in diverse societies and cultural contexts.[4] Here, the sensation of nerves, with grief and anger as its etiological explanation, resemble the kinds of embodied distress noted from other ethnographic contexts where nerves are bodily manifestations that communicate distress at the personal, familial, societal, and political levels (Low, 1994)

The discourse on "normalization" among Bosnians refers to recovery after the war on many levels of society and individual health and well-being, including restoring "normal" social and economic functions of family life. Moreover, as the narratives of people from small towns and rural areas in Bosnia indicate, "health" seems to be encoded in terms of sociality, in particular for the women, but also of work (the physical ability and the mental inclination to work); both are accompanied by light-heartedness. Social exchange and work are also seen to promote health; both stand in sharp contrast to the condition, at present among Bosnians, of unemployment and a sense of social isolation in the host country. The stories reveal that much of the suffering felt today is a result of the way the war has ruptured these balances in people's lives (defined as normality), in social relations, and in the ability to work and be economically independent, which forms the basis for the family welfare project.

Health, then, to these informants is an inclusive concept, integrating social and moral balance with physical ability and mood. Rather than pertaining to the individual alone, health (and its recovery) is embedded in social relationships and reciprocity. Some of the women, in particular the older ones, refer to the need to have others (preferably women) to talk to, to unload their suffering. Mimica (1997), in her evaluation of a psychosocial program for internally displaced people in former Yugoslavia, made a similar observation. The refugees rated the social interaction among themselves as more effective in promoting their well-being than the psychotherapy offered by the program. Sennemark (1997) cites as a coping strategy one elderly Bosnian woman in Sweden who, suffering bodily aches and pains and finding no relief in the medication prescribed to her, made repeated attempts to be admitted to hospital. Unsuccessful in obtaining a diagnosis and hospital care, she was finally admitted for some time in a rest home. She felt a remarkable recovery, being able to spend all her time with other women: "I get better when I'm around people, when I can talk to other women, to unload my worries when others listen."

Many such stories make no sharp distinction between bodily and emotional pain, and incorporate the social dimensions of distress. In particular the older generation, often presenting somatic symptoms such as heart problems, headaches, tiredness, sleeping difficulties, and other bodily pains and aches, talk about their condition as "nerves." Sennemark (1997) reports that a husband relates his wife's story of illness, explaining her repeated visit to the hospital emergency ward thus:

> "She suffers a grief. Now all those medication they've given her have worn her down. But there are no remedies for nerves, are there?" The woman herself adds: "All this pain, it won't go away. It's nerves. Especially at night the pain gets bad. Nothing can cure this illness. After what they did to my niece, killed in front of my eyes, I shall never recover." She finds relief being with other women, telling them her story.

The practitioners visiting this and other families as part of a therapeutic program were not seen as primarily providing treatment but were included in a more familiar relationship, resembling women's visiting patterns in their home villages.

Suffering and healing, as these ethnographic glimpses indicate, are seen as multidimensional, integrating bodily and emotional pains and responses with significant social relations (their ruptures but also their healing potentials) and relations of power. The body is a common and powerful metaphor used to express, confirm, or contest social and political orders, and illness or distress can be a subtle form of resistance to powerlessness. Such a holistic view is an important reminder to problematize the relationship between social and political maladies and the human experience of distress and physical disorder, and to maintain a critical look at the premises from which interventions are made in the area of refugee health; complex social experiences are easily reduced to an individual's physical or mental response, translated into a medical idiom. Defining refugees as an *a priori* high risk group for mental disorders, as part of one's own generalizing construction of refugee-ness (Malkki, 1995), and the tendency in some host countries to define all victims of war as traumatized (Eastmond, 1998b) are examples of such medicalization of human suffering.

Concluding Remarks

Research and clinical practice of refugees' health issues require a composite set of conceptual tools and methodological strategies. The strength of the contribution from anthropological theory and method suggested here lies in moving us beyond a narrow medical or psychiatric focus, and expanding its conventional realm of the individual. Exploring suffering and illness as socially and culturally mediated phenomena, with the contextualized approach of ethnography, can open up important avenues to the linking of sociocultural analysis to medical enquiry and therapeutic practice.

The holistic perspective takes account of the complexity of factors involved, exploring social, economic, political, and cultural dimensions interacting with the processes of body and mind. Ethnography's attention to the multiple dimensions of context and the exploratory nature of investigation implies long-term involvement in the everyday lives of the people under study. The limitation in terms of time and material covered with ethnographic methods is obvious but can be seen to be compensated for by in-depth understanding and rich ethnographic accounts. A local community approach is made more difficult by the changing and trans-local character of refugees' lives, as for many other people in complex and globalized social settings. Biographical narratives, centering on the individual in a changing social reality, can complement more conventional field methods such as informal interviews, conversations, and direct observation.

More recently, this perspective includes greater attention to social and political contexts in which disorders are produced and defined. The linking of power relations to biology, psychology, and culture is particularly relevant in the case of health aspects of forced migration and other forms of organized violence, expanding the models of both social science and medicine. Recognizing complexity, then, may avoid reductionist models, in which socially complex and multidimensional experiences are reduced to individual biology and psychology, and the translation of sociosomatic idioms into a medical language.

Furthermore, ethnography aims at capturing the problems investigated as people in their local worlds themselves understand and talk about them. The indigenous understandings and management of ill health in local cultural accounts provide a useful basis for a comparative framework. The cultural diversity and plurality of medical systems that form part of most societies today bring about increased sensitivity to culture and cultural variation, including those of practitioner and patient. Cross-cultural data throw valuable light on the variation in definitions of "normality," and in kinds of expressions, explanation, and therapeutic interventions. As cross-cultural enquiries and interventions, they sharpen our awareness of the cultural constructions that go into our own models and methods, against ethnocentrism and category fallacies.

A hermeneutic/interpretive approach to illness and human suffering acknowledges these as experiential realities, meaningfully constituted through culture, and thus represents a challenge to empiricism, objectivist models in bio-medicine as well as in the social sciences. A perspective that recognizes that all knowledge is socially produced and culturally constituted also forces us to examine the premises of our own scientific models and the implicit claims to universal relevance made by many Western-based theories on human processes of body and mind. At the same time, the multiplicity of voices and perspectives on human suffering, although a seemingly impossible combination of epistemologies, is essential to cross-cultural understanding. The social dramas of war, violence, and displacement, disruptions of social existence and multiple loss, cannot be captured by one single framework of understanding. Rather, they demand continued efforts to construct a broad and multifaceted basis for comprehension and intervention. Needless to say, this has considerable relevance beyond an interest in theory; it is a vital concern in the areas of application, including an informed public policy in the area of refugees and health.

From such an applied perspective, the qualitative dimensions of health and illness can thus constitute an important component in quantitative investigations in cross-cultural contexts: Eliciting and examining refugees' categories and explanations of distress and exploring the full range of local meanings associated with these provide a necessary basis to ensure relevance and validity for subsequent epidemiological or other quantitative studies. The ethnographic approaches can also be a vital tool in clinical assessments or treatment, expanding the restricted context of the clinical encounter as well as the bases of the clinician's understanding, thus bridging anthropological and clinical traditions.[5] Although not specifically dealt with here, ethnography is also a valuable tool to understand clinicians and clinical settings, the medical system and health care organization in which refugees become patients.

Notes

1. This means that a sentence or a word is translated from one language to another by a bilingual person and then translated back to the original by another bilingual person.
2. For a more detailed description of the use of personal narratives and life histories as an ethnographic method, see Eastmond (1996).
3. Narratives can also be used to capture the personal meaning of suffering or illness in relation to its wider social meaning. Good and Good (1980) recognized this tension, emphasizing that the meaning illness has for an individual is grounded in, but not reducible to, the network of meanings that illness has for a particular culture.
4. See Low (1994) for a review of these studies.
5. In my collaboration with a local refugee medical center, this takes the form of an ongoing dialogue between my fieldwork in refugee communities and the clinical practice of psychiatrists, psychotherapists, and physiotherapists. The clinical work is also connected to a professional team that covers the broader legal, social, and economic concerns of refugee patients.

References

Bringa, T. (1995). *Being Muslim the Bosnian way.* Cambridge: Cambridge University Press

Brislin, R., Lonner, W.,and Thorndike, R. (1973). *Cross-cultural research methods.* New York: John Wiley.

Corlin, C. (1990). Chaos, order and world view: Tibetan refugees in Switzerland. *Disaster, 15*:2:87-113.

Eastmond, M..(1989). *The Dilemma of exile. Chilean refugees in the United States.* Gothenburg: Gothenburg Studies in Social Anthropology.

Eastmond, M. (1991). *Evaluación del proyecto de la Fundación Salud para Todos.* Report for the Lions International/ Sweden.

Eastmond, M. (1996). Luchar y sufrir–stories of life and exile: Reflections on the ethnographic process. *Ethnos, 61*:3-4:231-249.

Eastmond, M. (1998a). National discourses and the construction of difference: Bosnian Muslims in Sweden. *Journal of Refugee Studies, 11*:2:161-181.

Eastmond, M. (1998b). From displacement to disorder: The medicalisation of refugees, Paper presented at the 6th IRAP Conference, (IASFM) Jerusalem, December.

Eisenbruch, M. (1990). The cultural bereavement interview: A new clinical and research approach with refugees. *Psychiatric Clinics of North America, 13*:4:715-735.

Eisenbruch, M. (1991). From Post-Traumatic Stress Disorder to cultural bereavement: Diagnosis of Southeast Asian refugees. Paper presented at the 2nd IRAP Conference, (IASFM) Oxford, January.

Eyton, J. and Neuwirth, G. (1984). Cross-cultural validity: Ethnocentrism in health studies with special reference to the Vietnamese. *Social Science and Medicine, 18*:5:447-453.

Good, B.J. (1994). *Medicine, rationality, and experience. An anthropological perspective.* Cambridge: Cambridge University Press.

Good, B. and Good M. J. D. (1980). The Meaning of symptoms: A cultural hermeneutic model for clinical practice. In Eisenberg, L. and Kleinman, A. (Eds.), *The Relevance of social science for medicine.* Dordrecht: Reidel, 165-195.

Good, B. and Good M. J. D. (1982). Towards a meaning-centered analysis of popular illness categories: "Fright-illness" and "heart-distress" in Iran. In Marsella, A. J. and White, G. M. (Eds.), *Cultural conceptions of mental health and therapy* . Dordrecht: Reidel.

Herbst, P. K. R.(1992). From helpless victim to empowered survivor: Oral history as a treatment for survivors of torture. In *Refugee women and their mental health: Shattered societies, shattered lives.* New York and London: Norwood.

Kleinman, A. (1977). Depression, somatization and the "new cross-cultural psychiatry." *Social Science and Medicine, 11*:3-10.

Kleinman, A. (1980). *Patients and healers in the context of culture.* Berkeley: University of California Press.

Kleinman, A. (1995). Pitch, picture, power: The globalization of local suffering and the transformation of social experience. *Ethos, 60*:3-4:181-191.

Lifton, R. J. (1993). From Hiroshima to the Nazi doctors: The evolution of psycho-formative approaches to understanding traumatic stress syndromes. In Wilson, J. P. and Raphael, B. (Eds.), *International handbook of traumatic stress syndromes.* New York: Plenum Press, 11-24.

Low, S. M. (1994). Embodied metaphors: Nerves as lived experience. In Csordas, T. J. (Ed.), *Embodiment and Experience.* Cambridge Studies in

Medical Anthropology. Cambridge: Cambridge University Press, 139-162.

Malinowski, B. (1944). *A scientific theory of culture and other essays.* Oxford and New York: Oxford University Press.

Malkki, L. (1995). Refugees and exile: From "refugee studies" to the national order of things. *Annual Review of Anthropology, 24:*495-523

Marsella, A. J and Kameoka, V. A. (1989). Ethnocultural Issues in the Assessment of Psychopathology. In Wetzler, S. (Ed.), *Measuring mental illness: Psychometric assessment for clinicians.* Washington: American Psychiatric Press, 231-256.

Mimica, J. (1997). Psychosocial projects: Evaluation issues derived from forced migrants' and helpers' points of view . Paper presented at the conference entitled, The Study of Forced Migration–Psychological, Legal, Humanitarian, and Anthropological Interventions (June). Hvar, Croatia.

Morsy, S. A. (1996). Political economy in medical anthropology. In Sargent, C. and Johnson, M. (Eds.), *Handbook of medical anthropology: Contemporary theory and method* (revised edition). Westport, CT and London: Praeger, 21-40.

Sachs, L. (1983). *Evil eye or bacteria: Turkish migrant women and Swedish health care.* Stockholm: Stockholm Studies in Social Anthropology.

Scheper-Hughes, N. (1992). *Death without weeping: The violence of everyday life in Brazil.* Berkeley and Los Angeles: University of California Press.

Sennemark, E. (1997). *Utvärdering av Bosnien-projektet..* MA thesis. Department of Social Anthropology, Göteborg University.

Skultans, V. (1997). A historical disorder: neurasthenia and the testimony of lives in Latvia.. *Anthropology and Medicine, 4:*1:7-24.

Stepputat, F. (1992). *Beyond relief? Life in a Guatemalan refugee settlement in Mexico.* Ph.D. dissertation. Copenhagen: Institute of Cultural Sociology

Tapp, N. (1989). The reformation of culture: Hmong refugees from Laos. *Journal of Refugee Studies, 1:*1, 20-37.

Tung, T. (1984). Indochinese patients: Action for Southeast Asians. As quoted in Eyton, J. and Neuwirth, G. (Eds.), Cross-cultural validity: Ethnocentrism in health studies with special reference to the Vietnamese. *Social Science and Medicine, 18:*5:447-453.

Woodcock. J. (1997). Group work with refugees and asylum seekers. In Mistry, T. and Brown, A. (Eds.), *Race and Group Work.* London: Whiting and Birch.

5

The Autobiographical Method of Investigating the Psychosocial Wellness of Refugees

Didier Bertrand

This chapter is the result of my research carried out with refugees who were awaiting transit and resettlement from a camp in Thailand. The purpose of the research was to understand the dynamics of social and identity restructuring in the camps as the roles that refugees played were changed and altered. I will examine in this chapter the methodological and ethical issues in controlling and analyzing the interactions that take place during biographical interviews between a researcher and an informant. These interactive elements are an integral part of the research process, which need to be taken into account in order to: 1) express and construct the real setting of the information collected, and 2) analyze how subjectivity may interfere in the research process.

- *Exploration* in which the main issues and the dilemma of the refugees are drawn out;
- *Analysis* of content, context, and interactions;
- *An expressive overview* of what the refugee and researcher are doing in search of meaning.

Autobiography is thus an approach that is used to investigate the psychosocial wellness of a person. It requires subjective testimony of a person's current well-being with respect to adversity and the manner in which one builds his/her life. Furthermore, the process results in the collection of a large amount of raw material that can be used in different ways, with different methods, and with different perspectives. The autobiographical interview introduces the complexity and meaning of the interviewee's actions. In a refugee camp, we listen to hesitant, uncertain people, observing their behavioral changes in an interactive environment in which they testify about their past lives.

The Setting of the Autobiographical Interview

I began interviewing refugees who had been accepted to be resettled in France. These interviews took place in the library of the Quebec school in the camp since I needed a quiet and rather neutral place, and at a time convenient for them, when they were not in school or their training programs, eating, or looking for water or wood for fuel. I started the interview sessions by explaining that I was doing a research about refugee life and expectations, and that the results might be used in France in order to train people working with refugees in assistance projects or persons in charge of resettlement policies.

Most of the refugees knew me as a former program field director. The first problems that I faced were the issues of credibility and reliability, such that refugees would trust me and feel comfortable enough to speak to me. We would sit on a mat at the same level as I would start the interview, presenting myself and my interpreter who spoke in Vietnamese or Khmer so that there was more proximity. I often explained that I was not able to understand all that was said in their native language and I apologized for it. Usually the interpreter, a refugee him/herself waiting for resettlement, was known to the refugees as a teacher of French language in the camp. I would also explain why I decided to interview this person since I would not interview all the refugees bound for France. The usual reason for my selection was that these refugees were facing a problem in learning French or had other difficulties. As part of my approach, I would explain that I wanted to understand if they had any problems that could be helped. In using the autobiographical method in the transit refugee camp, I had only one refusal, and that from a woman who claimed that her husband did not want her to talk to me. A few others failed to attend their scheduled appointments which were arranged in writing for them by the translator.

The Methodology of Autobiography

Use of the autobiographical approach focuses on the interactions of researcher and refugee, the management of emotional content during the interview, and an assessment of the biographical material gained during the interview process. Each of these dimensions is discussed below.

The Position Maintained by the Researcher with His/Her Informant

The autobiographical method which is used to conduct biographical interviews is generally known in the field of anthropology. In order to maintain his/her position, the researcher who conducts an autobiographical session should:

- Have the empathy to listen and understand the point of view of the person that is being interviewed;
- Demonstrate an unconditional acceptance and neutrality (impartiality);[1]
- Be as non-directive as possible in order to not modify the refugee's way of thinking.[2]

The researcher obviously does not simply "lend an ear" to what is being said, but he/she is subject to "emotional transference" as his/her role as researcher is affirmed when the refugee allows the researcher to speak. Or the refugee might put the researcher in an undesirable position that is not expected, such as spy, friend, helper, etc. Keep in mind that most of the refugees have never met a researcher before and the experience might be imbued with different meanings given their understanding of the situation as they relate their life stories to an unknown person. This calls into question the researcher's ability to deal with the situation, and the context of the process of "otherness" and transference that is being observed.

Counter-transference can be analyzed by first recognizing the researcher's involvement in this research method, which determines the degree of empathy for the informant. We should be aware that there is no absolute non-involvement, and different categories of findings influence the researcher's singular and collective identity, his/her functions, theory, or ideology which may provoke an emotional response. Thus, the refugee's narration often raises emotional content, transference, and counter-transference material of which the researcher must be aware.

The transference phenomenon operates at both the representational and personal affective levels. The counter-transference of the researcher is continuous. While working on our research objective, for instance, we often become defensive because of certain research elements which appear worrisome in the interview.

The questions of subjective, personal experience and involvement imply an analysis of the situation as well as a scope of knowledge. It is necessary to point out that the researcher recognizes the subconscious aspects of biographical material, where there are possibilities to fantasize, and the anticipated behaviors of the actors and the victims. These are all part of the first level of the researcher's involvement in the story and its analysis. The researcher's awareness of his/her thematic choice supports the answers that are expected.

First of all, research begins by renouncing and temporarily forgetting the preconceived knowledge that we have about the subject. Hence, one becomes sensitive and attentive to what is being said, although it might not respond to or be in accord with our questions and hypotheses.

The informant is obviously knowledgeable of the topic that he/she is speaking about, and the researcher is there to listen, understand, and if necessary to remind the person of what he/she is supposed to be speaking about. The researcher has to be aware of his/her own ignorance; it counters his/her status and dominant role as often represented by the refugee. In fact, the informant is the important person in the interview, and without his/her agreement nothing can start or be done. The researcher commences by asking the informant to speak so that he/she can progressively fit in the answers to the researcher's questions while telling his/her story. The researcher encourages the informant to speak by emphasizing the importance of subjectivity, by telling his/her personal story.

In the refugee camp, there were leaflets in different languages secretly distributed by refugees themselves in order to prepare them for resettlement interviews. These leaflets explained what to say and what not to say. At times, I had to remind refugees not tell me these standardized stories so that they would not censor their manner of thinking while in the presence of the researcher. By being flexible in the way the interview is conducted and being attentive and not patronizing, the researcher aims to allow the informants to speak for themselves. In this way, refugee informants might feel that they are learning from their own revelations as they become aware of and realize what they related during the interview. Questioning should be progressive and evolving. One should be careful to avoid overwhelming the informant, while maintaining a pleasant, warm, and hospitable exchange.

Carefully listening to all that is said by the informant allows the researcher, for instance, to understand the day-to-day worries of the refugees in the camp and also their reactions to living in a closed community. Notes from my research diary highlight my thinking about a refugee's life in the camp.

Before I came to the camp, I naively imagined a transit camp as a safe shelter after a tormented journey, a place where you can find some food, health care, education, and relative safety so it would be a good place to learn. I realized quickly that refugee's life in a closed camp is far different from what it looks like from the outside. This realization helped me to build one of the main hypothesis of my research—that the ones who face the most difficulties in learning French before being resettled are also the ones who face the most difficulties in adapting to the camp life. This brings an additional burden for them that disrupts their learning. So those refugees who oppose camp may be the very ones who should be the first to leave.

One must consider not only material issues, such as water and food distribution for refugees, but also their safety. Having a good social network is important in counteracting the effects of the stresses of everyday life, including the conflicts with and humiliations from local guards, the isolation within overcrowded shelters, the presence of promiscuity, the need to improve the minimal daily food rations, and the difficulties in learning another language. How can a refugee have time for anything else?

I cannot simply tell the informants, "Now you are in the camp and it is better for you. Tell me about the times when you were young." If I said this, I would limit my chances to collect valuable information. One should be very attentive to what is worrying persons being interviewed. With research of this kind, using questions of little interest or rattling off a list of questions, refugees will react negatively, refusing, avoiding, or failing to respond. This approach also compromises the accuracy of the interview process. Thus, the researcher should "move off the center stage" and be in a position to receive the information, listening to what the subjects wish to say. It is important that researchers place themselves in the refugee's shoes so that they can focus on and understand the logic, affect, sequence, and context of the autobiography.

Empathy and Neutrality: Managing Emotions and Their Implications

Certain conditions can allow the level of self-censoring to drop and the defensive responses become less obvious between the informant and the researcher. Reminding the refugees or war victims of memories which are sometimes traumatizing, the stories told can take a tragic turn by evoking a range of negative emotional responses. Nondirectivity permits the emergence of very deep feelings. The comments of some refugees who said that they had a headache after an interview reflects the mental strain of the interview. The autobiographical method that surveys a refugee's life may awaken many memories of loss and grief. Refugees may recall feelings of hopeless illusions and reality. There is no doubt that these situations evoke nothing pleasant. Instead, they serve as a reminder of very stressful events and times that have had serious consequences.

When a refugee mentions unhappiness and suffering, the researcher should listen to these words without feeling responsible for their cause. The informant is free to refuse an interview, as well as free to say whatever. It is very important to remind the respondent of this freedom to participate or not, to speak or not speak, and to terminate the interviews whenever they wish.

Since I am not a therapist, I was always afraid of interfering in the lives of refugees. It seems important not to rekindle their traumas as they are often in need of psychological support, therapy, and follow-up. I was not always able to reassure informants. If one of them needed support, it was necessary to be present, available, and responsible and not simply walk away once I had collected all my information for the interview. Ethically speaking in these cases, the researcher owes the informant help and, if available, should refer the person for appropriate medical or psychological help.

Over the months, I slowly became someone with whom people could talk and confide within the camp. Some of the refugees came to meet and speak to me, and they knew that I was interested in them and their lives. One can imagine how gratifying it is to find somebody with whom you can talk in a friendly and informal manner. Some of the interviews were followed by sharing meals together. This was done in order to rediscuss the themes which were discussed earlier, or ask other questions which might be bothering the informants. I was faced with other difficulties due to the fact that the position of the researcher in the camp is totally atypical. It was assumed that all Europeans were entrusted with some powers of decision-making, powers that often exceed their actual abilities. For example, a number of times refugees approached me in the streets requesting help to resolve their refugee status application problems with the United States. It was very difficult for me to convince them that I did not have any of the decision-making powers that other foreigners had in determining the fate of refugees. Even neutrality is suspect. I knew that, for some time, a rumor was spread in the camp that I was a spy for the embassy. Since these refugees had lived most of their lives under totalitarian regimes, it was easy to understand their misgivings about my research and misinterpretations about who made decisions. I had to cope with these suspicions and distrustful mentalities. In refugee camps, one should realize that such things are part of their survival strategy.

I have been able to help some of the refugees in a discreet way by talking with some officials or referring them to the right person such as a mental health worker or social worker. The absolute neutrality that some researchers insist upon would be viewed by refugees here as an unworthy and unacceptable indifference. In exchange for the information received, the researcher may assist the refugee through advice and recommendations. When doing this, it is important not to use a condescending tone. The researcher should be compassionate and careful about the risks of interfering.

In the process of testifying about their autobiographical stories, refugees have invited me to share both their past and present sufferings, such as exile, flight, traumas, illnesses, losses, and the horrible experiences of war. The researcher listens by being attentive to what is said and to what is not said, managing the emotional weight of the interview, which sometimes is not easy. For instance, a woman was telling me how her children were recently killed by pirates on the sea. How should one react to such long silences that interrupt the telling of the story? There are silences that are painful, a pain that cannot be expressed with words; silences that are full of the nostalgia of being away from one's country for a long time, a country that one loves and wishes to return to; and, silences that are full of horror, a part of a life that is too difficult to share.

Obviously, these autobiographies can make the researcher weep, be depressed, and, at the same time, feel a kind of euphoria created by a closeness to the victim that is being interviewed. As a consequence, the researcher may have the urge to console, comfort, and to hug. It is difficult sometimes to know what to do, how much compassion to show, and how much feeling to express. Following repeated interviews with trauma victims, the researcher may worry too much about the interviewee, wishing to help him/her make up for and undo the sufferings though some magical and fantastic power. Or the researcher may succumb to boredom, leading to difficulties in focusing on the questions at hand, listening attentively, and accurately transcribing what has taken place and said. During this process of collecting autobiographies, I found myself experiencing nightmares with some frequency. After an interview, it is not unusual that the researcher may not be unable to think or concentrate on anything else apart from the refugee's story that was just heard. The researcher bears an inverse trauma which is demonstrated by psychosomatic and avoidance symptoms and even intrusive thinking. The investigator certainly does not come out unharmed from the meeting, and has to try hard to control these undesirable emotional and physical symptoms.

Another entry in my diary captures my feelings as I began the biographical interviews:

> After my first day in the camp, I can see how very difficult my first interviews with Khmer refugees were, being aware of the defenses that I mobilized to avoid listening, especially to stories about the horrors of Pol Pot. I started the first interview in Thai language that I didn't speak or understand well. This placed some distance between the words and me. I was so worried to wake up with dreadful memories. I was also afraid that the first refugee that I interviewed would commit suicide because I gave him an opportunity to remember ... but he returned here the day after smiling as usual, and I was the one who left with worries and nightmares. I remember as well how difficult it was to come back to these tapes. Some of them remained on my desk for weeks. I deliberately avoided listening to them. I realized also after listening to the first interviews that I didn't let the person speak very long about their Khmer Rouge experience. I tried to steer them to another period of their life when they fled Cambodia and sought asylum in Thailand. But, wasn't this a way not to provoke a discussion of this trauma for the refugee that I was so afraid to touch the subject ... or afraid also to be traumatized myself by hearing the story?

Analyzing Autobiographical Material

To respect and maintain authentic research, the researcher has to stay in the background while recording what the refugee desired to say, or at least what the interpreter has translated from Khmer to French. Facts do not speak for themselves, but rather are analyzed as part of interactions, values, and meanings. The investigator plays an active role in the research and anticipation phase by conceptualizing the stories in order to capture their social and cultural value into a collective thesis (which constitutes a sociological synthesis). The work of an ethnopsychologist (which I consider myself) is to highlight through the use of autobiographical information the person, his/her psychosocial identity, and the context and meanings that help to explain the refugee's life, personal story, and cultural values.

The biographical story is a process that may travel to the depths of a refugee's life. It needs the prior recognition of the researcher as somebody who is able to receive the words that have been confided. The biographical interview is a field for dual experiences: in a certain way the refugee narrator makes his/her life public, saying "Look at me: see how well I am" or "See how I am suffering." These statements make it possible for us to understand the person's being. The refugee reveals something to the researcher, who is a spectator, i.e., listening and accepting the statement. The researcher can, however, introduce another reality by his/her questions, being careful not to break the mirror that has been established between the two.

We know that memory may be inconstant, whimsical, unreliable, and repressed, factors that call into question the truthfulness of words that refugees utilize to survive. The value of the autobiographical testimony is that its analysis is more than establishing truth and falsehood. While it is not a simple account of the real past and what we know already, autobiography seeks to establish the truth of the self and its meaning. Refugees already have had numerous experiences in the past with the police of their country of origin, the United Nations High Commissioner for Refugees (UNHCR) to establish their status as "refugee," and countries where they wish to resettle that they have been socialized into specific strategies to be accepted for resettlement. These acquired "stories" make it difficult for the researcher and often contaminate the biographic story. So, can the investigator expect that the interview process with refugees to be neutral? Can it really be? Even in France, social workers find it difficult to get a story that remains the same (names, relatives, events might change over time). Throughout their lives, refugees have masked a certain part of their story, or highlighted their professional experiences (in order to be selected), or persecutions (in order to get a refugee status), in an imaginary and creative way. Within the embassies of the countries offering resettlement, a paradoxical situation existed in that everyone knew that a refugee's story at application for resettlement was not one hundred percent true. However, all played the game well. The leaflets in Khmer, Vietnamese, French, and English that circulated in the camps, also gave refugees the expected responses that resettlement countries expected.

The made-up story is filled with realities of life. Refugees use various versions of their life story depending upon the situation and purpose. It is influenced by a number of complex factors with social and psychological origin, incorporating also elements of past, present, and future. We ourselves, for instance, when we write our *curriculum vitae* (CV) may tailor it for a particular person or position, adding, modifying, or omitting professional experiences and even academic degrees. It is something similar when a refugee reveals his autobiography. In particular, time participates in the social and identity construction of the reality of the refugee. The person's comprehension, conscience, and magnitude of the worldly horizon (which has different values in each society), testify to the capacities of the subject to find the meaning of his/her story. Beiser (1988)[3] put it this way:

... to concentrate on the present and cutting off from the past and future seems to be a survival strategy for the refugee which leads to the blindness to the world where one is not allowed to think of the past and does not consider what the future can bring. If this is a regular phenomenon in the camps, depression and mental illnesses can be risks that will accompany the unavoidable process of worldly reintegration at the time of reinstallation.

In fact, the ethnopsychologist is more interested in the way in which refugees see themselves and the manner in which they describe their story (optimistic, passive, or active: full of expectations, sufferings, or hope). Each person presents a unique story that captures the way it was lived and the way it is imagined or the way that he or she expects us to hear the story. Even the manipulations in story-telling is also part of one's culture.

When refugees relate their personal and collective stories that may be interesting and painful, they are involved in a process that permits them to find meaning in their long and perilous lives. By keeping a distance from what has happened and from the purpose of what was said, one can analyze the results to understand the affective involvement of the researcher and his role. The raw data of the autobiographic interviews that have been collected during the complicated development of the subject will be condensed, analyzed, and interpreted.

Analysis

Autobiography (a tool in which person A encourages person B to speak in order to get information written in the biography of B) is a tool of the researcher which should be placed above the knowledge of the person who is speaking and relationship between sexes. For instance, it is very difficult for us to conceptualize the importance of the change of a refugee's image that he/she experienced as a member of the community. The importance of collective identity clashes with our own ideas of the individualist subject, particularly the Vietnamese, since in the end it is not the individual who is telling his story to the world, but rather it is the group's voice that is hear. The oral narration becomes more a story of social life than of asserting oneself. In contrast to Western assumptions, all subjects do not play the role of the subject in their own story nor do they pose in front of the elements or events. Rather, they integrate themselves in these elements as part of their fate or their *karma* in a Buddhist understanding. Knowing about the strong reluctance of Asians to speak about themselves and their sentiments, I commented on in my diary while in the refugee camp:

Many refugees were accepted for resettlement in France because during the selection process, they spoke to a French person by emphasizing their position in the family, using such phrases as, "my father was ... in the ex-government." At first it sounded strange. I heard this as a way to avoid speaking about themselves and their choices as ego, but I realized that it had more to do with the way they defined themselves as an individual, i.e., how they linked themselves to others and mostly to the family.

There is no individual person as such, but we can observe complementarity and stability in the entire cosmic integration where the achievement of the individual is not the holder of his life and is not alone and not different from the others.

Autobiography was born as a literary form with the advent of the Western industrial civilization and the rise of the bourgeoisie. It is important to note that this kind of interview brings a cultural model of the subject which has to be adapted prudently in other civilizations and culture. For instance, in Asia the person is placed in a more holistic conception where complementarity and harmony are favored, whereas the Western model of the subject favors individual achievement and mastery of his/her life.

The assertion of the ego is entwined in ideology and cultural background reflecting on the conception of a human being and human development. By speaking of one's past or future, the subject places him/herself in a historical, social, and cultural constellation, in particular the family, in link with the supernatural. The individual is enmeshed in a conflict of times—that of the past (respect for ancestors), the future, and the family projects for which one is the bearer.

I believe that building an autobiographical profile helps to place the subject on a temporal axis where the present is seen as the outcome of previous alterations. But what I often find is that the temporal axis reflects a Western representation of time. For example, a Southeast Asian person has a cyclical time concept dissimilar to the Newtonian linear time frame. In order to better understand Khmer and Cambodian refugees, we have to examine the conception of the person and his/her development connected with Buddhism and folk beliefs. In terms of knowledge, the refugee's knowledge is understood and articulated with the knowledge of the researcher: one of the scopes of biographical research is to develop this double setting to move into scientific knowledge.

The discourse of the interviewee is the main element in establishing a perspective, more than a historical, ideological, or subconscious articulation of data about a complex object. This singular story is also saturated with "empty" words borrowed from social stereotypes, but the person telling the story, the aspects of his/her life, and what is precious or seen as worries, paradoxically appear suddenly in the margins, in the off-points of the dialogue which accumulates and builds up in relation to the supposed expectation of the other.

Only an integrated and multidisciplinary approach allows us to understand how subjects use, construct, define, and express meaning in their lives through their biographical story. In this way, we come to how they make intelligible the multiplicity of constraints that impinge on their choices and decision in politics, laws, economy, morality, values, and religion.

Conclusion

Autobiography can be used when we want to investigate a complex situation and when we presume that the facts we want to investigate are the result of a long-term process involving time and other factors. It is an appropriate investigation method as it opens and gives power to persons who are the most concerned about and effected by the problem that we intend to study. Also, autobiography can be used as an adjunct to other approaches, either qualitative or quantitative. Oftentimes, it allows us to draw representative samples from a larger population that may be studied in greater detail.

Autobiography in itself is completely subjective. It is from the individual subjectivity that we can gain more psychological understanding. It is, however, intended to lead to a strict and objective analysis of what is going on, beginning with the interactions between researcher and person interviewed, and progressing later to content analysis of data. A researcher may pursue a more objective assessment of the data through a structural analysis of a refugee's life, or through computerized statistical analysis.

The autobiographical method carries out an epistemological inversion as it attempts to understand situations and events by putting oneself in the point of view of the social actors who are experts of their own cultures. It allows better definition of how the subject lives with time, space, institutions, and an understanding of one's history of destructions, conflicts, destructuring, and restructuring. The researcher can then better understand the social and historical world which surround the refugee in a complex web of social interactions, role networks, expectations, orders, norms, values, and punishments. Initially, the importance of the economic, social, and cultural context appears, followed by a strong overlapping current that links the biographical story of the individual with the characteristics of his/her personality, family group, and institutional structures. The Vietnamese and Cambodian refugees who are survivors have specific life experiences where the elaboration of loss is linked with their Buddhist beliefs in which *dukha*, suffering, is inevitable, and the origin of life is conceived as the result of earlier life actions of *karma*. These explanations, however, are not the only ones that the researcher may systematically come to. An examination of a matrix of complex meanings will result in many findings.

In contrast to questionnaires, which give models of pre-established thinking and representations developed by the researcher, the biographical interview allows personal wordings and a very large scope for thinking and reflection. Answers are not proposed and subjects are free to give their own content, form, and length. The subject can use his/her own terms and ways of reasoning, which allow a subconscious approach and motivation in the emotive and irrational responses. Autobiography illuminates a sharp comprehension and intimacy with the subject, his/her internal conflicts, choices, and the paradoxes of life that one has to manage.

However, there are difficulties with this kind of research. One issue is that the researcher is directly concerned about his/her expectations and representations and also about his/her interactions with the subject. Another issue is the degree of empathy to be expressed to the person offering a testimony or confiding in the investigator. How best can the researcher regulate and modulate the exchange with the interviewee? Autobiography presents an array of problems for the researcher and while it may prove cathartic for refugees, there is a concern about how to establish and use trust in the storytelling process. Once trust is established and refugees agree to participate, the biographic process begins to progress smoothly. Telling their histories permits refugees a vehicle for explicating aspects of their personal changes and interpersonal actions of their life. With this method, refugees can better understand and appreciate the personal perspectives and sociopolitical and historical contexts, adjustments, and role shifts that they undergo in making decisions that affect their lives.

The scientific story is then built by a series of breaks and identifications in the process of storytelling, especially since the person's position or status is not predefined. The process evolves little by little as the story revolves around poles of recognition and acceptance where the researcher manages the differences around common points of interest. It is important that the researcher not forget that this life story is very valuable for the one relating the account because often the person needs to express the tale as testimony of the sufferings that have been survived.

The biographical method is, however, only one method among many that are complementary. For example, after I completed the autobiographical interviews and the analysis of the thematic content, I conducted a computerized, lexical analysis of the data, performed an analysis of cases, and then constructed a questionnaire that I subjected to correlation analysis and factor analysis. Only a plurality of readings, qualitative and quantitative, that are supported by specific reference models, can explain the complexity of a refugee's reality, allowing an understanding of the ways that the subject expresses and gives meaning to life. Autobiography is a first step to clinical understanding, and later steps may be found in its materials that may elaborate questionnaires and deeper investigations.

Autobiography can provide indications about the well-being of refugees through answering such questions as:

- What are the criteria that refugees utilize to describe well-being?
- How do they relate their feelings, thoughts, and experiences, positive and negative?
- How can refugee workers plan the appropriate services and programs to address the issues and problems that refugees have identified?

Every refugee has had a unique experience, and thus has a unique story. This individual relies upon strategies that employ cognitive and psycho-affective elements as well as other strategies that have proved effective in extremely complex situations. Refugees reveal many ideas, norms, and practices on which they learn to mold, form, and build their identity. Autobiography is one method to study a refugee's story that we use to comprehend the web of interactions, experiences, thoughts, values, and structures that give substance to the respondent's personal identity.

Notes

1. The collection of autobiographical stories presupposes that the researcher respects and believes the words of the subject.
2. Nonsuggestive and clear stimulations to a subject allows him or her to go into details during the interview. However, one should not be too intrusive in order to not create a block. Reformulating, especially when it concerns the interpreter, allows the ambiguities of the testimony and the areas which lack understanding to be brought out. It also shows that we are listening and understanding, while being aware that improvised reformulations can lead to a break in the narration. One should ask clear cut questions instead.
3. See Beiser, M. (1988). Influence of time, ethnicity, and attachment on depression in Southeast Asian refugees. *American Journal of Psychiatry, 145*:1.

Part III

CASE STUDIES OF
REFUGEE PSYCHOSOCIAL WELLNESS
Quantitative Approaches

In this section, we turn our attention to the use of primarily quantitative methods in order to investigate the psychosocial wellness of refugees. The literature concerning refugees is replete with studies that attempt to understand the psychological consequences of forced migration and its traumatic experiences and to explain the factors that lead to health adjustment in the aftermath of the experience. The next three chapters reveal distinct ways to tackle the study of refugee wellness.

In chapter 6, the reader encounters the investigations of Raija-Leena Punamäki whose purpose is to link political reality with psychological processes as she studies the suffering of Palestinian children, women, and ex-prisoners. Her emphasis is on psychological wellness that stresses strengths, such as mastery, goal-orientation, and the struggle for justice. Punamäki is interested in how these populations "mobilize all human capacities including political, social, and mental to encourage endurance." She speaks of "action research" where investigators use their findings not only for the advancement of knowledge, but also for the planning and implementation of service programs and for advocacy and policy.

Miriam Potocky-Tripodi examines data of the United States's national census to determine the economic integration of various refugee groups in the United States. Her studies focus on the relative adjustment of Southeast Asians, Central Americans, Cubans, Haitians, Eastern Europeans, including those from the former Soviet bloc countries as compared with non-immigrant/refugee groups. In chapter 7, she: 1) presents a theoretical model that guides her work in refugee adaption and economic integration; 2) discusses six factors that influence economic integrations; 3) describes the U.S. census and the database from which she drew her information; and 4) elaborates on her sophisticated methodology utilizing quantitative measures and statistical analyses to ascertain the adjustment of resettled refugees and immigrants.

The literature contains meager reference to what happens to refugees who have returned to their former homes. In chapter 8, Maryanne Loughry and her Vietnamese colleague Nguyen Xuan Nghia present their findings about refugee youth who were forcibly repatriated to their home areas. This study is characterized by use of cross-sectional analysis of the adjustment of this returning group of young people, who did not escape their country. Loughry and Nghia explain how they defined and measured psychosocial wellness and present the factors that influenced the mental health of returnees and their counterparts.

These three examples illustrate issues in doing quantitative research: definition, operationalization of variables, reliability and validity of measures, sampling, difficulties in collecting data, use of statistical analysis, and finally, the use and generalization of findings.

6

Measuring Suffering

CONFLICTS AND SOLUTIONS IN REFUGEE STUDIES

Raija-Leena Punamäki

Introduction

This chapter introduces my research experiences among Palestinian women, children, and political ex-prisoners and discusses some conflicting issues. First, I will present our research settings and questions and explore the theoretical models that depict the links between the sociopolitical reality and psychological experience. Then, I will respond to the critics of psychological research on traumatized refugees who object to it on political, ethical, and scientific grounds. They argue that the applied models ignore human resourcefulness, cultural diversity, and political context. My response is that psychosocial well-being is also a victim's human right. Research can expand our knowledge about the processes that facilitate recovery from trauma, and this knowledge, if properly translated into intervention, helps people to recover. Finally, I will present two significant findings from this research: first, the role of ideological commitment in promoting well-being in violent conditions; and second, the function of dreaming in processing and recovering from painful experiences.

The Setting

The violence which we have been subjected to is a nightmare. It all happened suddenly, and I still feel that the demolishing of our home cannot be true. When I am looking at the ruins of our house, I feel that something terrible has happened to us, but still, the ruins are not real to me. I have the feeling that somebody else is looking at the remains of our home, somebody who is not me.[1]

The interview is taking place in a green tent adjacent to the newly ruined stone house. A dozen chairs welcome visitors, as in a traditional Arab living room. Another tent, filled with mattresses, serves as the family's sleeping room. Among the crushed stone walls and cement floor the visitor can discern pieces of furniture, clothes, and a doll. Our hostess has just returned from visiting her two detained sons, and when we arrive she is sobbing quietly. She says:

> My detained sons are 15 and 16 years old. Finally I got a permission to visit them in Moscobiyye (a detention center in West Jerusalem). The youngest was crying, his stomach was aching, his pains were unbearable, and he could not walk or stand straight. He had been badly beaten by the interrogators. I had to carry him in my arms as if he were a little boy.... I said to him: "Prison is for men, you have to stand and be strong." What else could I, as a Palestinian mother, have told my son? What else?

I met this woman of fifty-four years of age in the West Bank town of Beit Sahour, in 1979. The Israeli army had destroyed three houses in the village in order to punish the families because their youngsters threw stones at the soldiers. Human rights lawyers were there protesting to the international press, a small group of Israeli peace activists came to show their solidarity, and Palestinian volunteers gradually rebuilt the family's home.

Experiences like this motivated my research among Palestinian women, children, and political ex-prisoners. The Palestinians lost their homeland in 1948, and in 1967 hundreds of thousands more were forced out of the West Bank to become refugees in Jordan and Lebanon. The Palestinians who live under Israeli military occupation are still being confronted with more land confiscations to make room for more immigrants into "Greater Israel."

The political conflict is thus the very basic issue in this psychosocial research. Palestinian lives are characterized by loss and violence, humiliation and suffering. Palestinians are also renowned for their persistent struggle for independence and for their refusal to succumb to foreign occupation. The victims' horrors exist side by side with the fighters' heroism, and this political double message is actively present in everyday life. The political conflict has its imprint on child development, parenting philosophy, and individual and collective attempts at mastery. As a researcher, my task is to reveal the phenomenon in its all richness, and to document and crystallize the human conflict of suffering and endurance.

The Question

In order to be able to provide psychological help to the civilians who live under such extreme conditions, it was necessary to find out how military violence affects family life, mothering, mental health, and child development. We aimed at analyzing the psychological processes and social factors that may protect civilian victims: to understand how people manage to blossom despite their objectively painful experiences.

Table 6.1 summarizes the main research questions, samples, measurements, and findings of our psychosocial studies among Palestinians. We examined the women's appraisal of their own resources, their coping strategies, their feelings of control, and the social support they received as protecting factors. As far as the children were concerned, the research focused on coping strategies and mastery over military violence, attitudes to war, peace, and the enemy, and their well-being. Together with the Gaza Community Mental Health Programme research team, we have tried to reveal the secret of child resilience during the Intifada violence, and studied cognitive capacity such as creativity and intelligence, quality of parenting, and attitudes to peace as mediating between exposure to trauma and psychological adjustment. The symbolic capacity of processing painful experiences seems to be especially salient for children's endurance, and therefore we studied the relationships between traumatic events and dreaming and playing. Our research on political ex-prisoners included epidemiological and qualitative studies, and we are currently attempting to find out about healing and rehabilitation practices among torture victims.

These research projects involved extensive fieldwork. We visited Palestinian homes and schools before and after the uprising, the Intifada, during and after the 1982 Lebanon war, and when the area became part of the Palestinian Authority. For me, the foreigner, the visits served as an intensive course in psychology, political science, and history. Patiently and vividly, Palestinians taught me the secrets of human suffering, endurance, and purposeful activity in the context of a national struggle.

Parents often expressed their worries about the impact of the ever-present violence and death on their children's development. They asked how they could promote their children's well-being, learning abilities, moral development, and healthy human relationships in the years to come. Many of the later research questions originated in these conversations. For instance, ex-detainees often told us how they suffered from nightmares, repetitive violent dreams, and sleeping difficulties. Consequently a research on the association between trauma and dreaming was designed. In the same vein,

Table 6.1 The Research Questions, Samples, Measurements, and Main Results of Psychosocial Research among Palestinian Women, Children, and Ex-prisoners

Research Aims	Sample	Measures	Main Findings
Factors affecting mental health of Palestinian *women* under military occupation; the role of appraisals, resources and coping	174 West Bank and Gaza; 30 Beirut Camps; 35 Galilee	*Traumatic events *locus of control *Coping; Unfinished sentences *Mental health *Interviews	Exposure to traumatic events increased the risk for mental-health problems, but also increased social-political activity as coping. Women appraised their environment as highly stressful, but also their own resources as relatively sufficient.
Children's (9-13 years) *attitudes* towards war and peace, across different political situations (e.g., before and during the Intifada)	128 West Bank; 40 Galilee; 204 Before and during the Intifada (West Bank)	*Attitude scale *Picture test for stress responses *Fear scale	The more children suffered personally from violence and loss, the more favorable attitudes they showed towards their own national struggle.
The content and effectiveness of *children's* (9-15 years) *coping strategies.* The association between personal and collective traumatic events and coping responses among *children* before and during the Intifada	66 Before the Intifada (West Bank and Gaza); 32 Beirut camps; 204 Before and during the Intifada (West Bank); 268 After the Intifada (Gaza)	*Picture test *Unfinished sentences *Self-esteem *Psychological well-being *Fear scale	The more children were exposed to violence and loss, the more active and courageous coping strategies they used. The active coping modes were not, however, effective in reducing children's mental health problems. The Beirut children's coping modes were overwhelmed by traumatic memories and desperate attempts to rebuild their destroyed world.
Association between Intifada traumatization and *children's* (10-11 years) mental health, cognitive and creative processes[1]	108 During the Intifada	*Political activity *Cognitive capacity *Creativity *Self-esteem *Neuroticism	The more traumatic experiences the children had and the more they participated in the Intifada, the more concentration, attention and memory problems they had. Children's political activity could not protect children from developing emotional problems.
The role of parenting in protecting children's mental health and encouraging resilience[2]	During the Intifada 108 children (10-11 years); After the Intifada 90 follow-up (13-14 years)	*Perceived maternal and paternal parenting	Good, i.e., loving and wisely disciplining parenting protected children's well-being by making them less vulnerable in two ways. First, if parenting was poor, i.e. rejecting and neglecting, exposure to trauma decreased children's intellectual, creative, and cognitive resources, which in turn, predicted psychological problems. Second, political activity increased psychological problems only if children experienced poor parenting.

1. In cooperation with Drs. Samir Qouta and Eyad El Saraj from the Gaza Community Mental Health Programme.
2. In cooperation with Drs. Samir Qouta and Eyad El Saraj from the Gaza Community Mental Health Programme.

Table 6.1 continued

Torture experiences, coping strategies and mental health among political prisoner[3]	40 before; 550 during; and, 79 + 128 after the Intifada	*Exposure to torture and ill-treatment *PTSD *Somatic symptoms *Coping with hardships *Appraisal of trauma *Narratives	The more experiences of torture and ill-treatment men had, the more they suffered from intrusive re-experiencing of trauma, withdrawal and numbness, and hyperarousal. Existential problems were not related to torture experiences. Duration of imprisonment, military's harassment, and marriage and economic difficulties all predicted intrusive re-experiences of trauma. The narratives revealed seven types of prison experience. Of them only one was exclusively negative, characterized by suffering and disillusionment. The others also included rewarding perceptions characterized as a struggle between strength and weakness, heroic fulfilment, developmental tasks, a normative stage in a man's life, growth in personal insight, and return to religion.
The role of dreaming in traumatic conditions among children and adolescents (6-15 years)	268 Gaza; 144 Galilee	*Dream diary *Psychological well-being *Child- and family related traumatic events	Compensatory dreams could moderate between trauma and psychological symptoms. Traumatic events were not associated with psychological symptoms among children whose dreams were bizarre, vivid and active, and involved joyful feelings and happy endings. Traumatic events were associated with mundane persecution and unpleasant repetitious dreams. These dysfunctional dreams were, in turn, associated with poor psychological adjustment. Contrary to the repression hypothesis, the more repressive coping strategies of paralysis, denial and numbing children used during the day, the more nocturnal dreams they recalled.
Trauma therapy process; the role of attachment, memory, coping and dreaming in predicting successful recovery among ex-prisoners	45 clinical group; 20 group counseling; 70 controls	*Significant events in therapy *Therapeutic bond *Dream diary *Remembering and appraising the trauma	No findings to date.

3. In cooperation with Drs. Samir Qouta and Eyad El Saraj from the Gaza Community Mental Health Programme.

research on children's play was motivated by parents' frequent worries and by their disapproval of children's war games. Adults could not understand why children incorporated violent scenes into their games (e.g., playing "soldiers and prisoners" and "Arabs and Jews") when these very scenes had caused them suffering. Therefore it was important to learn what kind developmental and adjustment function these games serve in traumatic conditions.

Theoretical Approaches

The argument that there is nothing more practical than a good theory also applies to psychosocial research among traumatized refugees. Revealing the dynamics between the subjective and objective is crucial in understanding the victims and the survivors. The researcher's *Weltanschau* and conceptualization of human nature affect the choice of theoretical model which, in turn, explains the link between sociopolitical reality and psychological processes. Research on traumatized refugees has been based, albeit often implicitly, on three conceptualizations. According to the impact model, exposure to traumatic events produces symptoms and disturbances in human relations, and hinders favorable development. The multifactorial model suggests that the impact of traumatic experience on adjustment is mediated by various personal, social, and political factors. Finally, the process model analyzes unique combinations of conscious and unconscious, cognitive and affective responses aiming at integrating painful experiences.

The Psyche as a Mirror

The impact model implicitly perceives human life as a reflection of the external reality. For instance, children living in violent conditions are assumed to behave aggressively, and experiencing trauma is equated with symptom formation. Research questions typically focus on how being a refugee and having war experiences influences symptoms such as PTSD and somatic complaints, and long-term social problems. The question is often presented in a highly emotional tone: "The research documents the impact of the horrors of war on children ..." (Goldstein, Wampler, and Wise, 1997). Results based on such simplistic concepts can hardly bring new insights, and the reader merely learns that war is not healthy for human beings.

Symptom-oriented trauma research neglects the observation that human beings actively construct their lives and attempt to make sense of their experiences, however horrible they may be. Furthermore, children and families seldom passively accept the hardships, but attempt to strengthen their own and collective resources and find creative ways to cope with and master them (Lazarus, 1991; Punamäki, 1986, Turner and Gorst-Unsworth, 1990).

Our research among Palestinian women and ex-political prisoners provides support for this criticism of the symptom-oriented approach. Their stories revealed that the objective reality of the military occupation with its violence, humiliation, and other horrors was not reflected directly in their psychological responses. Quantitative results further confirmed that the impact of traumatic events on women's mental health was mediated by how capable or helpless they appraised themselves as being, and by whether they used active or passive coping strategies. The following extract from an interview with a refugee woman of sixty-four years shows that exposure to trauma (house demolition, loss of family members) does not categorically lead to symptoms or lack of coping resources.

> Look at me. My home was destroyed. My sons were taken away to prison … Israel forbade us to rebuild our house. But we carried our old home here, stone by stone, and built it with the help of friends … When I am knocked down I'll grow stronger. The more I suffer, the firmer I stand. I believe that deep in their souls the occupiers sense it. They are afraid of our spirit. That is why they use more cruel means against us, but they know it will not help.

Reawakening Like a Sleeping Beauty

Multifactorial models take into account mediating factors, and researchers ask how and why painful experiences may lead to poor psychosocial adjustment. Whether a traumatic event causes symptoms depends, among other things, on the nature, severity, and acuteness of that event, on the meaning given to the experience, the available help and social support, and on the survivors' personal characteristics (La Greca et al., 1996). Multifactorial models typically use a wider range of outcome variables, i.e., instead of focusing on pathology or symptoms such as PTSD, the adjustment criteria include working and parenting capacity, intimate attachments (Kanninen and Punamäki, 1998) among adults, and learning capability (Rousseau, Drapeau, and Corin, 1996), coping resources (Kostelny and Garbarino, 1994), peer relationships, identity formation (Baker, 1990; Macksoud, 1996), and moral development (Elbedour, Baker, and Charlesworth, 1997) among children.

Our research on Palestinian women and children applied the multifactorial model. Accordingly, we hypothesized that a variety of factors concerning the person, the family and society can protect mental health, even if the experiences are overwhelmingly traumatic. Among women, active coping modes, sufficient resources, social support, and a happy marriage were assumed to be associated with good mental health in the face of traumatic events. Among children, loving and intimate mothering and fathering, creativity and cognitive capacity, as well as active coping strategies, were assumed to function as protective factors.

Parenting and coping resources turned out to be especially salient for families living in conditions of political violence. We found that constant experience of military violence, loss, and humiliation fosters unique parent-child relationships. On the negative side, mothers expressed guilt for not being able to protect their children from horrific and violent scenes, and felt that their children had to take political responsibility before they were fully mature. On the positive side, they reported that hardships increased family cohesion and affection, which could protect their children. We also found that political violence molded Palestinians' coping resources, reflecting the fact that they are both victims and survivors, both defeated and victors.

The multifactorial trauma research model is mistakenly called comprehensive. It is doubtful, however, whether adding all kinds of intuitively or theoretically relevant factors to the model reveals the "secret of human survival and recovery." Like the six good fairies donating beauty, wisdom, and goodness to Sleeping Beauty as her christening presents, various beneficial characteristics of this model are collected to predict good outcomes in the face of hardship. In the role of the seventh, non-invited fairy, poisonous characteristics predict vulnerability in facing trauma. There is a risk here of self-evident predictions; beneficial "fairies" bring good presents and harmful fairies bad ones.

The Comprehensive Process Model

We tend to perceive frightening and painful experiences as something alien in our lives, exceptional and probably happening to others. Impact and multifactorial research models portray trauma-related responses along these atomistic lines; a trauma befalls us and either breaks or strengthens us depending on how protected or vulnerable we are.

It may be just as reasonable to think that suffering, disappointment, and cruelty are inseparable parts of human life. People continuously deal with painful experiences by regulating their emotions and incorporating them as a part of their life experience. A successful struggle with traumatic memories may neutralize their negative effect.

Subsequently, it would be insightful to analyze the mental processes that contribute to healing. Processing trauma involves unique combinations of conscious and unconscious functioning domains, cognitive (e.g., thinking, remembering, imagining, or appraising) and affective (emotion, mood, and feeling) modalities that foster the integration of painful experiences as a part of healthy adjustment.

During our field work, the Palestinians gave us examples of their numerous ways of processing traumatic experiences. We observed how trauma had drastically changed their dreaming, remembering, and imagination processes, and their children's play. For instance, sleeping and waking realities dynamically interrelated in extreme conditions, as the following quotation from a fifty-eight year old village woman reveals:

> Last night I dreamt about my sons in prison, and I woke up screaming. That is why I am constantly tired, exhausted and afraid. Every night I dream about soldiers, destruction, killing, death and violence. I cannot sleep in the tent, I dreamed that soldiers came and set fire to it. I am half awake, I have to keep one eye open in case soldiers come.

Memories of childhood traumatic scenes were often fused together with the women telling us about their current violent experiences. This is what a thirty-four year old woman from a refugee camp said:

> I lost both of my parents in 1948 when we fled from Palestine. I still have dreams that they are alive and I am with them. I have always been fearful and sensitive. Now, when the soldiers are invading the camp and moving around, my life is becoming intolerable … I fear death. I cannot breathe, I fear that I will suffocate from horror … I only can walk around and my nerves are shattered … I am afraid that the same will happen as in 1948, that we will be thrown out of our homes …

In my opinion, description and observation do not contribute to our understanding of unique integrative mental processes among trauma survivors. Their experiences need to be analyzed in the context of general research focusing on cognitive and emotional functioning. Knowledge about dreaming and remembering is particularly useful. Research evidences suggest that dreaming and sleeping are especially affected by severe trauma such as concentration camp captivity (Lavie and Kaminer, 1991) and military combat (van der Kolk et al., 1984). However, dreaming may function as a crucial integrating process in traumatic conditions if survivors are helped to maintain healthy dreaming patterns, characterized by narratives, emotional expression, and content repertoires (Punamäki, 1997; 1998a; 1998b). The difficulty of incorporating symbolic material into dreaming presents a "trap" for trauma victims; the more they need the healing potential of dreaming, the more these processes are jeopardized. Hence, I would like to argue that recovery from trauma depends on the success of integrating cognitive and emotional, conscious and unconscious processes.

Research further shows that the timing of psychological responses to trauma is important; different kinds of responses are beneficial at the acute and later stage of exposure. For instance, denial of the event, numbing the associated feelings, and avoiding any reminiscence of the traumatic scene, may be rational and life-saving responses in acute danger, but may also impair later recovery (Horowitz, 1986). In the same vein, remembering repetitious horror dreams has been associated with mental health problems immediately after traumatic events (Brown and Donderi, 1986; Cartwright and Romanek, 1978; Punamäki, 1998b), but this kind of intensive dreaming has also predicted subsequent recovery and long-term adjustment (Cartwright and Lloyd, 1994).

Our present study focuses on the recovery process of tortured political ex-prisoners who are seeking help for their psychological suffering. Ex-prisoners constitute a considerable group of Palestinian society, one consequence of the Israel and PLO agreement in 1993 being the release of about thirteen thousand political prisoners. Among them are men who have been systematically tortured and ill-treated (Amnesty International, 1989; B'Tselem, 1991, 1994, 1998; Reyes (1995), and their rehabilitation presents a great challenge to mental health workers (El Sarraj et al., 1996).

The experiences of returning prisoners show how recovery proceeds in stages, and how the timing of an intervention may determine its success. Prison life involves a typical emotional double-bind situation. The men told us that torture, ill-treatment, and humiliation evoke powerful emotions, which they were forced to keep inside, suppress, or replace by feelings of endurance and heroism (Qouta, Punamäki, and El Sarraj, 1996). Expressing feelings of fear, anger, or revenge would simply have been life-threatening in prison. Upon returning home, they realized that adjustment to married life and their paternal role demanded a diametrically different behavioral and emotional repertoire. Expressing rather than suppressing emotions was now appropriate.

The process approach allows us to analyze these conflicts and human dilemmas on emotional, cognitive, and behavioral levels, between waking and dreaming realities, and conscious and unconscious attempts at mastery. It shows that psychological integration proceeds as stages across time.

Criticism and Conflict

Research as "an Imperialistic Enterprise"

Asking questions about traumatic experiences, psychological strengths, and vulnerabilities among refugees has been criticized from political, ethical, common-sense, and scientific points of view. Denouncing research as useless, politically incorrect, and immoral is based on two main arguments. First, the psychosocial approach tends to pathologize, psychologize, and medicalize refugee life by ignoring the fact that trauma survivors also show endurance and have chosen a purposive struggle for justice and a better life. Research victimizes the refugees rather than strengthens them. Second, because refugees' losses originate in political, social, and economic injustice, the consequent human suffering should be resolved in that context. Critics are concerned that focusing on individual tragedies prevents survivors from mastering their destiny and changing unjust conditions. They doubt the legitimacy of psychosocial research among traumatized people (Summerfield, 1996).

This criticism may be justified, but it is based on a narrow concept of psychological processes, and it perceives the experiential world as elitist, individualistic, and "dangerous." The rehabilitation of trauma victims is imagined as a kind of "Woody Allen" psychotherapy that forces a freedom fighter to talk about his relationship with his mother. Psychotherapy does not focus on weaknesses, however, but rather aims to enrich and strengthen people's capacities by helping them to make sense of the trauma and integrate painful and conflicting issues. Unconscious processes do not only involve negative impulses (such as uncontrollable aggression), but also carry seeds of creativity, expansive thinking, feeling, and sensuality. My argument is that, because trauma may comprehensively jeopardize victims' well-being, we must mobilize all human capacities, including the psychological, political, social, and spiritual, to encourage their endurance. The researcher's mandate is to produce such practical and insightful knowledge.

Traumatized people often suffer from nightmares, excessive fears, and concentration difficulties. If there is effective treatment available, it would be unethical to deprive survivors from it by arguing that "the trauma industry handicaps people's potential." Individual healing is not contradictory to the political and human rights struggle for justice. The criticism seems to be based on emotional concern and slogans rather than on thorough analysis of the interaction between mental processes and an unjust world. Understanding this interaction is crucial in fighting against both injustice and war, and against individual suffering.

Protecting Refugees from the Researcher

The field-work method has been criticized for ethical and security reasons. Posing questions to suffering people while not being able to remove their ordeal and injustice is considered immoral by some. Critics argue that traumatized people prefer to avoid and forget their painful experiences. Recalling killings, detention, and deportations can be harmful because it evokes unbearable and uncontrollable feelings. Finally, visits to the homes of human rights activists can attract the attention of the military and subsequently place the hosts at risk.

Our experiences of extensive field work, however, has shown that people experience interviewing in a variety of ways. Every visit seems to be different. At the positive end, we felt welcome, our work was considered worthwhile, and people considered it important that the "world would learn about their experience." Some people grew enthusiastic about allowing a stranger to share in the painful events and feelings:

> Wonderful! This brings some change to my daily routine. We seldom have the opportunity to speak about our feelings and experiences. My husband is in prison and I'm a mother of small children, and in general, I hardly ever can speak about myself, my own sentiments and real experiences … [a thirty-two year old woman from a refugee camp, West Bank]

On the negative side, we sometimes felt like vultures, armed with dozens of questions. Some people regarded the interviews as shear nonsense. Angrily or ironically they sometimes told us to "try yourself to imagine our life situation." They expressed doubts that revealing their experiences would bring them any benefits, and suspiciousness was always present.

> Please, you must use your imagination. How would you feel? Could you remain a calm observer, if you are enjoying the fruit of a vine tree, and somebody comes, cuts it down, crushes it by force into the ground, and then builds his house in your vineyard or in place of your olive trees? This is what happened to us when the occupiers came. And you ask whether I feel sad, angry or energetic? What do you think? I had only one choice, to join the Palestinian resistance. [A sixty-seven year old refugee woman]
>
> Are you mocking us? What is the meaning of these questions? All information collected about the lives of Palestinian people living under foreign occupation is used against us. The occupying force is very clever, one has to be careful. I do not want to answer these question because I do not want the occupiers to know my strong and weak points, so that they can plan their strategies to break us down. [A twenty-eight year old woman from a refugee camp]

Alien Cultures

Scientific criticism of our work has focused on political bias and deficiencies in the research settings on the one hand, and in our choice of quantitative methods to describe the human consequences of traumatic events on the other.

Research on refugees and war victims is highly a political and thus emotionally-loaded subject. The participants live in a situation in which one people is fighting against another. Subsequently, no sphere of life remains neutral, innocent, or politically intact. Until the peace agreement between Israel and the Palestinians in 1993, it was almost impossible to study Palestinians without being accused of biased political sympathies. A large proportion of the results of the early research was rejected in professional journals with pronouncement that "the other side should be studied," referring to the suffering of Israeli Jewish children and soldiers.

Our critics have further pointed out that our research is based on a narrow Western scientific approach, characterized by linearity of the time concept, separation between the psyche and the soma, and on spiritual and material worlds (Bracken, Giller, and Summerfield, 1995). It subsequently ignores the cultural and social diversity in the context of the everyday life of refugees.

Further, doubt has been expressed that refugees would universally respond to traumatic events by developing psychological symptoms. These doubters propose, for example, that in some societies, expressions of pain, such as nightmares or intrusive remembering, do not disturb people's everyday life because they are considered normal mental processes in that culture (Summerfield, 1996).

As far as refugees are concerned, it is difficult to assess this argument because we do not know to what extent mental processes are universal or culturally specific. The evidence of cultural dominance in explaining responses to trauma is based on anecdotes about how individuals from "other cultures" differently perceive and make sense of their experiences. Empirical research is needed to provide understanding of how personal, political, cultural, and biological issues interact and produce unique refugee experiences.

Stress and trauma seem to be universal in human life, but refugees are forced to encounter them excessively. It is essential to understand the relative importance of various aspects of their suffering. I faced problems applying "Western" stress and trauma models to depict the unique Palestinian struggle with Israeli military occupation. My work deserves criticism, for instance, for failing to integrate the historical genesis of the loss and trauma experienced in 1948 explicitly into the research model. The significance of this may be crucial in parenting practices, survival strategies, and memory regulation. Yet, every culture, including scientific and Western cultures, attempts to provide some tools for understanding people's purposeful activity and aspiration to change their destiny.

The Risk for Stereotyping

Political and psychological realities are intimately interwoven in Palestinians' lives. Splitting sociopolitical and psychological spheres creates stereotypical images of refugees, portraying them as either victims or heroes.

The victim image is promoted by well-meaning and worried people. They may protest against military violence and human rights abuse by showing victims as an embodiment of horrors and by predicting that their misery will affect generations to come. Their concern about the developmental potential of war children may be expressed by portraying them as a lost generation, as aggressive children, or as obstacles to peace. Discourse on war victims in the former Yugoslavia involves emotional expressions like such as "however, can anybody recover from such an assault?" This question is based on the idea that human development and behavior directly reflect the violent environment. Ambitious psychosocial research and healthy empirical curiosity can correct that misunderstanding of the nature of psychological processes.

Yet, it may be as dangerous and unrealistic to idealize suffering and struggling people. The hero image considers them as "supermen," ideologically motivated, and legendarily intact. This image corresponds, to some extent, with the Palestinian values of pride, heroism, and martyrdom. Some, although very few, participants in our study protested about such heroic treatment. One was a thirty-five year old town woman who said:

> Nobody likes to be merely an image. We, the Palestinians, are like other people, flesh, blood, mistakes, and hopes. You Europeans like to imagine us either as terrorists or as saints, according to your political sympathies. We also join in the game and present ourselves as heroes to the world press ... I visited my neighbor, whose boy was killed in the demonstration. I am a mother myself, and my son was killed, so I knew the agony of this mother. There I saw her sitting among strangers, a proud unnatural grin on her mouth, her eyes twinkling ... I could not enter the house ...

Both victim and hero images are misleading, contrasting with everyday reality, and they may harm efforts to create comprehensive rehabilitation for victims and survivors. Professionals working with refugees sometimes feel helpless when they meet traumatized families. Although it is human to be affected by another's suffering, feelings of impotency originate from the misperception that "normal people" cannot understand extremely painful realities. Professional inability reflects lack of knowledge rather than real empathy. Consequently empirical research should absolutely reveal the dynamics of how violence intrudes on child development, parenting and family relationships, and moreover, how the human being can recover from these intrusions.

Sharing the Work

A researcher is often haunted by worries about the futility of the research. My colleague Dr. Samir Qouta and I have recently been asking a hundred political ex-prisoners in Gaza to join our study and to tell us about their experiences. Our questions deal with prison and childhood events, human relationships, memories of imprisonment, and recovery from the traumatic events. The men wanted to know how their participation would help them and their families and promote their future prospects, which had been badly compromised by their long years in prison. They understood our academic enterprise, but they also wanted to experience some benefits. Their expectations were concrete, and included scholarships for students, jobs for the unemployed, and safety for human rights activists: "If we tell you about our experiences, are we going to get any help? Yes or no?"

Action research could provide an alternative to the apparent conflict between researchers' and participants' interests. This would involve: first, planning the study together with the survivors; second, bringing the primary results back to them; and third, possibly analyzing the results together with the participants or their "informants." The conclusions of the study would immediately be translated into practical action to improve the life situation of the participants.

Our research among Palestinians has been based on traditional academic sharing of work: researchers plan, collect, and analyze the data. However, the results have been brought back to the participants through local organizations. We have also often given more indirect feedback through publishing booklets for parents and survivors (Punamäki, 1990), and counseling human rights activists, teachers, lawyers, and parents. As a member of the Psychologists for Social Responsibility organization, I have initiated and managed a foreign-aid based intervention project based on the research results.(Punamäki, 1990).[2]

The field work and visits to the Palestinian families provided an opportunity for immediate feedback. Parents were highly concerned about the developmental prospects of their children. Collecting research data can, in our experience, easily be combined with providing information and individual consultation, and possibly alleviating participants' acute suffering.

There are some good examples of application of action research among victims of violence. Dawes and de Villiers (1987) consulted families exposed to human rights violations in South Africa. Their work included, among other things, preparing children for detention, consulting human rights lawyers, testifying in court, and, as a rule, reporting the findings to both the victims' families and human rights organizations. Chilean psychologists, for their part, have also created insightful professional practices that combine therapy, social support and networking, and political activity. Their experiences show that victims of political repression can be healed only by integrating their purposeful struggle against injustice as a natural part of the treatment (Becker et al., 1989; Lira, 1994). Others argue, however, that the integration of the political sphere into psychotherapy can function as intellectualization and detachment, thus hindering recovery.

Looking back at my research among Palestinian refugees, I notice that some changes are evident in the motivation, in the public to be addressed, and in the share of work with other professionals. My early research was primarily motivated by concerns about human rights, political injustice, and military violence towards civilians. Accordingly, the results were aimed at informing the general public and people who are responsible for civilian safety. For instance, our research on the frequency of torture and ill-treatment typically served both the need to document human rights violations and to learn about resilience among victims.

My current focus is more academic and only indirectly involves human rights and peace activism. The aim is to produce insightful and practical about psychological processes among trauma victims, which can be translated into therapy, consultation, and intervention. Concerning victims of human rights, for instance, reporting the extent of hardship is not scientifically interesting, and human rights organizations do that documentation more effectively. The researcher's mandate, in turn, is to assess the risks of developing symptoms of anxiety, depression, and PTSD that exposure to trauma may constitute among survivors. Lawyers, for their part, may use such evidence in their clients' demands for compensation and the denouncement of violation. The share of work shows that psychological understanding and defending victims' political rights are not contradictory.

Results

Finally, I would like to present two set of results combining the qualitative and the quantitative approaches. The first set focuses on the importance of ideological commitment in surviving in extreme conditions. The data were collected from 239 women residing in the occupied West Bank and Gaza, and in Beirut, before and during the Lebanon war. The second set of data focuses on the dynamics between waking and dreaming mental processes in coping with military violence. They are based on the documentation of dreams among 412 children and adolescents in Gaza and Galilee after the Intifada.

Ideological Commitment

The study of Palestinian women's mental health followed the stress model developed by Lazarus and Folkman (1984). Figure 6.1 presents the concepts and research methods used to collect the data at each step of the process. *The source of stress* refers to the traumatic events related to the military occupation, and the everyday, mainly economic, difficulties. Characteristic traumatic events under military occupation were the loss of family members through death or imprisonment, destruction of the home, army confrontations and harassment, and humiliation by soldiers and settlers.

Whether such hardships pose a risk to mental health depends, however, on the *primary appraisal*, i.e., whether the women estimated their experiences as a strain, "the last straw that broke the camel's back", or as a challenge, "it provided me opportunity to measure my potentials." *The secondary appraisal* refers to the women's estimation of their own resources to cope and to master the stress, in which they may consider themselves helpless or in control.

The next step in the stress process is the choice of *coping strategies* that may involve active efforts at changing the source of stress, accommodating it and/or using intrapsychic coping strategies, such as denial or day-dreaming. It is only if the appraisals and coping efforts fail that stressful experiences may result in mental health problems. Finally, *vulnerability and protective factors* describing the women's social resources are important mediating links between stress and mental health problems.

The results showed statistically what life had already taught us in the Middle East: traumatic experiences of violence, loss, and terror increase the risk of mental health problems among civilians. Yet, the human capacity to deal with hardships is impressive, and people tend to mobilize all available psychosocial resources to master the violence, loss and humiliation. More concretely, the more the women

Figure 6.1 Schematic Model of Stressful Person-Environment Interactions

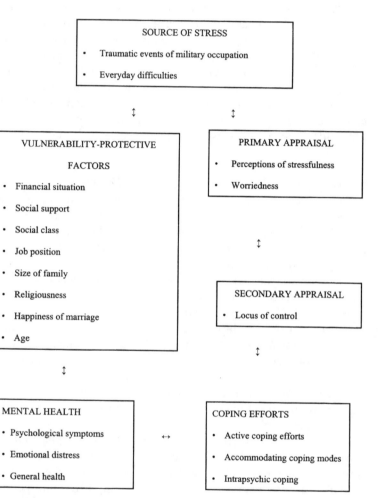

were exposed to traumatic events, the more they showed psychological symptoms of anxiety, depression, hostility, and general health problems. However, the women who strongly believed in their ability to control and influence the national cause, suffered less from mental health symptoms. Furthermore, a good financial situation, sufficient social support, a happy marriage, and religious commitment protected their mental health.

The finding that their belief in their ability to influence political destiny safeguarded women psychologically can be understood as an implication of ideological commitment. Ideological commitment here means a strong belief in their own resources, access to social support, and the inevitability of political participation. Such commitment constituted a special kind of cognitive-emotional schema that apparently functioned as a "protective shield" in painful situations. Nationalistic and ideological motivations were present at all stages of the stress process.

Primary appraisal of the relevance and harmfulness of events was determined in the political context of a victimized and struggling nation. Examples include: "I say to myself, as long as we are a nation under a hostile foreign power, we have to sacrifice." "Why should I cry because my son is in prison? We did nothing shameful, my son was taken because his good actions, our pride. He loves his country and defended his home." "How small my suffering is compared to that of other Palestinians, and what they have lost."

Secondary appraisal of available individual and collective resources is influenced by national history, people's own experiences and social norms and values, as the following examples suggest: "If we do not fight against injustice and struggle for our national rights, who will do it for us?" "Palestinians are strong, our children are studying even in prison." "I never thought that I could find so much strength in me, as I did when fighting against the soldiers who were terrorizing my family."

Coping with and mastery of stressful situations is facilitated by ideological assurance about continuing the resistance, having some prospects for the future, nationalistic pride, and social-political cohesion. People use coping resources provided by the collective aim, and adapt them to their own psychological make-up.

> Naturally, I have changed due to the military occupation. I think that in another political situation I would have been a devoted, although little-educated, Muslim woman. But history and my nation's fate do not give me peace. Confrontations with the occupying soldiers and personal losses have made me more conscious ... I am deeply aware of the life around me. I see clearly its motley character, pain, and also its beauty. I realize that my job here is to change the world, and this sense of necessity gives me the strength and a feeling of importance. [Woman of thirty-two years from a village]

Expressing symptoms is also attuned with the norms, values and political aims of the struggling society. Palestinian women appreciated heroism and condemned submission. The collective aims of achieving independence were preferred to or combined with individualistic ambitions.

I felt that it was not right to show my sorrow and despair to the occupiers. They would be too happy to break us down. When the Israeli soldiers destroyed our house, we did not cry but we were dancing and singing together with my friends: "We are strong, our spirit is high." For seven days my friends came round, and we continued our consoling and sad party.

We are people at the mercy of a militarily strong army. We have to be firm and united. We cannot afford to break down, give up or get frustrated. If that happened, they would finish us all.

Daytime and Nighttime in a Violent Environment

We documented children's symbolic processes of dreaming and playing in Gaza during the first weeks of the peace treaty between Israel and the Palestinians in 1993. The period was one of relative calm and, together with my Palestinian colleague Amal Judah, we could travel almost anywhere, including refugee camps and religious suburbs.

The Intifada had started six years previously in Jabalia refugee camp in Gaza. It aimed at ending the military occupation and establishing an independent Palestinian state on the West Bank and Gaza. Young people took very active roles in the resistance in organizing demonstrations, stone throwing, and strikes (Kuttab, 1988). The Intifada has been described as a collective therapeutic process that turned Palestinians from victims to masters of their destiny. However, it was also a war that the occupiers launched against Palestinian children, if the number of injured and killed are any indication. During the first four years of the Intifada, one child in twenty-two was seriously injured by gunfire, beatings, or tear gas in the Gaza strip, and one in forty-one on the West Bank (B'Tselem, 1994; Graff and Abdolell, 1991).

The dangerous and life-threatening circumstances demanded untold flexibility from the children's adaption capacities. Their dreaming revealed some of the processes through which they attempted to master the horrific experiences and regulate their frightening feelings. We found compensatory dynamics between their daytime activity and nighttime dreaming: the more active the child was during the day and the more he or she coped with military violence by displaying a lack of fear, the more avoidant and withdrawing his or her dreams were at night. In the same vein, if the children showed fear and used passive and withdrawing coping strategies in facing violence during the day, their nocturnal dreams typically incorporated active initiation and heroic themes. The dream extracts in table 6.2 show that active initiation dreams were characterized by the dreamer's meeting the challenges, dominant participation, and courage. The avoidant observer dreams, in turn, incorporated scenes of persecution and fear, and feelings of helplessness.

Table 6.2 Examples of Compensatory Relationship between (a) Passive Coping Strategies and Active Initiation Dreams, and (b) Active Coping Strategies and Passive Avoidance Dreams

Passive Coping Strategies	Somebody's house is destroyed by soldiers ... I wish that the soldiers' house would be ruined. People are under curfew ... I feel as if I am an imprisoned bird. There is a demonstration ... I go out and watch them. I see a soldier ... I feel frightened, but I hold myself and go home. I hear about shooting of my people ... My heart would be depressed and fear for my brothers. Somebody is taken into prison ... My hatred increases.
Active Initiation Dreams	I dreamed that the Jews knocked on our door and two of my brothers were at home. When I heard the knocking I knew that they were the Jews, and I informed my brothers and let them run away to the roof to the nearby house. They did so, and while they were running over the roof, I heard their sound and was afraid that the Jews would hear them, and think that they are wanted. So they would shoot them. I began praying and asking God to save them until they have run away. I woke up, and could not see the dream continuing. (Girl of eleven)
Active Coping Strategies	Somebody's house is destroyed by soldiers ... I will hinder the soldiers. People are under curfew ... I will be furious and sad. There is a demonstration ... I join them. I see a soldier ... I want to kill them and throw them with stones. I hear about shooting of my people ... I feel angry and sad. Somebody is taken into prison ... I carry a knife and go to the street.
Passive Avoidance Dreams	I dreamed that I was going to school. The soldiers faced me. So, I became frightened and woke up from my sleep. I dreamed that I was with groups of friends. We walked in the Gaza street and looked at its buildings. When we reached the main street, and saw an Israeli chasing a young man ... my friends followed and threw stones after him for a little while. I run away. Then we run away through a street blocked with barrels filled with tar. I hide in a small street until the soldiers went away. I woke up and I was worried. (Boy of ten)

Compensation dynamics allowed the children to express both courage and fear, both heroism and helplessness, and to integrate these feelings into their experiential life. Their mental struggle succinctly tells us how they courageously confronted military force during the day, but had to ventilate feelings of being helpless victims during the night.

A similar dynamic was revealed by results showing an association between frequent daytime repressive coping strategies and frequent remembering of nocturnal dreams. Accordingly, the children who coped with daytime danger by denying it and numbing their feelings during the day, frequently re-experienced painful events and fearful feelings in their dreams. Dreaming thus provided them with a night-time safe place (Hartmann, 1995) where they could afford to express the feelings that the traumatic events evoked, and to process images that were too provocative fully to acknowledge during the day.

These compensation dynamics between day and night realities manifest the basic dilemmas of being strong and weak, afraid and brave, and victim and victor. Most Palestinian children in the Gaza refugee camps were forced to tackle these dilemmas every day when living under foreign military occupation. In their dreams they could enjoy the possibility of changing roles: from a dangerous but courageous confronting of the enemy to the less vulnerable role of an observer. This elastic shifting between active and courageous, and passive and fearful roles communicates something about the human capability to employ all available resources to maintain mental health. It also tells us about the burden that military violence places on a developing child.

Role reversal was common in the Palestinian children's play during the Intifada and long afterwards. Children who had been witnesses and victims of soldiers' violence often repeated the frightening scenes in their playing. They played the part of a strong soldier in direct or disguised ways, the interplay between strength and courage forming the core themes. Playing and dreaming seem to share important developmental functions in dangerous environments: they enable children symbolically to master experiences that were originally overwhelming and uncontrollable. Children seek compensation for frightening experiences through shifting between activity and passivity, fear and courage, and horror and heroism across various conscious states.

The results concur with earlier observations that children tend to employ an imaginative exchange of roles in traumatic conditions. They identify, for instance, with a stronger person and, sometimes, even with an aggressor (Freud, 1965; Terr, 1983), which provides them with "a strong person schema" to replace "a weak person schema."

Conclusion

My research work was first motivated by feelings of grief, rage, and shame when witnessing house destruction, deportations, and the killing of Palestinians who opposed Israeli military rule. Feelings of impotence and empathy were so dominating that I had difficulty expressing my questions and crystallizing the psychological perspectives in the human rights struggle. When I went to the university, my erudite professor, Johan von Wright, commented on my text by remarking that I was still immersed in the reality of my research subjects, Palestinian women. A researcher must choose her role and take an analytical distance from the suffering, but without losing the palpation of that very life. Psychosocial research involves constant balancing efforts between distancing and connecting, theory building and description, and observation and active initiation.

Notes

1. This case and all others in this chapter come from my notes entered into my diary while doing research in refugee situations.
2. As a member of the Psychologists for Social Responsibility organization, I have initiated a foreign-aid based intervention project based on the research results. The project is called the Family Happiness Project which has been active in Beirut from 1985 to the present.

References

Amnesty International (1989). *Urgent Action Bulletin* (May 18, 1989). London: Amnesty International.

Baker, A. (1990). The psychological impact of the Intifada on Palestinian children in the occupied West Bank and Gaza: An exploratory study. *American Journal of Orthopsychiatry,* 60: 496-505.

Becker, D., Castillo, M. I. I., Cómez, E., Kovalsky, J., and Lira, E. (1989). Subjectivity and politics: The psychotherapy of extreme traumatization in Chile. *International Mental Health, 18:* 80-97.

Bracken, P. J., Giller, J. E., and Summerfield, D. (1995). Psychological responses to war and atrocity: the limitations of current concepts. *Social Science and Medicine, 40*: 1073-1082.

Brown, R. J. and Donderi, D. (1986). Dream content and self-reported well-being among recurrent dreamers, past-recurrent dreamers, and nonrecurrent dreamers. *Journal of Personality and Social Psychology, 50*: 612-623.

B'Tselem (1991). *Annual report 1990: Violations of human rights in the occupied territories.* Jerusalem: The Israeli Information Centre for Human Rights in Occupied Territories.

B'Tselem (1994). *Human rights violations in the occupied territories 1992/1993 information sheet.* Jerusalem: The Israeli Information Centre for Human Rights in Occupied Territories.

B'Tselem (1998). *!987-1997: A decade of human rights violations information sheet.* Jerusalem: The Israeli Information Centre for Human Rights in Occupied Territories.

Cartwright, R. D. and Lloyd, S. R. (1994). Early REM sleep: A compensatory change in depression? *Psychiatry Research, 51*: 245-253.

Cartwright, R. D. and Romanek, I. (1978). Repetitive dreams of normal subjects. *Sleep Research, 7*: 174.

Dawes, A., and de Villiers, C. (1987). Preparing children and their parents for prison: the Wynberg Seven. In Hanson, D. (Ed.), *Mental health in transition.* Cape Town: OASSSA Second National Conference Proceedings, September 1987, 3-30.

Elbedour, S., Baker, A. M., and Charlesworth, W. C. (1997). The impact of political violence on moral reasoning in children. *Child Abuse and Neglect, 21*: 1053-1066.

El. Sarraj, E., Punamäki, R. L., Salmi, S., and Summerfield, D. (1996). Experiences of torture and ill-treatment and posttraumatic stress disorder symptoms among Palestinian political prisoners. *Journal of Traumatic Stress, 9*: 595-606.

Freud, A. (1965). *Normality and pathology in childhood. Assessments of development.* London: Harmondsworth.

Goldstein, R. D., Wampler, N. S., and Wise, P. H. (1997). War experiences and distress symptoms of Bosnian children. *Paediatrics, 100*: 873-878.

Graff, A. and Abdolell, M. (1991). *Palestinian children and Israeli state violence.* Toronto: Near East Cultural and Educational Foundation of Canada.

Hartmann, E. (1995). Making connections in a safe place: Is dreaming psychotherapy? *Dreaming, 5*: 213-228.

Horowitz, M. J. (1986). *Stress response syndromes* (2nd edition). Northvale, NJ: Jason Aronson.

Kanninen, K. and Punamäki, R. L. (1998). Trauma therapy among torture victims: The role of attachment, defenses, and emotional processes in successful recovery from trauma. *Psychology Bulletin.* Journal of Psychology Resource Center, Department of Psychology, University of Western Cape.

Kostelny, K. and Garbarino, J. (1994). Coping with the consequences of living in danger. The case of Palestinian children and youth. *International Journal of Behavioral Development, 17:* 595-611.

Kuttab, D. (1988). A profile of the stone throwers. *Journal of Palestinian Studies, 17*: 14-23.

La Greca, A. M., Silverman, W. K., Vernberg, E. M., and Prinstein, M. J. (1996). Symptoms of posttraumatic stress in children after hurricane Andrew: A prospective study. *Journal of Consulting and Clinical Psychology, 64*: 712-723.

Lazarus, R. S. (1991). Progress on a cognitive- motivational -relational theory of emotion. *American Psychologist, 46*: 819-834.

Lazarus, R. S. and Folkman, S. (1984). *Stress, appraisal and coping.* New York: Springer.

Lavie, P. and Kaminer, H. (1991). Dreams that poison sleep: Dreaming in Holocaust. *Dreaming, 1*: 11-21.

Lira, E. (1994). *Psicología y violencia política en America Latina.* Santiago: Ilas.

Macksoud, M. S. (1996). The war experiences and psychosocial development of children in Lebanon. *Child Development, 67*: 70-88.

Punamäki, R. L. (1986). Stress among Palestinian women under military occupation: Women's appraisal of stressors, their coping modes, and their mental health. *International Journal of Psychology, 21*: 445-462.

Punamäki, R. L. (1990). *Give us our childhood. Parents and teachers guide for helping children in political violence* (Arabic). Helsinki: Finland.

Punamäki, R. L. (1997). Determinants and mental health effects of dream recall among children living in traumatic conditions. *Dreaming, 7*: 235-263.

Punamäki, R. L. (1998a). Correspondence between waking-time, coping, and dream content. *Journal of Mental Imagery, 22*: 109-126.

Punamäki, R. L. (1998b). The role of dreams in protecting psychological well-being in traumatic conditions. *International Journal of Developmental Behavior, 22*: 559-588.

Qouta, S., Punamäki, R. L., and El Sarraj, E. (1996). Experiences and coping strategies among political prisoners. Peace and Conflict: *Journal of Peace Psychology, 3*: 19-36.

Reyes, H. (1995). The conflict between medical ethics and security measures. In Gordon, N. and Marton, R. (Eds.), *Human rights, medical ethics, and the case of Israel.* London: Zed Books, 1-17.

Rousseau, C. E., Drapeau, A., and Corin, E. (1996). School performance and emotional problems in refugee children. *American Journal of Orthopsychiatry, 66*: 239-251.

Summerfield, D. (1996). *The impact of war and atrocity on civilian populations. Basic principles for NGO interventions and a critique of psychosocial trauma projects. Relief and Rehabilitation network, Network paper no. 14.* London: Overseas Development Institute.

Terr, L. (1983). Chowchilla revisited: The effects of psychic trauma four years after a school bus kidnapping. *American Journal of Psychiatry, 140:* 12: 1543-1550.

Turner, S. and Gorst-Unsworth, C. (1990) Psychological sequelae of torture: A descriptive model. *British Journal of Psychiatry, 157*: 475-480.

van der Kolk, B., Blitz, R., Burr, W., Sherry, S., and Hartmann, E. (1984). Nightmares and trauma: A comparison of nightmares after combat with lifelong nightmares in veterans. *American Journal of Psychiatry, 141*: 187-190.

7

Use of Census Data for Research on Refugee Resettlement in the United States

METHODOLOGICAL STRENGTHS AND LIMITATIONS

Miriam Potocky-Tripodi

Despite its heritage as nation of immigrants, the United States has an extremely limited systematic collection of immigration data (Levine, Hill, and Warren, 1985). It has been noted that, "There have not been innovative efforts to collect survey data on a scale comparable to those launched to study other national issues ... This leaves the census as the major, and often the only, source of data for the study of contemporary immigration" (Hirschman, 1994, p. 710). Consequently, there have been a large number of studies using census data to examine diverse aspects of immigration such as variations in language usage (Bills, Hernandez-Chavez, and Hudson, 1995); determinants of naturalization (Yang, 1994); patterns of marriage (Biddlecom, 1993) and fertility (Kahn, 1994); characteristics of immigrant children (Hirschman, 1994; Jensen and Chitose, 1994); the impact of immigration on residential patterns in metropolitan areas (Alba, Denton, Leung, and Logan, 1995); and various facets of immigrant economic adaptation such as educational attainment and labor market experiences (Poston, 1994; Simon, 1995), poverty (Jensen, 1991), public assistance utilization (Jensen, 1988), and home ownership (Alba and Logan, 1992). However, few of these studies have focused specifically on refugees, suggesting that refugee scholars may be underutilizing this potentially valuable data source.

I have conducted a series of studies over the past several years using data from the 1990 census to examine the economic integration of various refugee groups resettled in the United States. My first series of studies (Potocky, 1993; 1996a; 1996b; Potocky and McDonald, 1995) focused on Southeast Asian refugees in California, and my second series of studies (Potocky, 1996b; 1997) focused on Cuban, Nicaraguan, Haitian, and Soviet and East European refugees in Dade County, Florida (the Miami metropolitan area). In the following discussion, these studies will be used as a basis for illustrating methodological issues in the use of census data for research on refugees. The discussion will begin with a brief rationale, definition, and conceptual framework, which form the context of my research. This will be followed by an overview of the census and its advantages. Next, the potential uses of the census data for studying refugees will be described and illustrated, including identification of the limitations of the data. Finally, the discussion will conclude with a summary of the strengths and weaknesses of the census, and some suggestions for researchers who may wish to use the methods described.

Rationale, Definition, and Conceptual Framework

There are many aspects of refugee adaptation that are important areas for study. I have focused on economic integration because this issue is central to United States refugee resettlement policy. Current resettlement policy is codified in the Refugee Act of 1980 (P. L. 96-212). The goal of this policy is to assist refugees to become economically self-sufficient as rapidly as possible following their arrival in the United States. As a consequence of this policy focus, numerous studies have been undertaken to assess refugee economic integration as well as to identify those factors which influence it (Bach and Carroll-Seguin, 1986; Caplan, Whitmore, and Bui, 1985; Chiswick, 1993; Gozdziak, 1989; Logan, Alba, and McNulty, 1994; Majka and Mullan, 1992; Model, 1992; Perez, 1986; Portes and Stepick, 1985; Tran, 1991; Uba and Chung, 1991; Westermeyer, Callies, and Neider, 1990). My research falls within this body of scholarship.

One of the first issues that arises when working on this topic is how refugee economic integration is defined. The official policy definition focuses on public assistance utilization. A refugee is defined as being economically integrated if he or she is not receiving public assistance. I have argued (Potocky, 1996a) that this definition is too narrow to adequately represent the construct of economic integration, and that it should be expanded to include other indicators. Specifically, my definition is as follows:

> Minimal economic integration of refugees is attained if the economic status of the refugees is at least equal to that of any native-born minority group, as measured by poverty rates, employment, welfare utilization, home ownership, and similar economic indicators. (p. 255)

I developed this definition based on my analyses of the census data. I will describe this further below, when examining the uses of the data.

Once economic integration is defined and assessed, the next issue of interest is to empirically identify those variables that influence it. This requires a conceptual framework to guide the selection of variables for investigation. My research is driven by a comprehensive theory of refugee economic integration developed by Kuhlman (1991). The model postulates six categories of factors that influence economic integration:

A. Characteristics of refugees, such as demographic and cultural variables;
B. Flight-related factors, such as cause of flight and attitude toward displacement;
C. Host-related factors, such as economic and cultural variables in the host society;
D. Policies, including international, national, and regional/local;
E. Residence in host country, including length of residence and secondary migration;
F. Non-economic aspects of adaptation, such as acculturation and the host society's attitudes toward refugees.

My use of this framework is described below. Prior to addressing the specific uses of the census to study refugees, a general overview is necessary.

Overview of the U.S. Census

The U.S. Census is a cross-sectional survey that has been administered in various forms every ten years since 1790. While the original purpose of the census was to enumerate the population for the purpose of Congressional apportionment, its goals have since been expanded to include the collection of data on a wide variety of demographic and socioeconomic variables. The decennial census involves the administration of two questionnaires: a "short form," which is to be distributed to every housing unit in the country, and a "long form," which is administered to a sample of these housing units. The short form contains only questions regarding basic demographic information, whereas the long form contains these as well as many more items. It is the latter form which provides the data for all in-depth tabulations and research studies involving detailed analyses.

The census long form is a written questionnaire that is completed by one household member on behalf of the entire household. The questionnaire solicits data on over 125 demographic and socioeconomic variables. Particularly relevant to refugee researchers, it should be noted that instructions for completing the questionnaire are available in thirty-three languages. Thus, a significant effort has been made to reduce response bias due to language barriers.

The long form is administered to one in every six housing units in the country. The sampling strategy is designed to enhance representativeness by oversampling in sparsely populated areas and undersampling in densely populated areas. Subsequently, data from a subsample of this long-form sample are made available to individual researchers. This subsample is referred to as the Public Use Microdata Sample (PUMS) and is available in two sample sizes: 1 percent and 5 percent of the total population. These data are available for each state and counties and metropolitan areas within it. The 5 percent sample identifies even smaller geographical areas such as census tracts. Both the 1 percent and the 5 percent subsamples are obtained using a stratified systematic selection procedure. This procedure is complex. First, an iterative ratio estimation procedure is used to assign weights to each element of the long-form sample in order to produce total population estimates. Then, a total of 1049 strata are used to create homogenous subgroups from which the PUMS subsamples are drawn. These strata are derived from all possible combinations of the variables of geographical location, type of housing unit, family composition, race, Hispanic origin, home ownership, and age (U.S. Bureau of the Census, 1993).

The Census Bureau has undertaken extensive procedures to reduce sampling error. Procedures are also in place to reduce nonsampling errors such as missing data, inconsistent information from respondents, and recording errors. In the intervening years between each decennial census, the reliability and validity of the previous census are extensively evaluated, and pilot studies are conducted to improve the accuracy of the next census (U.S. Bureau of the Census, 1993).

The PUMS data are available on magnetic tape and CD-ROM. The files contain two types of data: household-level variables and person-level variables. The data are in ASCII format, which is convertible for analysis with statistical software such as the Statistical Package for the Social Sciences (SPSS). The files must first be processed on a mainframe computer due to the large file size; subsets of the data may then be downloaded for processing on a personal computer. The files are accompanied by a user's manual (U.S. Bureau of the Census, 1993) that fully describes the variables, their operational definitions, their locations in the file, and their codes. The PUMS files are available in most university libraries and local government offices in the United States.

Advantages of the PUMS

The PUMS essentially contains the unaggregated responses to the long form questionnaire for each housing unit in the subsample (excluding any data that might identify individuals or households). Thus, the PUMS provides for the following research capabilities:

> Public use Microdata files essentially make possible "do-it-yourself" special tabulations. Since the 1990 files furnish nearly all of the detail recorded on long form questionnaires in the census, subject to the limitations of sample size and geographic identification, users can construct an infinite variety of tabulations interrelating any desired set of variables. Users have the same freedom to manipulate the data that they would have if they had collected the data in their own sample survey, yet these files offer the precision of census data collection techniques and sample sizes larger than would be feasible in most independent sample surveys. Microdata samples will be useful to users (1) who are doing research that does not require the identification of specific small geographic areas or detailed cross tabulations for small populations, and (2) who have access to programming and computer time needed to process the samples. Microdata users frequently study relationships among census variables not shown in existing census tabulations, or concentrate on the characteristics of certain specially defined populations. (U.S. Bureau of the Census, 1993: p. 1.1-1.2).

Since refugees are such a specially defined population, the PUMS can be very useful for researchers in this area. The possible uses of these data to study this population will now be described.

Uses of the Census to Study Refugees

The use of the PUMS to study refugees is made possible by the inclusion of two key variables: place of birth and year of immigration to the United States. Thus researchers can select individuals from the sample based on these key variables in order to examine specific refugee groups of interest. For example, my research has focused on the following groups: Soviets and Eastern Europeans (i.e., persons from Hungary, Poland, Romania, and the former Czechoslovakia) who entered the U.S. after 1950; Cubans who entered after 1960; Haitians after 1970; and Nicaraguans and Southeast Asians (i.e., persons from Vietnam, Cambodia, and Laos) after 1975. These dates were chosen in order to identify persons who left their countries following the particular political circumstances that engendered massive refugee outflows.

There are two limitations here. First, the census does not include data on immigration status. There are many legal statuses for persons entering the United States (e.g., refugee, legal immigrant, asylee, parolee, entrant, etc.). Thus, it is impossible to identify those persons who entered the U.S. with the status of "refugee." Further, some of those individuals with this legal status may in fact not have personally experienced or had a well-founded fear of persecution, which is the defining characteristic of a refugee under the Geneva Convention and Protocol (United Nations, 1951; 1967). Conversely, some persons who would qualify as refugees under the Geneva definition are not granted that legal status by the United States. None of these data are collected by the census. Thus, research using census data is limited to identifying those individuals who come from so-called "refugee-generating countries." For purposes of brevity, I refer to these individuals as refugees.

The second limitation concerns year of immigration. This variable is coded in intervals of varying length (i.e., 1987-1990, 1985-1986, 1982-1984, etc., to "before 1950"). Thus, exact year of immigration is not available. This causes a slight decrease in the precision of analyses involving this variable. Additionally, this limitation can be a problem if a political circumstance occurred in a given country, causing it to become a refugee-generating country, during one year within one of the intervals. In this case, it would not be possible to distinguish those persons who immigrated immediately prior to the event ("nonrefugees") from those who immigrated immediately afterward ("refugees"). Further, because the code for the most recent period of arrival spans a four-year interval, it is not possible to study the early phases of the refugee experience, such as the transit period, the asylum-seeking period, and the period shortly after arrival. Essentially, the research is limited to the long-term resettlement phase.

After identifying the appropriate cases for the study, researchers must then select those variables from the data set which are relevant to their research questions or hypotheses. Since my research focuses on economic integration, I have selected those variables which are indicators of economic status, and those which are hypothesized to be correlated with economic status, based on the conceptual framework and prior empirical work. Table 7.1 shows the list of variables that I have employed in my analyses.

Table 7.1 Variables Used in Studies of Refugee Economic Integration

Indicators of Economic Integration	
Person level	**Household level**
Auspices of employment	Home ownership
Earnings income	Household income
Employment status	Housing costs
Hours worked per week	Number of autos
Employing industry	Number of occupants per room
Occupation	Number of workers
Poverty status	
Public assistance income	
Weeks worked in 1989	
Year last worked	

Correlates of Economic Integration	
Person level	**Household level**
A. Characteristics of refugees	
Sex	Number of persons
Age	Household headed by married couple
Ethnicity	Presence of nonrelatives
Place of birth	Presence of persons under age 18
Educational attainment	Presence of persons age 65 and over
Disability	Presence of subfamilies
B. Flight-related factors (None)	
C. Host-related factors (None)	
D. Policies (None)	
E. Residence in host country	
Length of residence in U.S.	
Secondary migration in past five years	
F. Non-economic dimensions of adaptation	
English speaking ability	
Language other than English spoken at home	
U.S. citizenship	
Presence of U.S. natives	

The list is divided into indicators and correlates of economic integration, and into household-level and individual-level variables. Further, the correlates are arranged according to the six factors of the conceptual framework; each variable is presumed to be an empirical indicator of the theoretical factor. It can be seen that there are no variables to represent factors (B) flight-related factors, (C) host-related factors, and (D) policies. Additionally, only a limited number of variables are available to represent factor (F) non-economic aspects of adaptation. This is another limitation of the census. It contains data only on micro factors (i.e., characteristics of individuals and households) and not on macro, or what may be termed environmental or contextual factors. Thus, research using the Census is necessarily conceptually constrained. In the present case, only a part of Kuhlman's comprehensive conceptual framework can be empirically investigated. However, Kuhlman (1991) noted that "a partial analysis is usually more feasible than a comprehensive one and can be most useful, provided the overall picture is kept in mind" (p. 19).

Once the refugee groups are selected and relevant variables identified, data analysis can proceed. There are three research objectives that can be achieved using census data: (1) population estimates; (2) descriptive statistics; and (3) correlational analyses.

Population Estimates

The census can be used to estimate the total population of persons from a given refugee-generating country currently residing in a given locality. Although the federal Internal Revenue Service and the Office of Refugee Resettlement collect some of these data, most of their data are for numbers of arrivals and state of initial resettlement. Since many refugees make secondary migrations, initial resettlement data provide only limited information. Thus, the census is very useful in this regard. To obtain a population estimate, the researcher simply selects the relevant cases from the sample, then weights each case by the factor which is assigned to it as a function of the sampling procedure (the factor is a variable in the PUMS file). For example, table 7.2 shows the sample sizes and total population estimates for the refugee groups in my studies. I used the 1 percent PUMS sample; therefore, as expected, each sample size is approximately 1 percent of the total population estimate.

Descriptive Statistics

The census data can be used to describe the demographic and socioeconomic characteristics of refugees and their households. These descriptive statistics consist of frequency distributions and measures of central tendency and dispersion. These statistics can be compared across groups to determine, for example, how various refugee groups differ on these characteristics, and how they differ from the native-born population. I have used this approach for two purposes: first, to assess the economic integration of refugees in rela-

Table 7.2   Sample Sizes and Total Population Estimates

Group	Sample Size	Population Estimate
State of California		
Southeast Asians	3,955	388,310
Dade County, Florida		
Cubans	3,969	390,440
Haitians	415	45,660
Nicaraguans	732	68,600
Soviets/East Europeans	58	6,545

Source: Potocky, 1993.

tion to each other and to the native-born population; and second, to assess, in a similar fashion, the economic integration of refugees who arrived in the U.S. as children and are now adults.

With regard to the first purpose, I was initially interested in how Southeast Asian refugees in California compared economically to native-born residents (Potocky, 1996a). The variables for analysis were the economic integration indicators listed in table 7.1. Recognizing that there are wide disparities in socioeconomic status among native-born ethnic groups in the United States, it was important to assess the refugees' status in relation to each native-born group. Thus, I grouped the native-born residents by ethnicity, and generated descriptive statistics for each group. Table 7.3 shows some of these data.

It can be seen that on most of the indicators, the economic status of the Southeast Asian refugees was lower than that of both the white and minority native-born groups. For example, they had a lower employment rate, higher public assistance rate, and lower yearly earnings. These findings led me to the conclusion that the existing policy definition of refugee economic integration (i.e., "not receiving public assistance") was inadequate to describe the economic reality of these refugees. If evaluated by this criterion, 75 percent of this population would be deemed to be faring well economically, a conclusion which is not supported by the other data. This led me to the development of the new, empirically-based definition described above.

My second descriptive research purpose concerned the economic integration of childhood refugees now in adulthood (Potocky, 1996b). I was interested in how they compared to those refugees who arrived when they were already adults, and also to their native-born peers of the same age range. I used the variables of age and year of immigration to select the appropriate cases for each group. This allowed me to identify those persons who arrived before and after age eighteen, to determine their age at the time of the 1990 cen-

Table 7.3 Personal Economic Characteristics of California Residents

Characteristic	Group Mean or %					
	Southeast Asian	White American	African American	Asian American	Native American	Hispanic American
Persons over 15 employed	44.5%	65.2%	57.8%	70.8%	59.5%	62.8%
Weeks worked in 1989 (employed persons over 15)	41.3	43.9	42.8	43.7	41.7	41.9
Hours worked per week (employed persons over 15)	37.1	39.0	38.9	37.3	38.6	38.2
Yearly earnings (employed persons over 15)	$16,632	$28,284	$21,394	$26,542	$19,256	$19,457
Persons over 15 who have never worked	31.9%	3.4%	8.5%	7.6%	6.4%	10.5%
Persons over 14 receiving public assistance	24.3%	3.7%	12.6%	1.7%	7.7%	6.8%
Percent of all persons living in poverty	34.1%	6.6%	19.9%	11.9%	16.8%	19.1%

Source: Potocky, 1996a

sus, and to identify age-matched native-born peers. I compared the groups on the person-level economic status indicators in table 7.1. Table 7.4 shows some of the results for the Southeast Asian group.

It can be seen that for most of the indicators, the economic status of the Southeast Asian childhood refugee arrivals was higher than that of the total adult population of Southeast Asian refugees. For example, a higher percentage were employed and a much lower percentage were receiving public assistance. However, the childhood refugee arrivals' status on most of the indicators was lower than that of their U.S.-born age-matched peers. For example, the percentage of childhood refugee arrivals living in poverty was higher than that of their native-born peers. Thus, these childhood refugees may be said to be in a transitional economic stage, having surpassed the adult arrivals, but not yet faring as well as their U.S.-born peers (Potocky, 1996b: 367-368).

I conducted the same analyses for the four refugee groups in Miami. The results showed that "in general, Cuban, Soviet/East European, and Nicaraguan childhood arrivals had higher economic status than both of their respective comparison groups" (Potocky,

Table 7.4 Economic Characteristics of California Southeast
Asian Childhood Refugees, Adult Refugees, and
U.S.-Born Peers

Characteristic	Childhood Refugee Arrivals	Group Total Adult Refugees	U.S.-Born Peers
Percent employed	55.1	44.5	72.7
Percent receiving public assistance	8.2	24.3	4.4
Percent who have never worked	23.1	31.9	5.7
Percent living in poverty	28.6	34.1	12.9
Years education (mean)	11.8	11.4	12.8
Percent enrolled in school	52.3	26.4	32.9

Source: Potocky, 1996b

1996b: 368). In contrast, the Haitian childhood arrivals had lower status than both of their comparison groups on most of the indicators.

Methodological Considerations

A methodological issue of importance in analyses of this sort is the determination of whether observed group differences are statistically significant. Typically, one would use an analysis of variance to answer this question. However, when using total population estimates such as those available from the census, statistical significance is not applicable since inferential statistics pertain to samples and not populations. Further, even if using the unweighted samples, the sample sizes are often so large as to make all differences, even small ones, statistically significant.

The solution to this problem is to use criteria of substantive significance instead of statistical significance. Substantive significance is used for evaluating "importance from a practical standpoint" (Rubin and Babbie, 1989: 457) or the "personal or social meaning" of the group differences (Bloom and Fischer, 1982: 396). Substantive significance "is primarily a subjective matter involving value judgments" (Rubin and Babbie, 1989: 306). Criteria of substantive significance are based on what are called effect sizes—that is, the actual magnitudes of the group differences, expressed in standardized form (Cohen, 1988). Thus, the researcher needs to determine *a priori* what effect size will be deemed to be substantively significant. For example, what difference in yearly household earnings between refugees and the native-born is meaningful? This determination is a judgment which should be based on considerations such as data from prior empirical studies; consultation with key individuals such as fellow researchers, service providers, or refugees themselves; and experience in the field. In the absence of such information, one may use conventions for small, average, and large effect sizes that have been proposed by Cohen (1988). The effect size approach as opposed to statistical significance testing is increasingly being advocated by some researchers (Orme, 1994; Schmidt, 1996).

A final point with regard to descriptive studies using the census is that PUMS data from prior decennial years can be used to assess changes in refugees' demographic and socioeconomic characteristics over time. Essentially, identical descriptive analyses would be conducted for each time point and then compared. Because the samples at each time point do not consist of the same cases, this constitutes a replicated cross-sectional survey design (Tripodi, 1985). Analyses of this type using the PUMS have been conducted by several immigration researchers (e.g., Jensen, 1988; 1991).

Correlational Analyses

The final research purpose for which the census may be used is to examine the correlations between variables, using either bivariate or multivariate analyses. I have used multivariate analyses to identify the most important variables (of those available in the PUMS) that influence refugee economic integration, and to determine the magnitude and direction of those relationships (Potocky and McDonald, 1995; Potocky, 1997). I will use the data from my study of Southeast Asian refugees in California (Potocky and McDonald, 1995) to illustrate the analytic methodology of this approach. This analysis was based on a subsample of the Southeast Asian refugees, those over age fifteen. Comparison groups such as those used above for descriptive purposes were not relevant to this analysis.

Independent and dependent variables. First, in congruence with my proposed expanded definition of refugee economic integration above, I operationalized this dependent construct by three variables from the census: employment status, public assistance utilization, and household income. Three separate analyses were conducted, one for each dependent variable. For the present purposes of illustration, I will focus only on employment status. This was operationalized as a dichotomous variable, i.e., "employed" and "not employed." The independent variables were the eighteen variables listed as correlates in table 7.1. In other words, those variables in the PUMS which were presumed to be related to refugee economic integration based on the above-described conceptual framework and prior empirical literature were selected for the analysis. The purpose of the analysis was to determine how these variables influenced employment status.

Variable definitions and coding. The analysis required recoding of some of the variables from the original coding in the PUMS. For the most part this consisted of collapsing categorical variables into dichotomous variables for practical reasons. For example, marital status was originally coded into five categories; for this analysis it was collapsed into two categories, "married" and "not married." For some other variables (e.g., years of education, length of residence, English-speaking ability) the original PUMS coding was used. Specific codes are shown in the Appendix.

Analysis Strategy. A logistic regression was conducted with all of the independent variables entered simultaneously into the equation. Logistic regression is the appropriate analytic method when the dependent variable is dichotomous (such as employment status in the present analysis) and there are multiple independent variables (as in the present analysis), one or more of which are continuous (such as age and education in the present analysis) (Morrow-Howell and Proctor, 1992). One advantage of the PUMS is that the large sample sizes available permit the researcher to conduct replication analyses. This is done by randomly splitting the sample into approximately equal halves. The logistic regression equation is computed on the first half of the sample and then verified on the second half. If the two results are similar, the validity of the findings is strengthened. This procedure was used in this analysis, as described below.

The analyses were based on the total population estimates. Thus, for the reasons described above, statistical significance was not meaningful. However, this does not affect the interpretation of the overall utility of the logistic regression equation, or the substantive significance of the effect of each independent variable.

Overall regression results. The usefulness of a logistic regression model can be evaluated by examining how well it classifies cases in regard to the dependent variable (Norusis, 1990). These classification results are shown in table 7.5.

For the computation sample, the model correctly classified approximately 75 percent of the cases. This represents an increase of about 20 percent in predictive accuracy over the prior probability of prediction, which is based on the observed distribution. Further, as

Table 7.5 Logistic Regression of Employment Status
of Southeast Asian Refugees:
Classification Results

Classification table for computation sample

	Predicted		
Observed	No	Yes	Percent Correct
No	73,242	20,267	78.3%
Yes	21,359	53,300	71.4%
Observed Distribution	56.3%	43.7%	
		Overall Percent Correct	75.3%

Classification table for verification sample

	Predicted		
Observed	No	Yes	Percent Correct
No	67,145	19,838	77.2%
Yes	19,513	50,739	72.2%
Observed Distribution	55.1%	44.9%	
		Overall Percent Correct	75.0%

Source: Potocky and McDonald, 1995

seen in table 7.5, the classification results for the verification sample
were nearly identical to those of the computation sample. Thus, it
appears that this eighteen-variable regression model has good utility;
in other words, the independent variables are useful in explaining
the differences in employment status in this sample.

Variable effects. The next issue of interest is the actual effect of each
independent variable upon employment status. These results are
shown in table 7.6.

In logistic regression, the odds ratio, e^b, "is the factor by which the
odds change when the ... independent variable increases by one unit"
(Norusis, 1990: B-43). If e^b is greater than one, the odds of the event
occurring are increased; if e^b is less than one, the odds are decreased,
and if e^b is equal to one, the odds are not changed. The standardized
logistic coefficient, R, is used for comparing the relative effects of the
independent variables. The larger the absolute value of R, the more
important is that variable's influence upon the dependent variable.

Table 7.6 Logistic Regression of Employment Status of Southeast Asian Refugees: Parameter Estimates

Employment Status[a] Independent variable	e[b]	R
Sex (0 = male; 1 = female)	.524	-.110[b]
Age (years)	1.004	.016
Place of birth (reference = Vietnam)		
Cambodia	.902	-.004
Laos	1.078	.000
Ethnicity (reference = Vietnamese)		
Chinese-Vietnamese	2.171	.092[b]
Hmong	.446	-.024
Laotian	.568	-.018
Cambodian	.847	-.007
Other	.207	-.044
Education (1 unit = approx. 1 year)	1.183	.174[b]
Length of residence (1 unit = approx. 3 years)	1.146	.056
Secondary migration[a]	.759	-.026
English ability (1 = very well; 4 = not at all)	.810	-.050
U.S. citizenship[a]	2.210	.114[b]
Disability[a]	.311	-.092[b]
Number of persons in household	.939	-.042
Household headed by married couple[a]	1.146	.018
Presence of nonrelatives[a]	1.348	.038
Presence of children[a]	.576	-.067
Presence of persons age 65 and over[a]	.751	-.036
Presence of subfamilies[a]	1.356	.034
Language other than English at home[a]	2.897	.045
Presence of U.S. natives[a]	.534	-.036

[a]0 = no, 1 = yes
[b]Five most important correlates

Source: Potocky and McDonald, 1995

The results indicate that having a household headed by a married couple, having nonrelatives or subfamilies in the household, having a household in which a language other than English is spoken, and having greater education, greater length of residence, greater English ability, and U.S. citizenship, all increased the odds of employment. Being female, being of an ethnicity other than Vietnamese and Chinese-Vietnamese, having made a secondary migration, being disabled, and having children, persons aged 65 and over, or U.S. natives in the household, all decreased the odds of employment. Age, place of birth, and number of persons in the household all had little effect on employment status.

The five most important correlates of employment status were sex, ethnicity, education, U.S. citizenship, and disability. Their specific effects were as follows: Females had about half the odds of being employed as did males. The odds of employment varied widely by ethnicity. For example, refugees of Chinese-Vietnamese ethnicity were over twice as likely to be employed compared to those of Vietnamese ethnicity. Each additional year of education increased the odds of employment by about 18 percent. Those refugees who had become citizens, compared to those who had not, had over twice the odds of being employed. Finally, those who were disabled had only one-third the odds of being employed, compared to those who were not disabled.

I conducted similar analyses for the other two indicators of economic integration (public assistance utilization and household income), and also for the other four refugee groups that I have examined. Taken together, the results yielded a number of implications for improvement of refugee resettlement policies, programs, and practices. Inasmuch as the focus of this paper is on methodology, I will not address these here.

Methodological considerations. The methodological issues attendant with correlational studies of this type are those which pertain to cross-sectional research designs in general. The main issue, of course, is that causal inferences cannot be drawn from such non-experimental designs. Nonetheless, these designs can be useful for identifying empirical relationships and testing hypotheses. The identification of empirically correlated variables can be useful in the development of subsequent longitudinal or experimental studies which can test those relationships causally.

Finally, it is possible to test competing causal models using correlational data, through the analytic technique of structural equation modeling. In retrospect, if I were to conduct the studies described here again, I would use this analytic approach. It would improve the analyses in two ways. First, it would assess how well the observable indicators in Kuhlman's (1991) theoretical model (i.e., the lower-case variables) actually fit together to form coherent latent constructs (i.e., the upper-case factors which are referred to as the measurement model in structural equation modeling). Second, it would provide a more detailed analysis by identifying the magnitudes of both direct and indirect relationships between the factors (what is referred to as the structural model in structural equation modeling). I plan to undertake such analyses in future studies.

Summary

The PUMS is a valuable data source for research on refugee resettlement in the United States. It has a number of strengths. First and foremost, it provides large probability samples that would not be feasible for individual researchers to obtain. Such samples greatly enhance the generalizability of the data. Second, a wide variety of demographic and socioeconomic data are collected. Third, the data can be considered to be highly valid and reliable due to the Census Bureau's extensive quality assurance procedures. Fourth, researchers can tailor their own analyses, including descriptive and correlational analyses that can include hypothesis testing. Fifth, it is possible to study subgroups of refugees, such as children. Sixth, one can examine trends over time. Seventh, due to the large sample sizes, it is possible to conduct verification analyses. Finally, research using the PUMS is inexpensive since the data files are available free of charge to university-affiliated researchers.

The descriptive and correlational approaches described can be used to design a variety of studies on different dependent and independent variables and the relationships among them. For example, using descriptive statistics, a researcher could examine the economic well-being or household compositions of older refugees from different countries. As another example, using the correlational approach, one could examine the predictors of different dependent variables such as citizenship (Yang, 1994).

Although the census data does not contain data on physical and psychological variables such as health, mental health, acculturation, and attitudes, it can nonetheless serve as a useful purpose for researchers examining these aspects of refugee adaptation. Specifically, researchers can collect demographic and economic data on their own samples and then compare these to the census data to determine the representativeness of their samples. This would enhance the generalizability of findings related to psychosocial adaptation based on non-census samples.

Like all data collection techniques and research approaches, the PUMS has some limitations. The major one of these is at the conceptual level. As with all secondary analyses, the data never contain all of the variables that are relevant to a given research question or hypothesis. As noted previously, the census does not contain data on contextual variables. Thus, any research questions concerning the impact of the sociopolitical environment upon refugees cannot be addressed using census data. A second limitation is that "true refugees" cannot be identified, nor can specific year of immigration. Additionally, only the long-term resettlement phase of the refugee experience can be examined. Third, it is not possible to conduct true longitudinal studies using the census. Finally, like all surveys, the census does not provide a "thick description" of refugee lives, such as would be gained from qualitative research.

In conclusion, I suggest a few recommendations for researchers who may wish to use the PUMS. First, they should read the literature of others who have used these data, in order to acquire a broader knowledge of the types of research questions and hypotheses that can be addressed, as well as the analytic approaches. Second, unless the researcher is extremely adept at working with large data files, it will probably be necessary to use the services of a computer consultant in the initial data processing stage in order to produce subsets of the files and convert them into the appropriate format for statistical analysis. Third, the researcher should become thoroughly familiar with the user's manual. Finally, the limitations of the data and the research design should be made explicit from the start.

References

Alba, R. D., Denton, N. A., Leung, S. J., and Logan, J. R. (1995). Neighborhood change under conditions of mass immigration: The New York City region, 1970-1980. *International Migration Review, 29*:625-656.

Alba, R. D., and Logan, J. R. (1992). Assimilation and stratification in the home ownership patterns of racial and ethnic groups. *International Migration Review, 26*:1314-1341.

Bach, R. L., and Carroll-Seguin, R. (1986). Labor force participation, household composition, and sponsorship among Southeast Asian refugees. *International Migration Review, 20*:381-404.

Biddlecom, A. E. (1993).The effect of immigration on the timing of first marriage. Paper presented at the annual meeting of the American Sociological Association.

Bills, G. D., Hernandez-Chavez, E., and Hudson, A. (1995). The geography of language shift: Distance from the Mexican border and Spanish language claiming in the Southwestern United States. *International Journal of the Sociology of Language, 114*:9-27.

Bloom, M., and Fischer, J. (1982). *Evaluating practice: Guidelines for the accountable professional.* Englewood Cliffs, NJ: Prentice-Hall.

Caplan, N., Whitmore, J. K. and Bui, Q. L. (1985). Economic self-sufficiency among recently-arrived refugees from Southeast Asia. *Economic Outlook USA, 12*:60-63.

Chiswick, B. R. (1993). Soviet Jews in the United States: An analysis of their linguistic and economic adjustment. *International Migration Review, 27*:260-285.

Cohen, J. (1988). *Statistical power analysis for the behavioral sciences* (2nd ed.). Hillsdale, NJ: Erlbaum.

Gozdziak, E. (1989). *New Americans: The economic adaptation of Eastern European, Afghan, and Ethiopian refugees.* Washington, DC: Refugee Policy Group.

Hirschman, C. (1994). Problems and prospects of studying immigrant adaptation from the 1990 Population Census: From generational comparisons to the process of "becoming American." *International Migration Review, 28*:690-713.

Jensen, L. (1988). Patterns of immigration and public assistance utilization, 1970-1980. *International Migration Review, 22*:51-83.

Jensen, L. (1991). Secondary earner strategies and family poverty: Immigrant-native differentials, 1960-1980. *International Migration Review, 25*:113-140.

Jensen, L., and Chitose, Y. (1994). Today's second generation: Evidence from the 1990 U.S. Census. *International Migration Review, 28*:714-735.

Kahn, J. R. (1994). Immigrant and native fertility during the 1980s: Adaptation and expectations for the future. *International Migration Review, 28*:501-519.

Kuhlman, T. (1991). The economic integration of refugees in developing countries: A research model. *Journal of Refugee Studies, 4*:1-20.

Levine, D. B., Hill, K., and Warren, R. (Eds.). (1985). *Immigration statistics: A story of neglect.* Washington, DC: National Academy Press.

Logan, J. R., Alba, R. D., and McNulty, T. L. (1994). Ethnic economies in metropolitan regions: Miami and beyond. *Social Forces, 72*:691-724.

Majka, L. and Mullan, B. (1992). Employment retention, area of origin, and type of social support among refugees in the Chicago area. *International Migration Review, 26*:899-926.

Model, S. (1992). The ethnic economy: Cubans and Chinese reconsidered. *Sociological Quarterly, 33*:63-82.

Morrow-Howell, N., and Proctor, E. K. (1992). The use of logistic regression in social work research. In Gillespie, D. F. and Glisson, C. (Eds.), *Quantitative methods in social work: State of the art.* New York: Haworth, 87-104. Also published in the *Journal of Social Service Research, 16*:1-2.

Norusis, M. J. (1990). *SPSS/PC+ Advanced Statistics 4.0.* Chicago: SPSS Inc.

Orme, J. G. (1994). Are effect sizes better than traditional hypothesis testing for evaluating research findings? Yes. In Hudson, W. W. and Nurius, P. S. (Eds.), *Controversial issues in social work research.* Boston: Allyn and Bacon, 237-240.

Perez, L. (1986). Immigrant economic adjustment and family organization: The Cuban success story reexamined. *International Migration Review, 20*:4-20.

Portes, A. and Stepick, A. (1985). Unwelcome immigrants: The labor market experiences of 1980 (Mariel) Cuban and Haitian refugees in South Florida. *American Sociological Review, 50*:493-514.

Poston, D. L., Jr. (1994). Patterns of economic attainment of foreign-born male workers in the United States. *International Migration Review, 28*:478-500.

Potocky, M. (1993). The economic integration of Southeast Asian refugees in California. Unpublished doctoral dissertation, University of Kansas School of Social Welfare.

Potocky, M. (1996a). Toward a new definition of refugee economic integration. *International Social Work, 39*:245-256.

Potocky, M. (1996b). Refugee children: How are they faring economically as adults? *Social Work, 41*:364-373.

Potocky, M. (1997). Predictors of refugee economic status: A replication. *Journal of Social Service Research, 23*:41-70.

Potocky, M. and McDonald, T. P. (1995). Predictors of economic status of Southeast Asian refugees: Implications for service improvement. *Social Work Research, 19*:219-227.

Rubin, A. and Babbie, E. (1989). *Research methods for social work.* Belmont, CA: Wadsworth.

Schmidt, F. L. (1996). Statistical significance testing and cumulative knowledge in psychology: Implications for training of researchers. *Psychological Methods, 1*:115-129.

Simon, J. L. (1995). *Immigration: The demographic and economic facts.* Washington, DC: Cato Institute.

Tran, T. V. (1991). Sponsorship and employment status among Indochinese refugees in the United States. *International Migration Review, 25*:536-550.

Tripodi, T. (1985). Research designs. In Grinnell, R. M. Jr. (Ed.), *Social work research and evaluation.* Itasca, IL: Peacock, 239-259.

Uba, L., and Chung, R. C. (1991). The relationship between trauma and financial and physical well-being among Cambodians in the United States. *Journal of General Psychology, 118*:215-225.

United Nations (1951). *Geneva Convention Relating to the Status of Refugees.* Geneva: Author.

United Nations (1967). *Protocol Relating to the Status of Refugees.* Geneva: Author.

United States Bureau of the Census (1993). *Census of Population and Housing, 1990: Public Use Microdata Samples Technical Documentation.* Washington, D.C.: U.S. Bureau of the Census, Data User Services Division.

Westermeyer, J., Callies, A., and Neider, J. (1990). Welfare status and psychosocial adjustment among 100 Hmong refugees. *Journal of Nervous and Mental Disease, 178*:300-306.

Yang, P. Q. (1994). Explaining immigrant naturalization. *International Migration Review, 28*:449-477.

Appendix

Variable Codes

Variable	Codes
Employment status	0 = not employed 1 = employed
Sex	0 = male 1 = female
Age	Years
Education	1 = none 2 = nursery school 3 = kindergarten 4 = 1st - 4th grade 5 = 5th - 8th grade 6 = 9th grade 7 = 10th grade 8 = 11th grade 9 = 12th grade, no diploma 10 = high school graduate 11 = some college, no degree 12 = associate occupational degree 13 = associate academic degree 14 = bachelor's degree 15 = master's degree 16 = professional degree 17 = doctorate degree
Ethnicity	1 = Chinese 2 = Cambodian 3 = Hmong 4 = Laotian 5 = Vietnamese 6 = All others
Place of birth	1 = Cambodia 2 = Laos 3 = Vietnam
Length of U.S. residence	1 = 0-3 years 2 = 4-5 years 3 = 6-8 years 4 = 9-10 years 5 = 11-15 years
Secondary migration in past five years	0 = no 1 = yes
Language spoken at home	0 = English only 1 = Language other than English

Variable	**Codes**
English speaking ability	0 = Speaks only English at home 1 = Very well 2 = Well 3 = Not well 4 = Not at all
Disability	0 = no 1 = yes
U.S. citizenship	0 = no 1 = yes
Number of persons in household	Number
Married-couple household	0 = no 1 = yes
Presence of non-relatives	0 = no 1 = yes
Presence of children	0 = no 1 = yes
Presence of persons aged 65 and over	0 = no 1 = yes
Presence of subfamilies	0 = no 1 = yes
Presence of U.S. natives	0 = no 1 = yes

8

Returnees to Vietnam

The Well-Being of Former Unaccompanied Minors

Maryanne Loughry and *Nguyen Xuan Nghia*

Introduction

Background

Vietnamese refugees first fled Vietnam in 1975 with the fall of Saigon. Subsequently more than one million people fled, and resettled in other countries. In 1988 in Hong Kong and 1989 in Southeast Asian countries, it was determined that the Vietnamese who were still leaving Vietnam would be screened individually for refugee status and given the right to appeal before being eligible for resettlement. This arrangement became known as the Comprehensive Plan of Action (CPA), and the Vietnamese were held in detention centers in asylum countries while awaiting their refugee status determination. Under the CPA more than 150,000 Vietnamese people lived in detention, 80,000 were resettled in new countries, and 72,200 returned to Vietnam (UNHCR, 1995). More than 3,000 of those who returned to Vietnam were children under eighteen years of age that had lived in the camps in Hong Kong and Southeast Asia since 1989 without parents or adult relatives, unaccompanied children.

This study is a continuation of research that started in 1992 with the systematic examination by Community Family Services International (CFSI) of the effects of detention on the psychosocial well-being of children (McCallin, 1992; Loughry, McCallin and Bennett, 1993) in Hong Kong. The goal of this study is to determine how the formerly unaccompanied children have adapted to Vietnam and their family following their years of absence in the detention centers of Hong Kong and Southeast Asia. This has been determined will be met by measuring the psychological and social well-being of a sample of former unaccompanied children who have returned to Vietnam and comparing these measures with those of children who never left Vietnam to seek asylum.

The study has two foci: first, a look at the problems that these children were experiencing; and, second, an examination of their system of social supports. In particular, we concentrated our attention on the protective factors in the children's environment that appear to assist them in proceeding through normal development even when in adverse settings. There are three broad categories of protective factors that have been identified as helpful to the children:

A. The attributes of the child including levels of sociability, intelligence, communication skills and internal locus of control;
B. Affectional ties with the family;
C. External social support systems that reinforce the children's coping efforts (Garmezy, 1991).

In this study the measures of perceived social support, self-efficacy, and external lifestyle have been used to see what role these protective factors may play in assisting the children to reintegrate into Vietnam. In other words, we expected that re-adjustment upon return to Vietnam would be mediated by the youth's social supports, self-efficacy, and lifestyle.

Cultural Issues and Measures of Well-Being

The study is a cross-cultural study of well-being. It is a particularly challenging study because there have been no other studies of well-being of Vietnamese in Vietnam. There have only been a few psychological and psychiatric studies conducted in Vietnam since 1975. To meet this challenge and in the hope of being culturally sensitive, the following steps were necessary. The study was conducted in close collaboration with Vietnamese staff from the Open University, Ho Chi Minh City. The Open University had recently concluded a number of sociological studies which had familiarized researchers with the sample group, facilitating the development of sampling techniques and social scales that would be relevant to this study.

The Open University staff also acted as cultural "interpreters," directing the study in culturally sensitive matters. This was particularly important because while the concept of well-being is debated in Western psychological circles, there is not an equivalent concept in the Vietnamese language. Lengthy discussion was necessary before the concept of well-being in the study took into account the cultural definitions of mental health, social needs, and wellness. The psychometric instruments were finally selected because jointly we agreed that they measured the dimensions of wellness: patterns of behavior, levels of social support, belief in one's ability, and standard of living. They were translated into Vietnamese and then back translated to ensure lexical equivalence (Eyton and Neuwirth, 1984). In addition to the psychometric measures, a smaller subgroup of the sample was interviewed in depth by the Vietnamese researchers. This was to facilitate the children supplementing the study with their own descriptions of the experience of the camps and their situation on return.

Methodology

Four hundred and three unaccompanied children returned to Thua Thien Hue. For our study we selected all the children who were under the age of twenty-one years at the beginning of the study. This was a total of 304 children. We sought to interview each of these children. At the conclusion of our study we had found and interviewed 208 unaccompanied returnee children (URC) under the age of twenty-one years. The remaining children had left Thua Thien Hue for work and study or had moved to a new location without a forwarding address.

To contrast the sample of unaccompanied returnee children we sought a sample of children who had not left Vietnam. To obtain this sample we invited each unaccompanied returnee child to nominate an acquaintance who was of similar age and may agree to be interviewed. This procedure produced a sample of 187 local children (LC).

Study Instruments, Questionnaires, Demographic Characteristics

In this study we collected demographic information of age, gender, educational background, present occupation, and socioeconomic status as well as the children's perceptions of their standard of living. The children who had been in the camps were asked about their departure, time in the camps, and care-giving arrangements. This questionnaire was specially designed to elicit relevant information about the children's lifestyle in Vietnam

Table 8.1 Description of the Two Samples

	Unaccompanied Returnee Children		Local Children		Total	
Gender						
– Male	102	49%	92	49.2%	194	49.5%
– Female	106	51%	95	50.8%	201	50.5%
– Total	208	100%	187	100%	395	100%
Marital status						
– Missing data	0	0%	1	0.5%	1	0.3%
– Single	168	80.8%	179	95.7%	347	87.8%
– Married	39	18.8%	7	3.7%	46	11.6%
– Divorced	1	0.5%	0	0%	1	0.3%
Average years of education	5.9		6.3		6.1	
Location						
– Rural	188	90.4%	160	85.6%	348	88.1%
– Urban	20	9.6%	27	14.4%	47	11.9%
Age	18.3		18.4		18.4	

1. Achenbach Youth Self-Report (YSR)

The Achenbach Youth Self-Report (YSR) was used to assess the participants' behavioral adjustment. The YSR was selected because it had been translated into Vietnamese and used in earlier studies with Vietnamese living outside of Vietnam (McKelvey and Webb, 1993). It was used to measure any problems that the children might have had based on the assumption that the children may have residual problems from their time in detention. The YSR is a questionnaire designed to obtain eleven to eighteen year olds' reports on their competencies and problems (Achenbach, 1991). For the purposes of this study, the seventeen item competency scale was omitted because many of the children were no longer attending school. The problem scale consists of 102 items about specific problems and sixteen items related to socially desirable behaviors. This scale consists of eight syndrome subscales: withdrawn, somatic complaints, anxious/depressed, social problems, thought problems, attention problems, delinquent behavior, and aggressive behavior. An additional syndrome, self destructive/identity problems, can also be scored for boys. Each subscale has a normal and a clinical range. The withdrawn, somatic complaints, and anxious/depressed subscales are grouped to form an *internalizing* subscale. The delinquent behavior and aggressive behavior scales combined form the *externalizing* subscale. The total score on the scale as well as the scores for the internalizing and externalizing subscales have a normal and a clinical scale. The YSR and its parent questionnaire, the Child Behavior Checklist (CBCL) had been used in cross-cultural research. The YSR has been translated into more than thirty-three languages, including Vietnamese (Achenbach, 1991). While the YSR scale was designed for eleven to eighteen year olds, it can also be used with nineteen to twenty year olds (Achenbach, 1991). Comparisons of scores of those outside the norms are made between respondents of the same age (Achenbach, 1991). Achenbach (1991) reports an overall scale test-retest reliability for the YSR of .81 with slightly higher stability for ages fifteen-eighteen years old (median r = .89). Validity for the use of YSR is made by correlations with the CBCL and the Achenbach Teachers' Report Form ® = .41 for boys and .45 for girls).

2. Social Support

The participants listed up to five individuals to whom "you can go to anytime you need help." They were asked how long they have known each person and to rate how supportive each person has been to them on a one-five scale of supportiveness. This procedure, developed by Weist, Freedman, Paskewitz, Proescher and Flaherty (1995) is based on larger measures of social supports and behaviors. Psychometric characteristics are not available for this scale.

3. Perceived Self-Efficacy

The participants completed a 20 item questionnaire designed to measure their perceived ability to cope with situations of daily living (Cowen et al., 1991). Children's belief in their ability to cope with life is an important adaptive value that differentiates stress-resilient children from stress-affected children. The participants responded to how sure they felt about managing 20 daily life situations using a Likert scale of sureness ranging from one-five, "Not at all sure" to "Very sure." Cowen (1991) reports a test-retest reliability of .65.

4. Exposure to Traumatic Events Scale

For those children who had left Vietnam, a 27 item Life Event Scale was specifically developed to measured the children's experience of events on their journey to Hong Kong and while in detention in Hong Kong. The children were asked to identify if they had been exposed to stressful conditions during their trip to Hong Kong: lack of food or water, sickness, robbery, boat breakdown, storm (typhoon), sexual abuse, beating, arrest/attack, intimidation/threatening, bad weather and sea sickness, separation from family. In addition, they identified if they had been exposed to stressful conditions while in the detention centers: sexual abuse, physical abuse, humiliation or intimidation, coercion, imprisonment, forced separation from family and friends, prostitution, suicide, substance abuse, hunger strikes, demonstrations, riots, tear gassing, forced relocation, weapon searches, gang conflict, murder, other forms of abuse. The children indicated on a four point scale if they had experienced (3), witnessed (2), heard about (1), or had no experience of each event (0). A total score was calculated by summing all 27 items.

5. In-Depth Interviews

Besides the questionnaire investigation, fifteen unaccompanied returnee children were selected for an in-depth interview. This interview was to supplement the quantitative facts of the questionnaire. It aimed at investigating the children's perceptions of their life in the refugee camps, their feelings about their present life, what is the cause of their success, and what is hindering them in the reintegration process. These fifteen children had been in the camps for lengthy periods of time.

Migration Experiences of Unaccompanied Returnee Children

The children left Vietnam between the ages of four and seventeen years of age (average age 12.69, standard deviation 2.5). Among them, 58.8 percent admitted that they journeyed to the camps of their own will, 26.1 percent by parental arrangement, and 15.1 percent by chance. When the children were asked the same question in the research of McCallin (1992), she found that 46 percent had journeyed of their own free will, 41 percent with parental consensus, and 13 percent by chance. When asked about care-giving arrangements in the camps, 73.5 percent reported that they actually lived with relatives, 8.7 percent with friends, and 17.9 percent alone—a fact that called into question the status of the children as "unaccompanied minors."

Traumatic Events

The children reported a large number of traumatic events on their journey to Hong Kong and in the detention centers. These are detailed in table 8.2.

Table 8.2 The Traumatic Events That the URC Have
Experienced on Their Journey to Hong Kong
and in the Detention Centers

A. On the Journey to Hong Kong

	Missing	Unknown	Heard About	Witnessed	Suffered Directly
1. Lack of water or food	1	11	5	17	174
2. Seasickness	1	3	1	45	158
3. Robbery	3	144	49	2	10
4. Boat breakdown	2	129	61	8	8
5. Storm	3	52	30	4	119
6. Being raped, abused	2	148	40	17	1
7. Physical assault	1	148	32	15	12
8. Detained, attacked	4	140	40	10	14
9. Threatened	9	126	34	15	24
10. Bad weather, enduring sickness	3	38	12	18	137
11. Being separated from relatives	8	152	21	12	15

B. In the Detention Centers

	Missing	Unknown	Heard About	Witnessed	Suffered Directly
1. Being raped, abused	3	142	49	9	5
2. Being beaten	1	69	47	66	25
3. Being insulted, threatened	5	96	34	52	21
4. Being forced to labor	3	126	40	33	6
5. Being imprisoned	2	74	47	82	3
6. Being separated from relatives, friends	3	112	25	31	37
7. Prostitution	3	175	26	4	0
8. Suicide	1	109	64	32	2
9. Drug addiction	3	165	31	8	1
10. Hunger strike	4	97	52	32	23
11. Demonstration	2	84	60	37	25
12. Violence	3	74	43	82	6
13. Being suppressed with tear gas	3	40	34	43	88
14. Being forced to transfer to other camps	1	92	40	46	29
15. Being searched for weapons	3	47	15	25	118
16. Gang conflicts	1	63	50	85	9
17. Killing of people	2	118	65	22	1
18. Other forms of abuse	8	168	25	5	2

The majority (84 percent) suffered lack of water and lack of food
on the journey, 58 percent met with storms, and approximately 5
percent ran into pirates. Some of the children tell of their meeting
with storms on their journey: [1]

Storms came while the engines were out of order which caused the feeling of sure death. All people aboard tied their hands to each other wishing that in death their corpses will drift to one spot. (URC 143)

It is frightening to remember it. The boat was like a leaf above the big waves. Everyone was afraid of dying in a shipwreck. It is still worrying to remember ... The incident even enters my dreams ... In my dreams there was much screaming ... Early after returning [to Vietnam] the screaming still appeared in my dreams, but now no more. (URC 141)

In the camps, 2.4 percent of the youth were raped or sexually abused, 12 percent were beaten, 42.9 percent were suppressed with tear gas, 15 percent witnessed suicides and 10 percent witnessed the killing of people.[2] The longer they stayed in the camps, the more they directly witnessed or experienced traumatic events ® = 0.29, p > 0.000). McCallin's work (1992) shows five factors causing stress to the children: 1) the length of stay in the camps; 2) the care-giving arrangement; 3) the age of the child; 4) the number of traumatic events experienced; and, 5) the centers where they lived. As we will see later, there also is in this study a significant correlation between the experience of traumatic incidents with present anxiety and depression of the unaccompanied returnee children ® = 0.20, p > 0.00), as shown in the analysis of the YSR scale (table 8.9).

While in Hong Kong, 65.6 percent stayed in the Shekkong Camp, 16.7 percent in Tai O Chau, 8.9 percent in Whitehead, 4.4 percent in Chimawan, 2 percent in High Island and 2 percent in Heiling Chau. Those who stayed in Shekkong and Tai O Chau camps experienced less traumatic events than others. The Whitehead detention center was characterized by violent occurrences. Those who stayed in Tai O Chau camp reported more exposure to traumatic events than those in Shekkong camp, yet in Tai O Chau camp the children reported feeling more comfortable because they could stroll outside the camp. In Shekkong after a disturbance in February 1992 causing twenty-four deaths, the counseling program implemented by Community and Family Services International (CFSI) assisted the children who experienced this disturbance. As for the Whitehead camp, the children were practically imprisoned with almost no privacy.

Those who stayed in High Island personally experienced on average 4.25 traumatic events, Whitehead 3.61, Chimawan 2.33, Tai O Chau 2.0, Heiling Chau 1.75, Shekkong 1.65 (p > 0.00). In table 8.3, we see that a majority of these children stayed in the camps for more than one year.

Table 8.3 Number of Years in Camps

Number of Years in Camps	Frequency	Percent	Percent Accumulated
– under 1 year	16	7.7	7.7
– 1 year	88	42.3	50.0
– 2 years	65	31.3	81.3
– 3 years	14	6.7	88.0
– 4 years	19	9.1	97.1
– 5 years or more	6	2.9	100.0

The life in the camps left strong impressions on the children. Though living in detention many of them thought that period of time was really useful for them:

> Life there was comfortable because people cared for our education though we were deprived of patriotic, parental, and fraternal sentiments. Life there was not bad, while in Vietnam we have to care even for our eating and clothing ... (URC 143)
>
> When remembering the life in the camp, one remembers the meals. Chicken wings and pate. It was merry to queue for food every day ... (URC 149)
>
> I think that life over there was spiritually not so comfortable, but we had sufficient entertaining activities ... Since repatriation, life is harder. As for schooling expenses, I feel worried because my parents have to work hard to assist me ... (URC 150)
>
> Life there is more joyful than here ... because we can enjoy schooling, amusement ... (URC 209)

But some others had different thoughts:

> In the camp, we had no freedom, we were not comfortable, we could not go out. Life there was complicated, but we accepted it for the sake of resettlement. Now it turned out to be impossible, so we returned to Vietnam, though it is hard but all right with spiritual comfort. (URC 144)

In general, they admitted that life in the refugee camps was physically more comfortable, less worrying than in Vietnam, but it was spiritually deprived and restrictive.

The years in camps also changed their perceptions and behaviors, leading to them feeling more mature. One of them typically says,

> in Vietnam we think only of earning the living, without traveling much, so we lack wisdom. In the camp we encountered many people, conducted a collective life, and came to know the personal characteristics of various people. Previously, I had no courage and fortitude to do anything, but now I am more brave, I can do anything, however hard it may be, as long as it is legitimate, not bad, I can withstand any criticism,

rumor. I have lived in various circumstances, either joyful or sorrowing, therefore I can overcome any difficult circumstances. Now I can survive alone in the mountains, because I am not discouraged before anything ... (URC 143)

Remembering the collective life over there which has enabled me to learn many things ... my bad actions are reduced ... I feel more confident ... after a period of time over there I became more proper in my behavior and more dignified and resolute in my speech ... (URC 150)

After few years of life in the camps, after passing through the screening process, and failing to be granted refugee status, 85.1 percent of the youth in the sample repatriated in the years of 1992-93. The returnees since 1994 account for only 8.7 percent of the children of this target sample in Thua Thien Hue province.

The Social Situation of Repatriated, Unaccompanied Returnee Children

The average family of the unaccompanied returnee children had 7.45 members per household; local children had 7.36 members. The small difference here has no statistical significance ($p > 0.69$). The above average number of persons in one household is typical of the poor households in the rural areas of Vietnam, particularly in the coastal areas. The families of the unaccompanied returnee children were more dependent on fishing for the family income, 61.2 percent compared with 47.8 percent. More of the local children came from an agricultural family, 12 percent compared with 3.5 percent.

There is no apparent economic difference between the unaccompanied returnee children's families and the local children's families. Both had similar housing and similar numbers of household goods. On average, the unaccompanied returnee children's family had 2.3 household goods and the local children's family had 2.6. This difference has a probability of ($p > 0.06$).

We calculated an *indicator of the standard of living* of the family by calculating a composite score based on the number of household goods, the type of family, and their estimation of the standard of living of their family.[3] Based on this indicator, we examined whether the economic status of the family had any effects on the measurement of the children's psychosocial well-being. There was not a significant correlation between the children's standard of living and their measure of anxiety and depression (table 8.9).

The great majority of the children returned to live with their parents after their repatriation. Of significance here is the number of unaccompanied returnee children who are living with either their spouses after their return. Some of the children became married in the detention camps. The percent of those who were then living with their marriage partners was higher than that of the local children, reflecting early marriage. These findings are demonstrated in table 8.4.

Table 8.4 With Whom They Stay before Fleeing and after Repatriation

	URC		LC
With whom they stay	Before fleeing away	After repatriation	Now*
– With parents	86.5%	72.1%	85.0%
– With mother	4.8%	7.2%	5.3%
– With father	1.9%	1.9%	2.1%
– With relatives	5.8%	6.7%	5.3%
– With others	0%	1.0%	0%
– With wife/husband	1.0%	10.6%	1.1%
– Alone		.5%	
Total	100%	100%	100%

* missing data = 2.2%

The occupations of the children can be classified into five main groups: 1) those who were studying; 2) those who were learning a vocation; 3) those who were working; 4) those who were unemployed; and, 5) those who were doing housework.

The rate of unaccompanied children who were unemployed is higher than that of the local children, and the rate of unaccompanied children learning a vocation is lower. It is important to note that many of the unaccompanied returnee children received assistance for vocational training from non-governmental organizations upon their return. After repatriation most of the unaccompanied returnee children were young. They were able to go back to school in Vietnam. Many of the older unmarried children attended vocational training.

Among the total of 208 children, 40.3 percent had attained level 1 education, 49.5 percent level 2, 4.4 percent level 3, and 2 percent were learning in colleges. The average level of education attained was grade 5.9. Of the unaccompanied returnee children, 4.8 percent were illiterate. Only 37 percent of the girls were studying or learning a vocation and the number of illiterate girls was double that of the boys. The average level of education of the boys was 6.3 years, while that of the girls was only 5.5 ($p > 0.01$). This difference in level of education is not reflected in the sample of local children, boys–6.5; girls 6.0 ($p > 0.19$).

Overall there is no significant difference between the education level of the unaccompanied returnee children (5.91 years) and the local children (6.31 years). However, the local children were staying at school longer and those local children undertaking vocational training were younger. There were more illiterate children among the unaccompanied returnee children. These results reflect the absence of opportunity for the returnee children, but highlight the significance of the education programs in the camps. Significantly more unaccompanied returnee children were unemployed. A proportion of both samples was currently undertaking vocational training either in government-run vocational training centers or privately. The choice of courses reflects both availability and the gender bias of the group. An equally large proportion of both samples was working

It is not surprising that over 40 percent were employed in fishing, because most of them lived in coastal villages and over 61 percent of their families lived mainly on income from fishing. The majority of those fishing were boys. The girls did sewing and hairdressing. Only 30.1 percent confirmed that their jobs were relatively stable, while 69.9 percent thought that their jobs were temporary and unstable. The local children believed that their jobs were stable (51.3 percent compared with 30.1 percent of URC).

The employed unaccompanied returnee children earned on average 9,398 dong each day while the local children report earning 12,508 dong.[4] However, this difference has no statistical significance. 22 percent of the unaccompanied returnee children worked less than four hours a day, 48 percent between four and eight hours, and 30 percent work more than eight hours. These rates among the local children were 7.6 percent, 63 percent, and 30 percent respectively. These rates do possibly indicate higher stability in the jobs done by the local children.

Investigating the spending of money earned also shows a difference between the unaccompanied returnee children and the local children. Of the unaccompanied returnee children, 39.7 percent spent all the money they earned, 19.2 percent spent a part and give a part to the parents or the guardians, and 41 percent gave all to their parents or guardians. Among the local children, the rates were 14.8 percent, 45.7 percent, and 39.5 percent respectively. The unaccompanied returnee children were possibly more independent and more self-supporting as shown in their spending.

The children were asked about their standard of living and the difficulties that they were meeting, and their responses can be viewed in table 8.5.

Table 8.5 Children's Evaluation of the Standard of Living of Their Families

	Standard of living			
	very difficult	*difficult*	*sufficient*	*well off*
URC	20.3	37.7	37.7	4.3
LC	9.2	35.7	50.3	4.9

While objectively there is no significant difference between the living conditions of the unaccompanied returnee children and the local children, the unaccompanied returnee children had a more negative perception of their families' standard of living. Of the unaccompanied returnee children, 23.3 percent estimated that the standard of living of their families was very difficult, while only 9.2 percent of the local children shared the same perception. The percentage of unaccompanied returnee children who thought that the standard of living of their families was sufficient was 37.7 percent as compared with 50.3 percent for the local children. These results may well reflect the unaccompanied returnee children's exposure to alternative lifestyles while in Hong Kong.

The unaccompanied returnee children were also more pessimistic about their present living situation: 44.2 percent stated that their present life was worse than a few years ago, while this rate was 34.1 percent among the local children.

Table 8.6 Observations of the URC and the LC about the Present Life of Their Families

	Observation about the present life		
	Better than before	*Same as before*	*Worse than before*
URC	16.5%	39.3%	44.2%
LC	28.1%	37.8%	34.1%

Present Difficulties

There is not much difference between the difficulties of the unaccompanied returnee children and the local children. The most outstanding difficulty is poverty. Of unaccompanied returnee children, 83 percent described their families as poor with insufficient money to pay school fees. The unaccompanied returnee children emphasized particular difficulties, such as difficulty with housing (12.7 percent as compared with 5.2 percent of the local children). Three unaccompanied returnee children (1.6 percent) said that since they have become too old after repatriation, so it is harder for them to study. Two unaccompanied returnee children met difficulties after losing all of their official papers after repatriation. Interestingly, the rate of local children mentioning the difficulty of crowded family conditions was three times higher than that of the unaccompanied returnee children. There is a gender difference in the children's perception. The girls reported greater difficulties in housing (16 percent), unstable jobs (21.3 percent), and family conflict (10.6 percent) than that of the boys who recorded rates of 9.5 percent for housing, 12.6 percent for unstable jobs, and 3.2 percent for family conflict.

Assistance

When asked whom did the children receive assistance from upon their return, 82.4 percent mentioned their family as the primary source of support for the children when faced with physical as well as with spiritual difficulties. Besides family support among the total of 208 respondents, over half (53.5 percent) mentioned the assistance of Nordic Assistance to Repatriated Vietnamese (NARV) and slightly less, 41.5 percent, the assistance of the European Commission Integration Program (ECIP). Four youth mentioned the assistance of World Vision and only eight acknowledged the assistance of the local authorities. NARV has assisted them in paying fees for vocational training, upgrading their accommodations and buying working implements such as sewing machines. Each was assisted by about US$200-300 for this. ECIP has offered credits for their families to do business, with some families borrowing up to twenty million Vietnamese dong (US$2000). Many received free health insurance from ECIP. Those who mentioned the assistance of World Vision commented about scholarships, the building of toilets for the families, and the purchase of working implements. In spite of this material assistance, the family was perceived as the strongest source of support.

They highly appreciated the assistance of the non-governmental organizations, as in the following typical case:

> While I was miserable for having no house to stay, NARV has given three million dong to build a small house and to use for the expenses of my child's birth. NARV personnel have come for encouragement after my child's birth ... NARV has assisted me for safe living. Additional assistance was offered for buying fishing nets. Therefore, last year I have earned one extra million dong ... (URC 144)

While many children have been assisted, not all of the children reported success with their businesses. Of significance here is the failure of the children to realize or acknowledge the assistance that they and their family have received from the local government authorities. All the children would have received assistance in being reunited with their family, registration, school, and jobs. The children were either unaware of these efforts or completely accepting of them. Their responses only focused on the assistance of the non-governmental organizations.

Aspirations

The children were asked what their hopes for the future were. Many of their responses were related to themselves, and few for their families. Most of their hopes were very practical. Significantly, the unaccompanied returnee children had much stronger aspirations than the local children to have money (14.4 percent compared with 6.5 percent) and reflected also in the desire to live overseas (10.3 percent compared with 3.3 percent). This possibly reflects the unaccompanied returnee children's beliefs that financial assistance will solve their future problems and that they have not abandoned all hope for a life in a resettlement country. The local children had stronger hopes for vocational training (14.1 percent compared with 9.2 percent).

Future Jobs

While a significant number of the girls in both samples have expressed a desire to be tailors, the unaccompanied returnee children preferred small trade (14.2 percent), driving (6.1 percent), and medicine or nursing (5.6 percent) as compared with 8.8 percent, 1.1 percent, and 1.1 percent for the local sample. These aspirations reflect a greater exposure to an urban lifestyle and to wider possibilities. They did not always reflect a realistic reflection on what is practical and possible.

There is no difference between how the unaccompanied returnee children's and the local children's descriptions of how they will realize their aspirations. Almost 25 percent of them did not know what to do to realize the above aspirations. Others comment that first they should continue with schooling (24 percent of the opinions), save money (21.5 percent), learn a vocation (18.7 percent), and continue in their present jobs (9.8 percent). The need for vocational guidance is very apparent from these responses.

The Psychosocial Well-Being of the Unaccompanied Returnee Children

As presented in the research methodology, the Achenbach Youth Self Report, the Social Support Scale, the McCallin Experience Scale (McCallin, 1992) and the Cowen Self-Efficacy Scales were used in investigating the present psychosocial well-being of the children. They were chosen as measures of the children's problems as well as possible strengths.

Table 8.7 Mean and Standard Deviation of Dependent Measures on the YSR Scale of the URC and LC by Gender

	Total (Boys + Girls)			Boys			Girls		
	URC	LC	Sig.	URC	LC	Sig.	URC	LC	Sig.
YSR- ss 1 withdrawn	6.02 (2.75)	5.80 (2.33)	0.63	5.51 (2.89)	5.44 (2.24)	0.84	6.50 (2.53)	6.33 (2.35)	0.62
YSR- ss 2 somatic complaints	5.64 (3.63)	4.68 (3.40)	0.01	5.03 (3.74)	4.35 (3.54)	0.19	6.22 (3.43)	5.00 (3.25)	0.01
YSR- ss 3 anxious/ depressed	10.42 (4.48)	9.94 (4.27)	0.28	9.51 (4.68)	9.35 (3.99)	0.80	11.29 (4.11)	10.51 (4.47)	0.20
YSR- ss 4 social problems	5.25 (2.48)	5.66 (2.19)	0.09	5.04 (2.56)	5.36 (2.15)	0.35	5.45 (2.40)	5.94 (2.2)	0.13
YSR- ss 5 thought problems	1.80 (2.17)	1.93 (2.39)	0.56	1.97 (2.3)	1.91 (2.57)	0.87	1.64 (2.03)	1.95 (2.21)	0.29
YSR- ss 6 attention problems	6.62 (3.31)	5.96 (2.82)	0.03	6.5 (3.48)	5.83 (2.75)	0.14	6.72 (3.14)	6.08 (2.89)	0.14
YSR- ss 7 delinquent problems	1.75 (1.68)	1.90 (2.19)	0.44	1.78 (1.83)	2.21 (2.61)	0.18	1.73 (1.56)	1.61 (1.64)	0.57
YSR- ss 8 aggressive behavior	4.23 (3.42)	5.42 (3.75)	0.00	4.65 (3.8)	5.91 (3.86)	0.02	3.82 (2.93)	4.94 (3.61)	0.02
Internal	21.47 (8.57)	19.93 (7.38)	0.06	19.49 (8.86)	18.61 (7.03)	0.45	23.36 (7.86)	21.22 (7.52)	0.05
External	5.99 (4.35)	7.33 (5.26)	0.01	6.44 (5.04)	8.13 (5.77)	0.03	5.55 (3.54)	6.55 (4.61)	0.08
YSR-Total	46.72 (17.12)	46.17 (16.69)	0.74	44.71 (18.97)	45.07 (17.20)	0.89	48.66 (14.97)	47.24 (16.20)	0.52

YSR Scale

Overall there is very little difference here between the scores of the unaccompanied returnee children and the local children who never left Vietnam. The female unaccompanied returnee children had more somatic complaints ($p > .01$), higher scores on the Internal Scale ($p >$

.02), and a higher overall YSR score (p > .05) than the local sample. On the other hand, the local children were significantly more aggressive than the URC group (p > .02) For boys it was a different picture. Both samples were the same on most all variable except that the local cohort was both more aggressive (p > .02) and scored higher on the External Scale (p > .03) than the URC group.

While the two samples in Thua Thien Hue were predominantly rural, it was possible to make a comparison between the rural and urban children in the sample. A significant difference was found between the two samples on the somatic complaint's subscale, the aggressive behavior subscale, and the external scale. This difference becomes more pronounced when the rural population is considered alone. The unaccompanied returnee children reported more somatic complaints than the local children (p > .00), significantly less aggres-

Table 8.8 Difference between Children in Rural and Urban Areas

	Urban			Rural			Total (Urban and Rural)		
	URC	LC	Sig.	URC	LC	Sig.	URC	LC	Sig.
YSR-ss1	6.85	6.22	.40	5.93	5.84	.74	6.02	5.89	.63
	(3.10)	(1.97)		(2.71)	(2.40)		(2.75)	(2.34)	
YRS-ss2	4.95	4.66	.79	5.71	4.68	.01	5.64	4.68	.00
	(3.45)	(3.64)		(3.64)	(3.38)		(3.63)	(3.40)	
YSR-ss3	12.85	9.77	.03	10.16	9.97	.68	10.42	9.94	.28
	(5.47)	(4.17)		(4.30)	(4.30)		(4.48)	(4.27)	
YSR-ss4	4.35	5.33	.09	5.35	5.71	.15	5.25	5.66	.08
	(2.21)	(1.66)		(2.50)	(2.27)		(2.48)	(2.19)	
YSR-ss5	1.95	2.51	.42	1.79	1.84	.84	1.80	1.94	.56
	(2.52)	(2.21)		(2.14)	(2.41)		(2.18)	(2.39)	
YSR-ss6	6.50	6.33	.83	6.63	5.90	.03	6.62	5.96	.03
	(2.86)	(2.65)		(3.36)	(2.85)		(3.31)	(2.82)	
YSR-ss7	3.00	2.93	.92	1.63	1.73	.57	1.76	1.91	.44
	(2.38)	(2.83)		(1.54)	(2.03)		(1.68)	(2.19)	
YSR-ss8	6.65	7.00	.79	3.97	5.16	.00	4.23	5.42	.00
	(5.10)	(3.97)		(3.11)	(3.67)		(4.36)	(3.76)	
Internal	23.20	19.88	.13	21.22	20.50	.14	21.46	19.93	.06
	(9.69)	(7.16)					(4.36)	(7.38)	
External	9.65	9.92	.89	5.60	6.89	.01	5.99	7.33	.01
	(6.90)	(6.17)					(4.36)	(5.26)	
Total	51.15	49.55	.76	46.25	45.60	.72	46.73	46.18	.75
	(19.75)	(16.90)		(16.81)	(16.65)		(17.12)	(16.69)	
Self Efficacy	65.10	66.59	.75	65.22	67.79	.05	65.21	67.62	.06
	(15.13)	(16.79)		(12.47)	(11.35)		(12.71)	(12.24)	
Social Support	14.35	15.04	.72	14.93	15.09	.76	14.87	15.08	.68
	(7.79)	(5.44)		(4.63)	(4.73)		(5.00)	(4.82)	

sive in behavior (p > .00), and have a lower score on the external scale that is a composite of the delinquent behavior and aggressive behavior subscales (p > .01). These differences may be observed in table 8.8.

No significant difference was found between the unaccompanied returnee children and the local children on the anxiety depression subscale. The McCallin (1992) study had reported an increased level of anxiety and depression among the children in the camps over time. This was not evident in the present study, though some differences were found within the unaccompanied returnee children's sample.

Table 8.9 Correlation between YSR-ss3-Anxiety/Depression Subscale and Dependent Measures

Dependent Measures	Correlation	Level of Significance
– Experience of traumatic events	0.20	0.00
– Social support (ss.)	- 0.17	0.02
– The length of stay in detention	0.04	0.58
– Attitude towards current living conditions	0.24	0.00
– Perception of living standard	- 0.09	0.18
– Level of living standard	- 0.09	0.17

Their anxiety and depression were closely related with their evaluation of the living conditions of their families, which were improving or deteriorating, with their parents' attitude after repatriation. The noteworthy part is that the standard of living is not related (® = -0.09, p > 0.17), and the number of detention years is also not affected (® = 0.03, p > 0.58). The children who had personally experienced more traumatic events had higher levels of anxiety and depression, and children who did not like their current living conditions were significantly more depressed.

1. Perceived Self-Efficacy Scale

Overall the boys were statistically more self-confident and sure of themselves in dealing with new experiences and difficult circumstances than the girls were. Female unaccompanied returnee children were less self-confident than the local girls were. Results of this analysis is found in table 8.10.

2. Social Support Scale

The Social Support scale shows no difference between the unaccompanied returnee children and the local children: the average score of the unaccompanied returnee child is 14.89 and 15.08 for local children (p > 0.71). There is also no difference of statistical significance

Table 8.10 Mean and Standard Deviation and Dependent Measures on the Perceived Self-Efficacy Scale of the URC and LC by Gender

Group/Gender	Mean	Standard Deviation	t-value	Significance
URC				
– Boys	68.22	12.79		
– Girls	62.31	11.99	3.44	.00
LC				
– Boys	68.89	11.02		
– Girls	66.38	13.26	1.40	.16
Total				
– Boys	68.54	11.96		
– Girls	64.22	12.73	3.46	.00

between boys and girls (boys 15.28, girls 14.52). However, the Social Support scale shows the relation with the following elements: There is a small but significant negative correlation between the unaccompanied children's scores on the withdrawn, somatic complaints, anxious/depressed, thought problems, delinquent behavior's subscales, and the children's perception of their level of social support. The higher the children scored on levels of social support, the lower the children's behavior problems. The children's attitude to their standard of living was more negative when they had less social support.

Some Observations and Conclusions

Effects of Life in Refugee Camps and the Reintegration of the Children in Vietnam

While the unaccompanied returnee children have lived for an average of two years in harsh confined conditions, without their parents, and at a vulnerable age, this study has found no significant difference between the returnee children and their local counterparts who never left Vietnam. It would appear that three to four years after their repatriation, the children have resumed life with their parents and have integrated into the fabric of Vietnamese society.

The unaccompanied returnee children have described traumatic experiences on the journey to the camps and within the commotion and the restraint life of the refugee camps. They still remember the events on their journey: storms, lack of food, lack of water, confrontation with piracy, being shipwrecked. They remember the fighting, the

Table 8.11 Correlation between Social Support Scale and Other Dependent Measures

	URC + LC		URC		LC	
	Correlation	Level of significance	Correlation	Level of significance	Correlation	Level of significance
-YSR - ss1 withdrawn	- 0.10	0.03	- 0.15	0.03	-0.05	(ns)
- ss2 somatic complaints	- 0.12	0.01	- 0.22	0.00	-0.01	(ns)
- ss3 anxious/depressed	- 0.11	0.03	- 0.17	0.02	-0.04	(ns)
- ss4 social problems	-0.07	(ns)	-0.13	(ns)	0.01	(ns)
- ss5 thought problems	-0.07	(ns)	-0.16	0.02	0.02	(ns)
- ss6 attention problems	-0.02	(ns)	-0.09	(ns)	0.07	(ns)
- ss7 delinquent behavior	- 0.18	0.00	- 0.16	0.02	-0.2	0.01
- ss8 aggressive behavior	0.03	(ns)	- 0.07	(ns)	0.01	(ns)
–Internal scale	- 0.14	0.00	- 0.21	0.00	-0.04	(ns)
–External scale	-0.09	(ns)	- 0.12	(ns)	0.07	(ns)
–Total	-0.14	0.00	-0.24	0.00	-0.03	(ns)
–Standard of living	0.20	0.00	0.25	0.00	0.15	0.04
–Perceived self-efficacy scale total	0.14	0.01	0.17	0.01	0.09	0.20
– Educational level	0.05	(ns)	0.05	(ns)	0.04	(ns)
– Age	0.04	(ns)	-0.04	(ns)	-0.04	(ns)
–Number of persons in the family	- 0.00	(ns)	- 0. 02	(ns)	0.02	(ns)
– Perception of the present life*	0.12	0.02	0.18	0.01	0.03	(ns)
– The standard of family living	-0.09	0.05	-0.17	0.02	-0.02	(ns)

* Spearman Rank correlation

drunkards, the killings, the gambling, the search for weapons, suppression with tear gas in the camps. These are still considered by them as the worst incidents in the period of detention. However these seem to have become less significant with time, and the memories have faded in their minds.

In the in-depth interviews, the children reported both negative and positive impressions. While feeling spiritually empty because of their separation from their families, they were able to study, to learn some trades such as sewing, computing, and languages without school fees. They enjoyed the communal activities with friends and many are still appreciative of the assistance that they received from the non-government agencies in the camps. They also admitted that life in the camps has changed them. The camps gave the children the opportunity to contact with people from different life circumstances. They reported that this has enabled them to be wiser, quicker, more mature, more brave, more self-supporting, and more confident in human relations.

Though failing to resettle in another country has caused disappointment and moments of desperation, they have not entirely despaired. Many of them have mentioned their belief in their destiny, the human lot, a concept deeply rooted in the belief of the Vietnamese. This explains their failure to resettle. This also encourages them very much. Most of the children report feeling consoled by the support and stability of their family.

Stress and Anxiety

Overall, the scales measuring some aspects of the children's psychosocial well-being present no significant difference between the unaccompanied returnee children and the local children. However, the results do indicate that life in the refugee camps without parents has had some effects on the well-being of the children, particularly the returnee girls. They appear to be more somatic complaints and to me more anxious and depressed than their male counterparts, the unaccompanied returnee boys. Both the male and female unaccompanied returnee children are less aggressive in their behavior than the local children, implying a passivity that they may have acquired in the camps. There are indications that the children who have repatriated to the urban areas show different patterns of response compared to those in the rural areas. A follow-up to this study will be made in Ho Chi Minh City to examine this pattern.

Some of the unaccompanied returnee children had more anxiety and depression than others. The level of anxiety and depression seems to be influenced by the children's worries about their present life. In particular they commented on their economic status: the families were poor, they did not have money for school fees, they were unemployed, with unstable jobs, and they had difficulty with housing. Some of them married early and this required more effort, particularly with the speedy changes in the economy of Vietnam. In the in-depth interviews, some children said that in the detention life they did not have to worry about eating, but after repatriation they have had to work hard for food. In some aspects, it is the totally dependent life in the camps that may have generated the present stressful situation. In spite of these difficulties, the children reported that the attitude of parents towards them after repatriation has been warmly supportive and this has enabled them to adjust back to Vietnam.

The majority of these children were coastal dwellers, living in poor residential areas along rivers. After the years dwelling in the refugee camps, they have had some exposure to the urban environment and to people from different parts of Vietnamese society. This has caused them to be more mature and increased their aspiration for advancement. In the aspiration for future jobs, many of them preferred popular jobs in urban areas. Some of the unaccompanied returnee children declined to resettle in their former rural areas. They tried to reside in urban areas with jobs such as industrial sewing and construction work. They only returned to their families to follow the traditional trades of fishery and agriculture, after their failure to find work and suitable housing in the city.

Lessons Learned

There is little difference between the well-being of the two sample groups on the measures used in this study. However, difficulties were encountered with these measures. Many of the items on the scales had to been explained at length to the children who were either illiterate or without significant formal education. Most of the children found some of the items difficult to answer because they could not understand the relevance of the questions or were unfamiliar with being asked such questions. The directness of the questions on a questionnaire is not very familiar in the Vietnamese culture where sensitive topics are approach more gradually. Many children also tired during the interviewing and had to be encouraged to continue. Overall though, the researchers in their own reports concluded that the study had measured dimensions of the well-being of the children. There will be further analysis of the children's interviews. A more comprehensive content analysis of these interviews will provide supplementary information and possibly additional dimensions of the children's concepts of their well-being.

While this study has been a study of the well-being of children who have repatriated to Vietnam. It is also an insight into the present situation of many children in Vietnam, especially those living in rural and coastal areas. This study shows that the children are surviving in difficult circumstances—circumstances that increase their vulnerability to leave school early, to marry when young, and even to flee their country when the opportunity presents itself.

The study leaves no doubt that the greatest assistance that the children have received to reintegrate back into Vietnamese society has been the assistance given by their families. The families have provided the moral support and practical assistance that has been necessary for the children to feel that they can face the challenge of resuming their life in Vietnam. Behind the scenes we know that there has been a great deal of assistance from local government authorities, non-governmental agencies and the United Nations High Commissioner for Refugees. This study does not always reflect these efforts because the children tell the story of repatriation here. They are not always aware of the assistance that has been given them both in the camps and upon their return. What the study does show is that this assistance has been successful. The children have successfully repatriated and reintegrated.

The study also indicates that many of the children have returned to very poor conditions. This is particularly evident in the coastal areas of Thua Thien Hue. It would seem that many left because of this poverty and possibly fared well in the camps because of the relatively better living conditions. This did not compensate for the absence of their parents, though a relative accompanied most of the children while they were in detention.

Notes

1. All of the case material reported in this chapter come from the authors' field notes and diaries. The number in parentheses following the case vignette refers to the number of the case.
2. Many of the children were in the Shekong camp when twenty-four people died in riots.
3. An implement = 1 point; kind of house: thatch roof = 1 point; tin roof = 2 points; estimation about the standard living: very difficult = 1; well-off = 4 (table 8.12).
4. 10,000 dong are equal to US$1.

References

Achenbach, T. M. (1991). *Manual for the youth self-report and 1991 profile.* Burlington, VT: University of Vermont Department of Psychiatry.

Cowen, E. L., Work, W. C., Hightower, A. D., Wyman, P. A., Parker, G. R., and Lotyczewski, B. S. (1991). Toward the development of a measure of perceived self-efficacy in children. *Journal of Clinical Child Psychology,* 20:169-178.

Eyton, J and Neuwirth, G (1984). Cross-cultural validity: Ethnocentrism in health studies with special reference to the Vietnamese. *Social Science and Medicine, 18*:5:447-453.

Garmezy, N. (1991). Negative life Events and Stressed Environments. *Pediatric Annals, 20*:9:459-456.

Loughry, M., McCallin, M., and Bennett, G. (1993). *Women in detention.* Geneva: International Catholic Child Bureau.

McCallin, M. (1992). *Living in detention: A review of the psychosocial well-being of Vietnamese children in the Hong Kong detention centers.* Geneva: International Catholic Child Bureau.

McKelvey, R. and Webb, J. (1993). Long-term effects of maternal loss on Vietnamese Amerasians. *Journal of the American Academy of Child and Adolescent Psychiatry, 32*:5:1013-1018.

United Nations High Commissioner for Refugees (1995). *Information package on the comprehensive plan of action on Indo-Chinese refugees (CPA).* Geneva: UNHCR.

Weist, M. D., Freedman, A. H., Paskewitz, D. A., Proescher, E. J., and Flaherty, L. T. (1995). Urban youth under stress: Empirical identification of protective factors. *Journal of Youth and Adolescence, 24*:705-721.

Part IV

CASE STUDIES OF REFUGEE PSYCHOSOCIAL WELLNESS

Mixed Approaches

In this final section we present three chapters that utilize both quantitative and qualitative methods to explore the psychological dimension of refugee flight and migration. One approach is a careful consideration of context and culture, allowing for the "voices" of the refugees to inform the development of quantitative measures. The other approach is the use of alternative strategies to confirm findings, a process referred to as "triangulation." The case examples in this part address both the development of instruments that are culturally and contextually sensitive, and the use of both qualitative and quantitative methods as a means of confirming the study results.

Chapter 9 presents an interesting and detailed illustration of the use of qualitative techniques to design measures for use in a quantitative study. The authors, Ilene Hyman, Morton Beiser, Sam Noh and Nhi Vu, focus on the impact of pre- and postmigration stress in the lives of resettled Southeast Asian children, especially their mental health. Through the use of case studies and focus groups, three dimensions of stress were found: 1) school adjustment; 2) parent-child relationships; and 3) inter-personal conflict. The authors conclude that the findings illustrate the need to consider cultural and contextual appropriateness when assessing stressful life experiences in immigrant or refugee youth as well as the utility of distinguishing developmental, culture-specific, and situational stressors as conceptually separate domains.

In chapter 10, Colin MacMullin and Maryanne Loughry discuss their mixed-method approach to the study of Palestinian children's worries. While the literature is dominated by adult-focused investigations into children's concerns, they present the results of a child-focused study in which children in Beach Camp, Gaza were asked to list and describe the things that worry them. Focus groups were established in which the children elaborated upon these worries, discussed their coping strategies, and suggested advice they would give to younger children who might face similar concerns in the future. MacMullin and Loughry offer suggestions for the utilization of their methodology.

Finally, Joseph Westermeyer has studied the Hmong people for more than thirty years, both in their native Laos and later in resettlement in Minnesota. As a psychiatrist and anthropologist, he has applied his clinical, quantitative and qualitative expertise to his investigations that have pursued: 1) an understanding of clinical research across cultures; 2) the evaluation of checklists and scales as measures of psychological response and symptoms; and, 3) the development of measures that are culturally-appropriate to the Hmong population. Westermeyer gives a sensitive description of the influences in his work in chapter 11 and relates how he designed his research at different stages of migration. In the study of the Hmong culture, their social and emotional adjustment, and degrees of psychopathology, he has established a research approach that captures elements of both quantitative and qualitative methodology.

The interested student, researcher, and even practitioner can learn much from these authors' discussion. Both qualitative and quantitative methods have obvious strengths and limitations, but used together, we see that they can support each other in the development of hypotheses, formulation of research strategies, and verification the findings.

9

Perceptions of Stress in Southeast Asian Refugee Youth

IMPLICATIONS FOR THE DEVELOPMENT OF
CULTURALLY APPROPRIATE MEASURES

Ilene Hyman, Morton Beiser, Sam Noh, and *Nhi Vu*

Clinical and research findings suggest that the risk of developing mental health problems such as alcohol abuse (Morgan, Wingard, and Felice, 1984), drug addiction (Amaral-Dias, Vicente, and Cabrita, 1981), delinquency and depression (Burke, 1982), Post-Traumatic Stress Disorder (Kinzie, 1986; Sack, 1985), and psychopathology (Kinzie, Sack, and Angell, 1986) is higher for children in refugee families than for their host country counterparts. Explanations have tended to center on the direct experience of trauma such as warfare, loss, the danger of escape, and the depriving experiences of refugee camp incarceration. However, children born to refugee families in resettlement countries, or who migrate at such young ages that they directly experience little premigration trauma, also suffer higher than expected rates of psychopathology (Freyberg, 1980; Kestenberg and Brenner, 1986). Research with adult refugees highlights the importance of postmigration stresses in the genesis of psychiatric disorders (Canadian Task Force on Mental Health Issues Affecting Immigrants and Refugees, 1988). Both observations suggest a need to study the postmigration stresses faced by children in refugee families. Stress event lists must be tailored for the specific populations under investigation (Turner and Wheaton, 1995). Commonly used inventories of life events and "hassles" are probably inappropriate for studies of the impact of stress on the mental health of children in refugee families. These instruments, developed for populations living under more or less predictable conditions, fail to capture the range of pre- and post-migration situations experienced by refugee children. The fact that dominant culture provides the referent framework for most stress inventories, although many refugee children are members of visible minority groups, is another source of difficulty. Inventories developed for use among dominant culture youth typically do not include stresses related to feelings of marginalization and discrimination, common to many new immigrant and ethnocultural groups.

The current publication from the Refugee Youth Project (RYP) at the Center for Addiction and Mental Health, Clarke Division, and the University of Toronto's Department of Psychiatry describes the development of a stress measure sensitive to the experiences of children of the "Boat People"[1] refugees from Southeast Asia. The study illuminates the unique experiences of children in these refugee families and also illustrates the use of qualitative techniques in the development of culturally and contextually appropriate measures of stressful experience.

Background

In response to the "Boat People" crisis, Canada admitted 60,000 Southeast Asian refugees between 1979 and 1981. The RYP is a study of risk and protective factors affecting the mental health of the children of a cohort of refugee adults who participated in the Refugee Resettlement Project, a ten year longitudinal investigation of the Southeast Asian experience in Canada (Beiser, 1999).

Since the pioneering work on stress and deleterious health outcomes that resulted in the development of the Life Events checklist (Hawkins, Davis, and Holmes, 1957; Holmes and Rahe, 1967), social scientists have continued to expand and validate measures of health-related stressors (Johnson, 1986; Compas, 1987). Similarly, most stress measures for children and adolescents employ checklists (Coddington, 1972a; Coddington, 1972b; Yeaworth et al., 1980; Compas, 1987; Kohn, Lafreniere, and Gurevich, 1990).

Measures developed for use with adolescents can be criticized on several grounds. First, since they have usually been generated by adult researchers and mental health professionals who cannot help but conceive of stressors from their own perspectives as adults, they may fail to tap the experiences that are salient from the viewpoint of the young (Compas, 1987). Second, although some investigations have used adolescents to help generate item pools, they have often failed to address culturally specific stressors (Cervantes, Padilla, and Salgado de Snyder, 1990; Solberg, Villarreal, and Kavanagh, 1993). Third, most inventories include a core list of stressors that, in the opinion of researchers, calls for varying degrees of social readjustment (Yeaworth et al., 1980; Compas, 1987; Kohn, Lafreniere, and Gurevich, 1990). Typical items include, the death of a loved one (a parent, sibling, or close friend), parental separation, failing in school, problems with alcohol, breaking up with a girl/boyfriend, and moving to a new school. Researchers often attempt to economize on length by dropping or combining items (Turner and Wheaton, 1995). Since the theoretical or empirical rationale for selecting (or dropping) items is rarely communicated, item comprehensiveness and face validity are often open to question.

Studies of the perceived stressfulness of events highlight the importance of cultural context when using standardized checklists (Askenasy and Dohrenwend, 1977; Newcomb, Huba, and Bentler, 1986). In one international comparative study (Yamamoto et al., 1987), the investigators found that children in six different countries experienced a similar number of events. However there was a great deal of inter-country variation in their rating of stressfulness. For example, the median scale value for perceived stressfulness of eight events explicitly related to school activities (e.g., "being kept back in the same grade," "receiving a poor report card," "not making a perfect score on a test," "getting up in front of the class to give a report") was highest for Egyptian children, followed by Japanese, intermediate for U.S., Australian, and Canadian children, and lowest for the Filipino group. The authors attributed the findings to the strict disciplinary practices in Egypt including physical punishment, imposition of fear, and inculcation of guilt.

The development of measures such as the Hispanic Stress Inventory (HSI) (Cervantes, Padilla, and Salgado de Snyder, 1990) and the College Stress Inventory for Hispanics (Solberg, Villarreal, and Kavanagh, 1993) attest to a growing recognition of cultural differences in the stress experience itself. Both versions of the HSI (one developed specifically for Hispanic immigrants and the second for U.S.-born Hispanics) include items dealing with, for example, cultural/family conflict (e.g., "some members of my family have become too individualistic," "family relations are becoming less important"). The College Stress Inventory for Hispanics, derived from a scale specifically designed to assess experiences of minority graduate students, included such items as, for example, "fear of failing to meet family expectations," "difficulty with faculty/peers on the basis of your ethnicity."

Method

Qualitative methods assist in identifying research themes and ensuring comprehensiveness (Strauss and Corbin, 1990). The RYP research team selected a qualitative approach to explore the experience of stress in Southeast Asian youth and to identify culturally specific items for the RYP stress inventory. The study began with seventeen individual interviews and six focus groups. The purpose of the individual interviews was to learn more about the life experiences of Southeast Asian youth in Canada from their own perspectives. Focus groups were used to explore and establish the commonality of issues emerging from the individual interviews. Although unstructured, the individual and focus group interviews routinely covered the following: premigration history and experiences (where appropriate), early adjustment experiences in Canada, adjustment problems specific to school life, experiences in family relationships, and issues relating to minority status and ethnic identity. The adolescents were not questioned directly about "stress" but rather were encouraged to identify concerns and experiences in each of the domains identified.

A young Vietnamese woman who had come to Canada as a child refugee was the principal interviewer for the in-depth assessments. She interviewed seventeen youth between the ages of 10 and 24 (mean = 16), five of them in the Vietnamese language. The interviewees were recruited from schools, community organizations, and popular meeting places for Southeast Asian youth in downtown Toronto. To obtain a representative sample, the research team followed a quota sampling approach: attempts were made to interview youth in each two-year age category between 10 and 24, to interview equal numbers of boys and girls, and to interview respondents identified as doing very well in school or on the job, as well as school dropouts. Hong Fook Mental Health Services, a prominent Southeast Asian community agency, helped RYP staff recruit youth for four of the focus groups. Participants were invited to join a get-together to "share experiences and discuss needs." Three of these groups consisted of between 15–20 teenage participants. The fourth was a smaller group made up of 5 adolescents. Two other focus groups (6-8 students) were organized with a local elementary school which had a large Southeast Asian student body. The focus groups were led by the same Vietnamese researcher who had conducted the individual interviews, together with another member of the Project team. Each interview lasted between one and two hours. After securing the permission of the participants, all interviews and focus groups were recorded, transcribed, and where necessary, translated into English.

Findings

Using an approach based on grounded theory (Glaser and Strauss, 1967), the authors continually reviewed the information collected in the interviews and focus groups in order to identify common themes. For heuristic purposes, these were categorized as: School Adjustment, Parent-Child Relationships, Intra-Personal Conflict. Findings were then used to generate items for a stress measure appropriate for Southeast Asian youth. Examples of new items that were developed for and incorporated into the RYP stress measure are included in each section.

School Adjustment

For most of the study participants, adjustment to a new school was the most common and difficult experience. Two main themes emerging from the data are concerns faced by many immigrant youth during the process of acculturation and resettlement. These are marginalization and cultural conflict.

Marginalization

Lack of English fluency was a major source of school stress. It contributed to feelings of insecurity about making new friends, to self-consciousness about speaking in a group, to fears of being made fun of or being laughed at by others, and to academic difficulties. Many of the youth reported "feeling different" from the other students and "not fitting in." Often, teachers' well-intentioned efforts to make the new student feel welcome paradoxically created feelings of self consciousness. In the words of an 18 year old woman:

> It was hard, it was really hard. I felt like I stood out a lot because obviously I was very different. And all the teachers kept telling everyone to be nice to me. I guess they meant well, but that doesn't make you feel good, because it shows that you don't belong and you know you're different from everyone else, and I didn't like that.

Lack of English proficiency created academic frustration. A 19 year old female student described her feelings:

> Other people, they would take only half an hour to study for a test. You had to study for two or three hours ... Many times, it's like you couldn't do as well as others, so you got discouraged and you cried.

Feelings of estrangement and intimidation were especially strong among youth in schools that contained few other Vietnamese students. As one 19 year old Vietnamese female expressed, "In the beginning there was no one to help. Because there were no Vietnamese in school, only Westerners." Others, especially boys, reported "not feeling safe" in situations where there were few members of their own ethnic group. Conversely, the security offered by fellow ethnic group members is illustrated by the following remarks made by a 15 year old Chinese-Vietnamese male.

> I know that even if I was somewhere and there were some Orientals behind me, and I didn't know them, I know that there was a pretty good chance if I got into a fight ... I'd get help from them. I feel more secure that way.

Cultural Conflict

Refugee youth had to adjust to school systems functioning according to unfamiliar cultural values. For example, the youth portrayed teachers in Vietnam as stricter and more authoritarian than teachers in Canada. According to one respondent, asking a teacher questions or for help would have been considered a sign of ignorance and a cause of embarrassment in a Vietnamese classroom. Students who had been exposed to a Vietnamese system in which incorrect answers led to punishment were understandingly reluctant to answer questions in their Canadian classrooms. Another difference observed was that in Vietnam it was considered unacceptable to answer a question with "I don't know." A 15 year old Chinese male who said that he felt "more Chinese" than Canadian at school reflected on the conflict between the relatively authoritarian atmosphere of Asian schools and the Canadian system's emphasis on classroom participation.

> I am not like the Canadian kids; They talk so much. You know they make remarks to the teacher and stuff and I am not like that.

Another observed that Vietnamese schools emphasized learning facts. This student found it difficult to get used to answering the opinion type of questions posed by Canadian teachers.

Measurement Implications

The stress measure developed for the RYP consisted of three inventories relating to the domains of School, Family, and Social Life. Respondents were addressed as follows: "This section is about the types of experiences young people may have at school/with family etc... For each one, please tell me whether you experienced it *during the past 6 months,* and if you did, how good or bad it made you feel: *very bad, somewhat bad, neither bad nor good, somewhat good, very good.*"

In an attempt to capture stresses related to feelings of marginalization and cultural conflict in schools, the researchers added two items to the RYP stress measure; "A teacher treated you differently from the other students" and "You felt like you didn't fit in at school."

Parent-Child Relationships

Two prominent child-parent themes emerged from the individual and focus group interviews: communication difficulties and high parental expectations.

Communication Difficulties

Although communication problems with parents are common during adolescence, the interviews suggested that linguistic, intergenerational, and cultural factors accentuated this difficulty in Southeast Asian families. Many students blamed the lack of common language at home. Although the first language of respondents was usually that of their parents, many of the youth quickly adopted English as their preferred language of communication, thereafter using it with siblings and friends. Some children who were born in Canada or who arrived at very young ages may have never become proficient in their parents' first language. Others lost whatever proficiency they may have achieved. Since much of the social and school lives of youth took place in English, difficulties articulating these aspects of their lives with their less fluent or non-English speaking parents were extremely prevalent. To illustrate:

> Sometimes I speak to my parents in English. I say things better in English than in Vietnamese, especially when it comes to dating and all those stuff. And sometimes you can't put the same thing in both languages. I think I speak Vietnamese most of the time. Just common things around the house, but then we don't really go into deep discussions or anything. I wish that either I could speak Vietnamese better, or they could speak English better so that we can talk. (15 year old Vietnamese female)

Unequal language fluency was only one among several sources of communication difficulty. Differential levels of acculturation to host society values created intergenerational and cultural strains. Parents and children often held different expectations about autonomy and freedom. Often these differences could not be articulated. Respondents' descriptions of their parents with terms such as "very strict," "not open to new ideas," and "behind the times," reflect these intergenerational differences. Disagreements about dating behaviors, going out with friends and staying out overnight, were frequent. Young women in particular complained that parental over-protectiveness restricted their freedom outside the home. An 18 year old female respondent explained that she was reluctant to have discussions with her mother; Experience had shown her that these were of no use: "She's much more strict, overprotective. She's not open to new ideas, new opinions."

Youth were also sensitive to differences between Southeast Asian parents' patterns of interaction with their children and what they observed in non-Southeast Asian households. Contrasts were particularly marked in the area of communicating personal thoughts and feelings. Many of the Southeast Asian youth were keenly aware that their parents were not emotionally or physically expressive and did not freely share personal information about themselves. Several respondents expressed a desire to learn more about the past experiences of their parents, notably about their flight from Southeast Asian; they had learned however, that certain things were not discussed with children.

> Many times you see them [parents] keeping sad things to themselves, so you're sad with them, but you don't really know what it is you're sad for. With the Westerners, the parents can tell them everything, from small to big things they can talk about them all. With Vietnamese there are many things you can't talk about. (19 year old Vietnamese female)

Communication problems were probably also responsible for the perception by some youth that their parents were not interested or did not want to be involved with their children's lives. Long working hours often left parents little or no time for their children. As one 15 year old respondent described her mother, "she goes to work and she's not home to take care of my brother and sister and that's like 5 days in a row 'cause she has to go to work from 3 to 12 and they're here with me." Even if parents were "available," youth often felt reluctant to burden them with problems. In part, this is situational: many parents who work long hours have little time left to devote to their families. In part, this may be an adaptive choice: refugee youth may feel reluctant to burden mothers and fathers with problems that seem unimportant compared with their parent's need to make a living in a strange country and to deal with a past filled with suffering that the children only dimly comprehend.

Parental Expectation

Many youth felt that their parents imposed exceptionally high expectations on their children. As one respondent said, "It's like pressure to be better than the rest and if you try it's not good enough." Fathers were often described as having even higher expectations than mothers, as well as being more distant and authoritarian.

Respondents also complained that their parents pressured them by comparing their performance, unfavourably, with that of children in other families, saying for example, "Oh you know, they get straight A's and stuff like that." Often this pressure was implicit rather than explicit. Unspoken cues were sources of pressure as potent as overt comments. As one respondent remarked, "They don't have to say anything. I know what they want from me. I already know."

Lack of positive feedback from parents coupled with the perception of excessive demand compounded an already tense situation. An 18 year old Vietnamese woman said, "I always find that whenever you have something good, let's say you receive high marks in school, you tell them. They're not encouraging like the parents I know that are not Vietnamese. Instead of being encouraging, they say that 'you could do better.'" A Chinese-Vietnamese male (15 years old) remarked about his father, "He's never given me a word of encouragement. Like he never does that, but that's the only thing I ask for sometimes."

As a result some participants felt "unacknowledged," "not valued." One 16 year old Vietnamese female said, "He never compliments me so I don't think he really cares."

Measurement Implications

These findings suggested several stress items to capture both situational and culture specific relationship-related stresses between youth and their parents. These included: "You had trouble talking to your mother/father because of a language problem," "You had arguments with your mother/father about dating/rules," "A parent was too busy or didn't have enough time for you," and "Your parents were often tired out and/or sad." Items chosen to reflect stress emanating from high parental expectations were: "A parent pressured or pushed you to do well," and "A parent was disappointed because you didn't do well."

Intra-Personal Conflicts

Many of the youth reported internal conflicts traceable to intergenerational differences in acculturation and values, and to ambivalence concerning ethnic identity.   .

Acculturation and Values

Most of the youths expressed respect for their parents' values and a desire to maintain their Southeast Asian language and way of life. However they were also attracted to sometimes incompatible Canadian values and practices. For example, they valued the "open" style of communication they observed in Canadian families, as well as privacy, autonomy, and celebration of Canadian normative events like birthdays.

The incompatibility of Western values emphasizing self-fulfillment and traditional patterns of subordinating the self to the interests of the family was a source of internal conflict. In younger children, the conflict might manifest itself as the choice between playing with friends after school or doing homework, and for young adults, in the choice of a profession. Reacting to pressure to pursue a career in medicine, one 15 year old Vietnamese male stated, "As much as I want to go into subjects like History, I don't want to disobey him [his father] because pleasing him is everything to me."

Generations of immigrant children have grown up with a need to express gratitude to their parents or repay them for sacrifices made in order to provide their children with a better life in Canada. As one 15 year old Chinese male commented, "my dad and my mom have actually wasted their lives for me. And to me, if I don't give them a good life in return, I'll feel guilty for the rest of my life." At the same time, the youth expressed the wish that their parents could trust them more to make their own decisions.

Ethnic Identity

Many youth expressed ambivalence about their ethnic identities. Some were very conscious that other Canadians viewed Vietnamese in a less than sympathetic light: "I find they don't have a very good image of us. For instance all the shootings, all the drug dealings, all the killings, the fights in cafes, it gives us all a bad name." (19 year old Vietnamese female) "Today there are a lot of stereotyping around. If you're Oriental, you look like a guy who'd be in a gang. That's how it divides." (19 year old Vietnamese male)

Other Southeast Asian youth, particularly those who had grown up in Canada, felt little identification with Southeast Asian culture. As one 16 year old Vietnamese female said, "There's nothing that I do that is Vietnamese. I've been raised in a different culture. I do speak Vietnamese to my parents but we barely ever speak."

Many of the youth were also aware of the personal challenges created as a result of being part of a visible minority group. These included dealing with discrimination and recognizing the need to work harder in order to succeed. One respondent said:

> The fact that I'm a racial minority makes a difference. It makes my struggle a lot harder than a racial majority. I know even if I'm well educated, the fact that I'm Oriental, if you want to get into the world, it'll be harder. No matter what kind of education you get, it's going to be harder because you're a racial minority. (15 year old Vietnamese male)

Another articulated a similar vision:

> To tell you the truth, over here, the Vietnamese people only want a little bit of a good reputation. But the fact is that even if you are lawyer, you will only get a bit of respect. So, let us alone! What are we to them? We are only the commoners. (Male focus group participant)

Measurement Implications

As a result of these discussions, the following culture-specific items were recreated for the RYP stress measure. The items "You didn't get enough privacy," "You embarrassed your parents or your family was ashamed of you," and "A parent treated you unfairly because you were a boy/girl" are believed to reflect salient intra-personal stresses resulting from intergenerational differences in acculturation and values.

Discussion and Summary

Cross-cultural measurement is challenged on the one hand by the need to ensure sensitivity to the culture and situation of specific groups under study, and on the other by the desirability of incorporating elements that permit inter-group comparisons. The Southeast Asian youth stress measure attempts to address both challenges.

Qualitative techniques were used to identify the range of salient stressors encountered by youth in Southeast Asian refugee families. Stressors deriving from three domains—school, family, and social life—could be reclassified in one of three conceptual categories: universal, culture-specific, and situational.

Developmental concerns such as emancipation versus the need to maintain relationships with one's family trouble many, if not all, youth growing up in Canada. Since these are universal concerns, items from stress measures in common use can be incorporated into the RYP inventory, thus providing a common core for inter-group comparisons. It seems a reasonable hypothesis that differing levels of acculturation to Canadian ways by parents and children will serve to intensify universal developmental struggles such as the conflict between autonomy and intimacy. A common measure of such stresses makes comparisons between specific groups such as Southeast Asian youth and their dominant culture counterparts feasible.

Other stresses may be inherently linked to specific ethnocultural beliefs and values. For example, because of a deep sense of filial obligation and the recognition of parents' sacrifices made in order to establish a better life for their children in Canada, some Southeast

Asian youth felt compelled to subordinate their own career choices to the wishes of their parents. Scholars have noted that filial piety is an important tenet of Asian Confucianist cultures (Hsu, 1971) and a deeply held value among Asian immigrant communities in the U.S. (Kim, Kim, and Hurh, 1991). Other examples of culture-specific sources of stress for Southeast Asian youth include an extreme focus on scholastic achievement as a route to success and the tendency to grant freedom and relief of responsibility more readily to males than to females.

The RYP study also identified stresses specific to the experiences of settlement and acculturation that probably apply to youth in many immigrant communities. For example, Southeast Asian youth identified feelings of marginalization, primarily due to the language barriers, feelings of insecurity and self-consciousness in social and educational settings, and experiences involving discrimination.

RYP findings support the need to ensure the cultural appropriateness of stress measures especially when assessing this construct in immigrant or refugee youth populations. Many of the stresses identified by the RYP study do not appear as part of the inventory of stresses on popular measures used with young people. Other key issues in stress measurement are summarized here. (For a more in depth review, see Turner and Wheaton, 1993.) These include:

1. *Types of Stressors to Include* – Research suggests that chronic stresses and demands of daily life "hassles" may predict adverse health reactions more effectively than major life events (Kohn et al., 1990; Rowlison and Felner, 1988).
2. *Stress Appraisal* – Two theoretical frameworks have guided most of the instrument development in this area. These are the "stimulus-orientation model" in which stress is seen as resulting from experiencing any of a number of situations that are threatening or that place excessive demands on the individual, and the "cognitive-orientation model" in which stressfulness of events is highly dependent on a person's perception of those events and stress may result from experiencing both pleasant and unpleasant events (Mullis et al., 1993). Current research supports the need for cognitive appraisals of events in addition to number of occurrences. Studies further indicate that events appraised as negative are more highly correlated with dysfunction than events appraised as positive or neutral (Mullis et al., 1993; Compas, 1987).
3. *Confounding* – Confounding or contamination arises when items used in a measure reflect the disturbance in mental or

physical health they are intended to predict. For example, as items dealing with increases in drug or alcohol use may be stressors or reactions to stress, Kohn et al. (1990 and Kohn and Milrose (1993) suggest that researchers avoid using items directly reflecting physical or mental health or subjective distress.

4. *Psychometric Properties* – Stress measures should be evaluated for predictive validity, or the ability to predict mental health outcomes; concurrent validity, or the existence of stress independent of the relationship to outcomes produced by the stress (using other concurrent indicators of stress); and test-retest reliability.

The stress measure developed for the RYP was designed to address many of these issues. By including new stress items, it provides valuable information on the nature of stresses (including "hassles") experienced by Southeast Asian youth, and also on cross-cultural variations in perceived stressfulness. The psychometric properties of the RYP stress measure and its relationship to mental health will be the focus of future publications.

Nearly 164,000 refugees, approximately 23 percent of whom were youth under the age of 19, were admitted to Canada between January 1989 and September 1994 (Citizenship and Immigration Canada, 1994). This flow is expected to continue. Despite the stresses they encounter along the developmental path, most children and youth in refugee families cope with the challenges of Canadian society. Despite the obvious diversity of refugee populations, many of the issues raised by this study are relevant to refugee youth, regardless of their country of origin, age, gender, and culture. The development and implementation of intervention programs to address these issues can benefit newcomer youth and hosts alike.

Notes

1. The term, "Vietnamese Boat People," is misleading on two counts. First, Southeast Asian refugees included many ethnic Chinese living in Vietnam. Second, most escaped their home countries over land, not by boat.

References

Amaral-Dias, C. A., Vicente, T. N. and Cabrita, M. F. (1981). Transplantation, identity and drug addiction. *Bulletin of Narcotics, 33*:21-26.

Askenasy A.R., and Dohrenwend B. P. (1977). Some effects of social class and ethnic group membership on judgements of the magnitude of stressful life events: A research note. *Journal of Health and Social Behavior, 18*:432-439.

Beiser, M. (1999). *Strangers at the gate.* Toronto: University of Toronto Press

Burke, A. W. (1982). Determinants of delinquency in female West Indian immigrants. *International Journal of Social Psychiatry, 28*:28-34.

Canadian Task Force on Mental Health Issues Affecting Immigrants and Refugees (1988). *Review of the Literature on Migrant Mental Health* (cat. no. Ci96-37/1988E). Ottawa: Ministry of Supply and Services.

Cervantes, R. C., Padilla, A. M., and Salgado de Snyder, N. (1990). Reliability and validity of the Hispanic stress inventory. *Hispanic Journal of Behavioral Sciences 12*:76-82.

Citizenship and Immigration in Canada (1994). *Refugee claims in Canada and resettlement from abroad–statistical digest.* Ottawa: International Refugee and Migration Policy Branch, November.

Coddinton, D. R. (1972a). The significance of life events as etiologic factors in the diseases of children. I-A survey of professional workers. *Journal of Psychosomatic Research, 16*:7-18.

Coddinton, D. R. (1972b). The significance of life events as etiologic factors in the diseases of children. II-A study of a normal population. *Journal of Psychosomatic Research, 16*:205-213.

Compas, B. E. (1987). Stress and life events during childhood and adolescence. *Clinical Psychology Review, 7*:275-302.

Freyberg, J. (1980). Difficulties in separation-individuation as experienced by offspring of Nazi Holocaust survivors. *American Journal of Orthopsychiatry, 50*:87-95.

Glaser, B. and Strauss, A. (Eds.). (1967). *The discovery of grounded theory, strategies for qualitative research.* Chicago, Aldine Publishing Company

Hawkins, N.G., Davies, R., and Holmes, T. H. (1957). Evidence of psychosocial factors in the development of pulmonary tuberculosis. *American Review of Tuberculosis and Pulmonary Diseases, 75*:768-780.

Holmes, T. H. and Rahe, R. H. (1967). The social readjustment rating scale. *Journal of Psychosomatic Research, 11*:213-218.

Hsu, F. (1971). Filial piety in Japan and China. *Journal of Comparative Family Studies, 2*:67-74.

Johnson, J. H. (1986). Life events and their relationship to health and adjustment. In Johnson, J. H. (Ed.), *Life events as stressors in childhood and adolescence.* Newbury Park, Sage Publications, 13-150.

Kestenberg, J. S. and Brenner, I. (1986). Children who survived the Holocaust: The role of rules and routines in the development of the superego. *International Journal of Psychoanalysis, 67*:309-316.

Kim, C. K., Kim, S., and Hurh, W. M. (1991). Filial piety and intergenerational relationship in Korean immigrant families. *International Journal of Aging and Human Development, 33*:233-245.

Kinzie, J. D. (1986). Severe post-traumatic stress syndrome among Cambodian refugees: Symptoms, clinical course, and treatment approaches. In Shore, J. H (Ed.), *Disaster stress studies: New methods and findings.* Washington, American Psychiatric Press, 124-140.

Kinzie, J. D., Sack, W. H., and Angell, R. H. (1986). The psychiatric effects of massive trauma on Cambodian children. *Journal of the American Academy of Child Psychiatry, 25*:370-376.

Kohn, P. M. and Milrose, J. A. (1993). The inventory of high-school students' recent life experiences: A decontaminated measure of adolescents' hassles. *Journal of Youth and Adolescence, 22*:43-55.

Kohn P. M., Lafreniere. K. and Gurevich. M. (1990). The inventory of college student's recent life experiences; A decontaminated hassles scale for a special population. *Journal of Behavioral Medicine, 13*:619-630.

Morgan, M. C., Wingard, D. L., and Felice, M. E. (1984). Subcultural differences in alcohol use among youth. *Journal of Adolescent Health Care, 5*:191-195.

Mullis, R. L., Youngs, G. A. Jr., Mullis, A. K. and Rathge, R. W. (1993). *Adolescent stress: Issues of measurement. Adolescence, 28*:267-279.

Newcomb, M. D., Huba, G. J., and Bentler, P. M. (1986). Life change events among adolescents: An empirical consideration of some method-ological issues. *Journal of Nervous and Mental Disease, 174*:280-289.

Rowlison, R. T. and Felner, R. D. (1988). Major life events, hassles, and adaptation in adolescence: Confounding in the conceptualization and measurement of life stress and adjustment revisited. *Journal of Personality and Social Psychology, 55*:432-444.

Sack, W. H. (1985). Post-traumatic stress disorders in children. *Integrative Psychiatry, 3*:162-164.

Solberg, V. S., Villarreal, P., and Kavanagh J. (1993). Development of the college stress inventory for use with Hispanic populations: A confirmatory analytic approach. *Hispanic Journal of Behavioral Sciences, 15*:490-497.

Strauss, A. L. and Corbin, J. A. (1990). *Basics of qualitative research: Grounded theory procedures and techniques.* Newbury Park: Age.

Turner, R. J., and Wheaton, B. (1995). Checklist measures of stressful life events. In Cohen, S., Kessler, R. C., and Gordon, L. U. (Eds), *Measuring stress: A guide for health and social scientists.* New York: Oxford University Press, 236.

Yamamoto, K., Soliman, A., Parsons, J., and Davies, O. L. (1987). Voices in unison, stressful events in the lives of children in six countries. *Journal of Child Psychology and Psychiatry, 28*:855-864.

Yeaworth, R. C., York, J., Hussey, M. A., Ingle, M. E., and Goodwin, T. (1980). The development of an adolescent life change event scale. *Adolescence, 15*:91-97.

10

A Child-Centered Approach to Investigating Refugee Children's Concerns[1]

Colin MacMullin and *Maryanne Loughry*

Introduction

Psychological interventions aimed at helping children who experience difficulties associated with forced migration require a substantial understanding of the inner concerns of these children. We really need to know precisely what it is that the children are worried about. Further, children's own theories about how they best cope with difficult circumstances, and how other children might successfully manage similar concerns, also provide an important source of knowledge for both the researcher and the practitioner.

However, to date, the study of children's worries has typically centered around children's responses to predetermined lists of events *thought by researchers* to be worrisome to children. This research has suggested that children and adolescents worry most about family, social relationships, and school (Simon and Ward, 1974); and academic school work, money matters, and social efficacy (Millar and Gallagher, 1996)

Such research has been criticized for failing to give children the opportunity to suggest the kinds of events and circumstances that really worry them as opposed to responding only to items suggested by the researchers (Henker, Whalen, and O'Neil, 1995). More recently, Silverman, LaGreca, and Wasserstein (1995) have suggested that the views of children be sought from semi-structured interviews, which could provide the children with opportunities to generate lists of their own specific worries.

This approach is clearly needed in Gaza, which has produced a very important body of child research over the last ten to fifteen years. However, again, much of this research has employed adult-constructed instruments and procedures that were designed to test hypothetical relationships, such as those between traumatic events and anxiety, or the impact of mediating variables such as parenting style on such relationships (see for example, Punamäki, 1989; Qouta, Punamäki, and El Sarraj, 1995). Further, the current literature leaves us with a view of Palestinian children as traumatized by the experiences of the occupation and the Intifada. However, the occupation and the Intifada ended in 1992. Are the children of Gaza still traumatized? Are they still worried by nightmares and concerned for the physical safety of their families and themselves? What are children in Gaza currently worried about?

The present studies sought to answer these questions by employing a four-part method that built upon the suggestions of Silverman et al. (1995). In the first instance, children were asked to merely list the things that worried them. A questionnaire was then constructed from the children's own lists of worries. Next, the children were surveyed with this questionnaire. Finally, focus groups were held in which the children were asked to elaborate upon their concerns, discuss the strategies that they use to cope with these worries, and to provide advice to younger children on how they might best manage similar kinds of problems.

Method

Subjects

The study was undertaken in two UNWRA schools in Beach Camp, Gaza in September 1998. The subjects were 287 children (141 boys and 146 girls) aged 11 to 16 years (mean 13.5 years).

Procedure

The data were collected by two Palestinian research assistants: a male working with the boys and a female working with the girls. An earlier study (MacMullin and Odeh, 1999) had suggested that the presence of a foreign researcher may influence the responses of the children (see discussion below).

Preliminary activities involved gaining permission from UNWRA officials and school principals to conduct the research and informing parents of the study. The research itself was undertaken on three consecutive days and involved four stages: (1) collecting lists of children's worries, (2) constructing the Inventory of Children's Worries, (3) administering Inventory and preliminary analyses, and (4) conducting follow-up focus groups.

Collecting Lists of Children's Worries

The researchers spoke to each class of children as a whole class. The children were provided with an explanation of the study: one which sought to find out what children in this particular grade worry about. This was followed by an amplification of the concept of "worry." Here the children were told that a worry was "something that really concerned them," "something that made them unhappy," and "something that they thought about a lot." The Arabic word *qalaq* was used for this concept. The children were then provided with sheets of blank paper and asked to record their own lists of the things that they or other children worry about. The children were told that their responses would be confidential.

Constructing the Children's Worry Scale

All of the children's statements of worry were pooled and then sorted into categories suggested by the items themselves. Examples of frequently suggested worries from each category were selected for use in a questionnaire–The Inventory of Children's Worries (ICW). The ICW, which contained 40 items, sampled worries from both boys and girls, and drew examples from each age group.

The instrument asked two questions about gender and age, and then presented by the stem: (in Arabic) "During the last six months, how often did you worry about these things." This was followed by the 40 items, each with a four-point Likert-scale from *galiban* (often), *ahianan* (sometimes), *qalilan* (little), and *nadiran* (rarely).

Inventory of Children's Worries

The Inventory of Children's Worries was administered to the same classes of children who were surveyed on the previous day. The children were reminded of the purpose of the study and told that the research had so far yielded a list of 40 different things that children had said they or others worry about. Each child was then given a questionnaire and asked to estimate the frequency with which he/she might have worried about each item over the last six months. Instructions were given about responding to a four-point scale and the children were encouraged to make use of the full range of the scale.

Focus Groups

On the third day, the researchers returned to the same schools and met with focus groups of six to eight children. The teachers and principals were asked to select children for the groups who could best help the researchers learn more about the nature of the things that children had indicated were worrying them.

In each school, the children sat with the researcher around a table in a quiet room. The researcher chaired the discussion and helped the children pass a portable tape-recorder around and across the circle as each person made her or his contribution. These sessions lasted approximately forty-five minutes during which time the researcher posed questions that sought more information about: the nature of the children's worries, how they were presently coping with these things, and the advice they would give to younger children who might face similar sorts of problems in the future.

Results

The Inventory of Children's Worries

As can be seen in table 10.1, the children were worried about a wide range of issues from the macro to the micro. Concern about political corruption, the dirty state of the streets in Beach Camp, and the children's personal futures dominated the list. Also high among the children's worries were concern for the plight of children in Iraq, anxiety about car accidents and the dangers to children playing in the streets of the camp, and worry about the deteriorating health services in Gaza.

It is interesting to note that possible indicators of trauma such as difficulty in sleeping, nightmares, and fear of the dark were ranked low on the list. The children also recorded low levels of worry about feeling lonely, helpless or sad.

Gender and Age Differences in Worries

There were significant differences between the worries of boys and girls. However, there were no apparent developmental differences noted in the study. This latter point could be explained by the narrow band of age in the sample (265 of the 287 children were either 13 or 14 years of age). The differences in girls' and boys' worries can be seen in table 10.2.

Table 10.1 Frequency of Children's Worries: Response to the Inventory of Children's Worries

Worry	Rank	Mean	SD
Corruption	1	3.53	0.94
Dirty streets	2	3.51	0.75
My future	3	3.47	0.96
Death of Iraqi children	4	3.41	2.27
Car accidents: children in streets	5	3.35	1.58
Lack of places for entertainment	6	3.29	2.14
Deterioration of health services	7	3.28	0.96
Failing exams	8	3.24	1.48
Bad manners of young children	9	3.21	1.95
Israeli occupation	10	3.18	1.93
Poverty and economic situation	11	3.18	0.94
Gaza having too many children	12	3.13	2.39
Palestinian notions of women	13	3.10	1.94
Lack of school facilities	14	3.09	2.29
Spread of bad morals	15	3.04	1.63
Smoking	16	3.01	1.31
Noise/Noisy streets	17	3.00	1.03
Women bedecking themselves	18	3.00	1.44
Violence and bad relationships	19	2.99	1.07
Myself/my family getting sick	20	2.93	1.18
Myself/my family being kidnaped	21	2.88	1.85
War	22	2.85	1.83
Parent getting angry at me	23	2.83	2.15
Israeli-Turkish alliance	24	2.79	2.58
Crowded homes	25	2.76	1.50
Early marriage / Forced marriage	26	2.72	1.46
Internal political situation	27	2.72	1.16
Feeling lonely	28	2.68	2.12
Being sad helpless and weak	29	2.68	1.98
Dying	30	2.56	1.81
No privacy	31	2.55	1.20
My looks (too short, too thin)	32	2.54	2.24
Teacher or principal beating me	33	2.54	1.29
Relationships with opposite sex	34	2.48	1.63
Discrimination against girls	35	2.41	1.47
Not being able to sleep	36	2.37	2.30
Family members beating me	37	2.25	1.51
Parents quarreling	38	2.21	1.45
Night-time and the dark	39	2.18	1.99
Homework	40	2.03	1.58

Chronbach Alpha .74

Table 10.2   Significant Differences in Boys' and Girls' Worries

Worry	Boys' Means (SD) (N = 141)	Girls' Means (SD) (N = 146)	F (1,282)	P
No privacy	2.13 (1.19)	2.94 (1.07)	36.62	.001
Teacher/principal beating me	2.71 (1.22)	2.39 (1.33)	4.32	.038
Smoking	3.22 (1.09)	2.82 (1.48)	6.55	.011
Parents quarreling	2.01 (1.26)	2.40 (1.59)	5.29	.002
Discrimination of girls	1.97 (1.13)	2.82 (1.63)	26.16	.001
Women bedecking themselves	3.21 (1.11)	2.78 (1.67)	6.66	.010
Relations with the opposite sex	2.05 (1.26)	2.90 (1.83)	20.88	.001
Failing exams	2.98 (1.09)	3.50 (1.74)	8.99	.003
Sad and helpless	2.23 (1.36)	3.10 (2.36)	14.47	.001
How society looks at girls	2.80 (1.18)	3.38 (2.43)	6.60	.010
Bad manners young children	2.91 (1.32)	3.51 (2.46)	6.95	.009
Parents angry at me	2.35 (1.32)	3.30 (2.63)	14.62	.001
Feeling lonely	2.42 (1.41)	2.93 (2.74)	4.22	.041
My appearance	2.16 (1.19)	2.92 (2.87)	8.54	.004
Israeli-Turkish relations	3.30 (1.09)*	2.30 (3.38)	11.05	.001

* Greater frequency for boys; all other items show a greater frequency for girls

The girls reported a greater degree of worry than did boys. This was the case for 11 of the 40 items in the scale. However, boys worried more than the girls about being beaten by the principal or teachers and smoking. They were also more concerned about the strengthening of the alliance between Israel and Turkey and women bedecking themselves.

Focus Groups

While the Inventory of Children's Worries provided a listing and a rank ordering of children's worries, and an indication of the similarities and differences in the concerns of girls' and boys', the discussions that were held in the focus groups provided the researchers with a much greater depth of understanding about these concerns. The following themes emerged during the focus group discussions:

1. Homework, Exams, and Punishment

The first issue to be discussed concerned homework and the possibility of failing exams. The younger girls appeared to be most concerned about these things. Failing exams was linked with worry about being "punished and beaten." Comments such as: "Good students do not worry about being punished" and "Beating up by the teacher is sometimes necessary for the student to become a good student" indicate some acceptance of punishment for failing to complete work or for failing exams.

The older girls did not report as much concern with punishment associated with homework and exams as did the younger girls. Instead, they reported more strategies for organizing their time: "I do my homework regularly, so that the exam will be easier." "I organize my time preparing my homework rather than watching television or playing." Similarly, the older boys did not report worries about punishment in relation to failing exams or failing to complete homework. Rather, they accepted that punishment was to be expected: "Students should do their homework so they will not be punished." "I think that our teachers beat us because they want us to study and understand." "When the teacher beats up the students, he does that for our own sakes. He likes us, that's why he punishes us, like our fathers."

2. Overcrowding

Concerning homework, one boy did express concern that: "Our house is so noisy and overcrowded ... we have ten persons in a small house and my older brother listens to the music the whole day and it's difficult for me to do my homework at home."

Overcrowding and the lack of areas to play were themes common to each of the focus groups. While on one hand a number of children suggested going outside to play as one of their strategies for coping with their worries, this inevitably led to discussion about the dangers of the streets. One child summarized the situation like this: "Playing outside is a good solution for our problems. But, the PNA is destroying the playgrounds to build houses. We play in the street because we don't have playgrounds." Another child added: "If we have big playgrounds, we can solve all of our problems."

3. Concern with the Palestinian (National) Authority

Comments about the PNA (which others refer to as the PA) were particularly prevalent. Indeed, while *corruption* was listed as the most worrisome issue in the quantitative part of the study, it also came to the fore in the focus groups. These discussions revealed three groups of issues: (a) general disillusionment with the PNA: "Before the PNA entered, the situation was better. We were expecting so many nice things from the PNA. Our PNA is underdeveloped." "With the arrival of the PA we hoped things would get better. As a matter of fact they are getting worse," (b) a view that the PNA are not competent: "The PA can't build roads properly. My father is a laborer.

When he was constructing a new road, he noticed that the water pipes were placed very close to the sewerage pipes which will end up polluting the water," and (c) a view that jobs and privileges are distributed on a system of patronage: "When a person is appointed, he knows someone high up in the PA office," "Nowadays, everything needs "*wasta*," "If you want to be a policeman, you have to know someone who works with the PNA to get that position."

4. Concern about the Environment

One particularly important worry, for which the children did not appear to have personal solutions, concerned the dirty state of the streets and the beach. This issue, which emerged as the second most worrisome from the questionnaires, was also raised with much passion in all of the group discussions with comments such as: "I don't like to go to the beach, it's dirty." "Yes, the sea is dirty too." "Gaza is dirty." "The street are dirty and the beach is dirty." "They throw sewerage in to the sea." "Why don't we keep our beach and sea clean?" "Why don't we keep our country clean?" "We should clean up Gaza." "I dream to see my country clean and free."

5. Relationships with Israel

Each of the focus groups discussed relationships with Israel. Common to all groups were criticism of Israel's continued occupation of East Jerusalem and expansion of settlements in the West Bank. There was a strong sense of pessimism among the children with comments like: "Peace will not succeed because of the Jewish settlers in Nitsareim and other places in the West Bank." "The Israelis talk about peace but put people in jail, and continue to demolish houses in Jerusalem." "I don't think any treaty can be successful."

6. Other Issues

Two other issues to emerge concerned the discrimination of girls within families and worry about early and arranged marriages. On the first issue, the strongest voices could be heard among the boys with comments like: "In some families you find discrimination between boys and girls, and it hurts both parties [boys and girls]. The father prefers the boy than the girls, and this makes injustice, depression and frustration. This affects the young people."

Both boys and girls spoke about marriage. Many of the older girls voiced wishes to choose their own husbands, but accepted that this was not possible: "My sister likes our neighbor. They always meet on the roof and talk. They like each other a lot. I am afraid that my mother will find out, because she will get very angry." One of the boys said: "Sometimes parents force their kids to marry somebody whom they don't like and after that the problems start between the couple and their children will suffer." Another boy ventured the view that: "Parents should not force their children to marry too early or to someone they don't like just because they want to get rid of them."

The issue of early marriage was clearly of concern to many of the children in the study. These sentiments were summed up by one boy who said: "I see in my family, that the father forces his children, boys and girls, to get married early when they are still young." Another boy added: "I think that 20 is a good age for marriage, not earlier."

Strategies for Coping and Advice for Others

The most common strategies suggested by the children for coping with their own worries involve finding ways of distracting themselves from their concerns. These included: going down to the sea and walking along the beach, watching television, playing outside, and the most often cited strategy—reading books. One child summarized these sentiments when she said: "I watch television, but I am miles away." Seeking distractions was also the most often cited suggestion that children had for their younger siblings. As one boy put it: "I'll advise them to read a story to get away from the problem."

A second group of strategies suggested by the children involved praying and reading the Quran: "To pray helps me and to read the Quran helps me." "When I worry, I listen to music or read the Quran or sleep."

A third and final group of strategies involved talking over the concerns with other people such as: sisters, brothers, mothers, fathers, teachers, cousins and friends. When asked particularly who they might turn to when worried, the most frequently cited people were mothers.

Discussion

There are two areas for discussion in this paper: the results of the present studies and their implications for research and practice in Gaza; and the methodology *per se* and its applicability in other settings.

The procedures adopted in this study have been useful in identifying a wide variety of issues about which these particular children worry. These range from macro issues such as politics, war, and religion through to micro issues such personal friendships and exam anxiety. The procedures have also highlighted differences and commonalties among the worries of boys and girls, and to a lesser extent, developmental differences in children's worries.

The first point of interest is to note that the issues about which the children worry most are mainly societal and group concerns such as dirty streets, Israeli occupation, war, corruption, death of Iraqi children, and the lack of medicines in the hospitals. High on the list of worries were also societal concerns about behavior such as women not wearing the veil, people taking drugs and alcohol, people swearing in the street, and the bad manners of young children. The trend in the relative importance of the children's concerns moves from the collective to the individual.

The issues that appear to be of least concern to the children are personal concerns such as being beaten and having no pocket money, and concerns about their parents' relationships such as quarreling and getting divorced. As was the case with the highest ranked concerns, here again, we see a marked contrast with the types of worries reported by children in individualistic cultures such as those in the United States (see Silverman, et al., 1995) and Australia (see Christie and MacMullin, 1998). In these countries, concerns appear to move from the individual to the group, to the global (Triandis, 1994).

One area where boys expressed greater levels of concern than did girls was being beaten by their fathers and by teachers and principals. The explanation for the gender difference is clear; the boys are beaten more often. However, as noted earlier, while the boys reported high levels of beating, both in the initial stage of the research and in the focus groups, they nonetheless rated this as one of their least troublesome concerns. This is an example of what Fiske (1990) refers to as "authority ranking" which is one of two social patterns that mark collectivist cultures. The other is "community sharing."

Hence, both the children's focus on community concerns above personal concerns and their acceptance of the need for authority and punishment can be interpreted as expressions of a traditional, homogeneous culture that values the collective above the individual. Further to this, when a society has shared a common history of war, forced migration, military occupation, Intifada, and ongoing political conflict, as has been the case in Gaza, this sense of collectivism is only strengthened.

One particular characteristic of collectivistic societies that has been discussed by Moghaddam (1998) is that of *locus of control.* Moghaddam argues that people in traditional, collectivistic societies are more likely to believe that their destinies are determined by factors beyond their control than people living in individualistic societies. This could explain why the children in this study had so few strategies for coping with their worries and very little advice to offer their younger brothers and sisters. Apart from one child's advice about spending time on organization as a way to prevent problems with homework and exams, and another's about talking over concerns with family members, all other ideas centered on : (1) accepting things the way they are, (2) seeking out diversions such as play, reading, watching television, or walking; and (3) prayer and reading the Quran.

Here it would seem that those who would seek to help children with their worries (social workers, teachers, or school counselors) could provide children with simple strategies for preventing or tackling those worries that are within their control. These might include worries about homework and exams, difficulties with friends and quarreling with siblings. One particular worry that could be tackled by the children, with the help of adults, is the concern about dirty streets and dirty environment. This was the children's second greatest concern. Here, a small scale project to take charge of the cleaning of one particular area (for example, the street outside of the school) and perhaps the development of a public education campaign by the children could give them a sense of being able to make a difference in a small way. This has been tried in Gaza, and from the evidence of this study, it is certainly worth trying again.

As mentioned earlier, the present study failed to detect any evidence of trauma among the children. If the children were still experiencing difficulties as a direct result of the political violence of the occupation and Intifada then we might have expected higher levels of worry about nighttime, sleeping, and nightmares than were recorded. Clearly, the children are concerned about their political and economic circumstances, but this concern does not appear to express itself in dysfunctional ways.

Beyond gaining insight into the nature of some of the things that worry these children in the Gaza Strip, the present study has also been useful in exploring a method that seeks to gain information about children's worries, without resorting to lists of concerns constructed by adult researchers. However, it was clear from an earlier study by MacMullin and Odeh (1999) that there could be a number of potential threats to the validity of these procedures.

Firstly, in the MacMullin and Odeh study which sought to identify the worries of younger children in the Gaza Strip, the Australian researcher was present at all times during the collection of data. In retrospect, it is thought that this may have prompted the children to think that they must provide the foreigner with an understanding of the political struggle that they are facing. This may have been reinforced by the presence of the teachers and principals, one of whom applauded a student's highly political speech at one stage during the preliminary discussions. These discussions, in which the researcher sought to explain the concept of *qalaq* (worry) may also have set the children thinking in a particular direction. As a consequence, in the present study, the foreign researchers stayed out the classrooms, leaving the data collection to their local counterparts. Efforts were made to ensure that the teachers and principals left the children to complete the exercises privately. Care was also taken not to elaborate the concept of worry by providing illustrations about the kinds of things the researchers are expecting of the children. This was done by talking about the experience of worry, rather than the particular circumstances that prompt it.

While these procedural changes may have reduced threats to validity, potential threats to reliability may be harder to counter. For, by their nature, these procedures are likely to produce different results each time they are employed. Political events such as the Wye Plantation peace talks and the on-going sanctions against Iraq clearly affected these particular children's responses at this time. Similarly, in MacMullin and Odeh's study, the children's concerns about kidnaping are likely to have been heightened by a recent incident in the children's neighborhood. This need not give concern if the purpose of the procedures is to construct an inventory to help the professional practitioner determine what people are currently worrying about in order to help them with those worries. However, as it stands, such an inventory has limited research potential for it deals merely with single content items that may not be of concern to other groups with whom the researcher might want to make comparisons.

This difficulty can be overcome by subjecting the data to test-item and principal-components analysis and in so doing identify clusters of worries that may constitute particular sub-scales. These procedures were used by Christie and MacMullin (1998) in a similar study in Australia which produced a six-factor solution allowing the construction of six meaningful subscales of worries. When used to produce a Children's Worry Scale, these procedures allow analysis of constructs at a higher level than the single item. Hence, applied to the present study, one could compare the scores of boys and girls on subscales such as school concerns or family worries. In order to use such a scale to make comparisons with groups drawn from different populations, it is necessary to exclude idiosyncratic items such as "worry about lack of medicines at the hospital" (explained by an intensive media campaign at the time of the study) and retain the more universal examples of children's worries.

While administering a Children's Worry Scale to a new sample will facilitate group comparisons, it will bring with it the risk of overlooking problems unique to the new group. Hence the procedures described here can be used for the construction and use of either situation-specific inventories or more universal scales. The method chosen will depend on the purpose of the study.

A further limitation of the present study concerns the selection of children for the focus groups. Recall that teachers and principals were asked to identify articulate children who could best help the researchers gain a deeper understanding about the things that they and other children worry over. These children were not necessarily representative of the sample and their understanding of other children's worries and the strategies that others use to cope with such concerns may not be accurate. Nonetheless, this is one of the trade-offs of qualitative research. What is gained by the deeper insight provided by the articulate children more than compensates for the loss of generalizability that accompanies a selected sample.

The procedures described here have their limitations. However, they do give researchers and practitioners a method for investigating the worries of children that promises to provide more information, than earlier approaches that have relied solely on more psychometrically robust, yet less child-centered techniques.

Notes

1. The authors would like to acknowledge and thank Dr. Jumana Odeh of the Palestinian Happy Child Centre and Dr. Samir Ragout of the Gaza Community Mental Health Centre for their assistance in collecting the data.

References

Christie, E. and MacMullin, C. E. (1998). What do children worry about? *Australian Journal of Guidance and Counseling, 8*:1:9-24.

Fiske, A. (1990). *Structures of social life.* New York: Free Press

Henker, B., Whalen, C. K., and O'Neil, R. (1995). Worldly and workaday worries: Contemporary concerns of children and young adults. *Journal of Abnormal Child Psychology, 23*:6:685-702.

MacMullin, C. E. and Odeh, J. (in press). What is worrying children in the Gaza Strip? *Child Psychiatry and Human Development.*

Millar, R. and Gallagher, M. (1996). The "Things I worry about" scale: Further developments in surveying the worries of post-primary school pupils. *Educational and Psychological Measurement, 56*:972-994.

Moghaddam, F. M. (1998). *Social psychology: Exploring universals across cultures.* New York: W. H. Freeman and Co.

Punamäki, R.-L. (1989). Factors affecting the mental health of Palestinian children exposed to political violence. *International Journal of Mental Health, 18*:2:63-79.

Qouta, S., Punamäki, R.-L. and El Sarraj, E. (1995). The relations between traumatic experiences, activity, and cognitive and emotional responses among Palestinian children. *International Journal of Psychology, 30*:3:289-304.

Silverman, W. K., LaGreca, A. M., and Wasserstein, S. (1995). What do children worry about? Worries and their relation to anxiety. *Child Development, 66*:671-686.

Simon, A. and Ward, L. O. (1974). Variables influencing the sources, frequency, and intensity of worry in secondary school pupils. *British Journal of Social and Clinical Psychology, 13*:391-396.

Triandis, H. C. (1994). Culture and social behavior. In Lonner, W. J. and Malpass, R. S. (Eds.), *Psychology and culture.* Boston: Allyn and Bacon.

11

Qualitative and Quantitative Research among Hmong Refugees

An Analysis[1]

Joseph Westermeyer

Introduction

This self-analysis of my work from the last three decades has the following goal: to assess the interplay between qualitative and quantitative methods used to study the Hmong people, their culture, and certain aspects of social adjustment and psychopathology. Initial work with the Hmong began in Laos during 1965 to 1975 (Westermeyer, 1971), and continued with Hmong refugees in United States from 1976 to the current time.

Several mentors shaped this particular approach to melding qualitative and quantitative research. The first of these influences, throughout the 1960s, was my anthropology advisor, Perti Pelto, who emphasized two points:

1. Inundate yourself in the culture, observing and participating in the people's way of life. Avoid projecting your own preconceptions onto them. This should lead to areas of special interest.
2. Construct a means for further investigating those aspects of their culture that interest you. Consider using a variety of methods and samples, including quantitative measures.

Pelto's beliefs and methods strongly influenced his former students, to the point that they prepared a compendium of their works written in Pelto's honor (Poogie et al., 1992). For that compendium, I prepared a chapter on my studies of opium use and addiction, emphasizing Pelto's influence (Westermeyer, 1992).

A second influence was the work of psychiatrist-anthropologist Alexander Leighton (1981). Leighton's work reflected both his anthropological, community-based observations outside of clinical settings, and his work as clinician-psychiatrist in cross-cultural settings. The focus for one of his earlier works was an unusual sociocultural setting that bore certain similarities to my work with Hmong: the remote isolation camps set up for Japanese Americans and immigrants in the United States during the Second World War.

A third influence was the psychiatrist Bertrum Schiele in the Department of Psychiatry at the University of Minnesota. Schiele was at the forefront of the psychopharmacology research during the 1960s and 1970s—an era that greatly stimulated the development of psychiatric rating scales to evaluate quantitatively the effects of psychotropic agents on psychopathological conditions. This era in turn stimulated the development of rating scales and scheduled interviews for use in general populations, to assess the distribution of psychiatric symptoms in non-clinical populations.

A fourth influence was James Butcher, a colleague and psychologist who translated psychometric instruments across languages. Butcher, with the Italian psychiatrist Pancheri, undertook perhaps the most difficult psychometric translation imaginable, the Minnesota Multiphasic Personality Inventory (MMPI), with its many historical and cultural items (Butcher and Pancheri, 1976). He also worked with collaborators from Latin American and Asia in translating, renorming, and restandardizing various psychometric instruments (Butcher and Spielberger, 1985; Butcher and Garcia, 1978).

These influences began and continued during my several studies conducted among the Hmong. The first of these studies began in 1965 in Laos. It began with Pelto's "cultural inundation: " a method partly experiential and partly observational, which lends itself more to qualitative rather than quantitative investigation. This phase in the work laid an important, even critical foundation for the later quantitative work. It was also intensely and inevitably personal, coming as it did in my twenties when I was still developing my own persona and life-way.

Cultural Inundation: Laos, 1965-1975

"Cultural inundation" or living within a foreign culture is a time-honored rite of passage in anthropological studies. In addition to being a challenging initiation, it also provides critical training functions, such as:

- Developing the cross-cultural researcher, personally and professionally;
- Fostering the ability to make compromises and to alter preconceived notions regarding theory or method while in the field (i.e., to be influenced by the experience, the data, and the people themselves);
- Acquiring skills to collect data cross-culturally, which involves working with language and translators, learning the "politeness" behavior of the people being studied, and being able to observe behaviors and events in a structured fashion;
- Being able to handle one's own data and to assess the data of others, based on day-to-day "field" experience.

My first trip to Laos was carefully planned. I went voluntarily as a physician to work with displaced persons needing medical care and public health services. (My wife and small daughter also went, albeit perhaps not so voluntarily.) This venture occurred in the midst of Second Indochina War, in which the Americans and their allies were succeeding the French as a major foreign presence. As French power waned during the early 1940s, the peoples in the region resumed a political and military struggle to decide governance over this culturally diverse area. My motivation in going to Laos, as I discerned it at the time, was three-fold: to collect data for a master's degree in anthropology, to have a cross-cultural experience as a physician, and to make a humanitarian contribution.

With Professor Pelto, I had planned to study psychosomatic responses of persons exposed to and fleeing combat violence. As it turned out, I was far too busy as a physician in the midst of those combat/flight situations (sometimes fleeing myself!) to study individual responses in any kind of detail. However, the hospital at which I spent much of my first year was in the midst of "Hmong country," providing an opportunity to live and working among the Hmong. Opium poppies in splashes of white, red, and purple grew resplendent on the encircling mountains. Poppy farmers were quite willing to discuss this predominant cash crop. And I encountered scores, then hundreds (and eventually thousands) of addicted patients in my clinical work. As a consequence of these problems and opportunities, I switched the topic of my research (undertaken during evenings, weekends, holidays, and slack times) to opium production, agro-economics, use, and addiction—a topic that has continued to occupy me up to the present day (Westermeyer and Chitasombat, 1996; Westermeyer, 1997). Like Leighton, I had the opportunity of functioning concurrently as fielder observer and as a clinician, with each role contributing knowledge and insight to the other.

When not working at the Sam Thong Hospital in northern Laos, I traveled to a few dozen villages (mostly Hmong) for various medical purposes (e.g., epidemics, refugee gathering points, collection sites for wounded militia and military). This village work, along with my work at the hospital, provided abundant opportunity to eat with them, stay in their homes, live and work with their families, celebrate their rituals and annual festivals, and share their travails. Although I became fluent primarily in Lao, the *lingua franca* for the country, I learned sufficient Hmong to understand their grammar, syntax, and pronunciation, to take a medical history, to conduct a brief social conversation, and to make my needs known (e.g., thirsty, tired). During my initial two years in Laos, I spent approximately one year living in Hmong settings, plus additional time working with the Hmong and other Laotian people[2] in a variety of medical and public health endeavors. Subsequently, I spent another twelve months in Laos during six separate trips over the next eight years. During each of these trips, I continued my interactions with Hmong people, although conducting more focused research projects during those later trips and using gradually more quantitative measures.

Over time I came to feel both comfortable as well as effective living and working among the Hmong. Their behaviors, interactions, and decisions became a part of my own repertoire, as I sought to live among them and follow their customs in conducting my own life. By the same token, I became sufficiently aware of their viewpoints to understand those ways in which my own values and customs (and medical practice) did not comport well with their values and customs. At times these could be negotiated, and they were willing to accept my baffling customs (e.g., boiling my drinking water, administering life-saving blood transfusions, conducting postmortem examinations in certain cases). At other times negotiations tended to be futile (e.g., dissuading relatives from removing a seriously ill, but treatable patient from the hospital so that he or she could die in an "auspicious place"). I enjoyed my days with the Hmong to the point of preferring the sometimes dangerous, often exhausting work among them, to the more complex, easier, and safer life among the Lao and the international community in the capital city of Vientiane. In sum, this experience with the Hmong over a decade met Pelto's goal of "inundation in the culture."

During this time, there was ample opportunity to study how the Hmong dealt with migration and flight from danger. As "migrants of the mountains," in Geddes terms (Geddes, 1976), the Hmong were accustomed to regular migration. Their reliance on slash-and-burn agriculture, their use of migration to solve interpersonal and political problems, and their constant reshaping of alliances led to regular relocations within the Annamite Mountains of Asia, even in the best of times (Bernatzik, 1970; Lemoine, 1972). Thus, they had traditions for coping with relocation to familiar ecological settings.

Flight from the North Vietnamese invasion of northern Laos produced some problems with which the Hmong were acquainted. These challenges consisted of moving an entire village and all of its people to a distant mountain, trekking for days or even weeks regardless of weather, and then setting up a new village within a few days—all the while protecting oneself and one's family from the elements. However, flight from modern military invasion introduced novel stresses:

- The Hmong did not choose the timing of the flight, so that crops in the field or rice bins overflowing with the next year's sustenance might be left behind;
- Chicken, pigs, and cattle would likely be abandoned, although they might retain horses (at least if the village were not suddenly attacked at night);
- Escape had to be rapid to keep ahead of pursuing soldiers, who were young men not burdened by children, the elderly, the ill, and wounded;
- As infirm members became too weak to continue, they were often abandoned to die along the side of the trail;
- For those abandoned, seriously wounded, or terminally ill, their deaths could not be properly mourned, nor their bodies properly buried;
- It was not possible to make a trip or two back to the original village site, as was common in peace time, in order to bring blankets, cooking utensils, farm implements, and even sawn timbers to provision and construct the new house on the next mountain.

People walked away from their homes with the clothes on their backs, perhaps some rice in a sack, any sidearms (usually a flintlock rifle, a cross-bow, and/or a long knife or machete), and perhaps a few cooking utensils. Infants and very small children could be carried, but larger children and the elderly had to bear the burden of the mountain trails with fit adults, keeping up as best they could. Mortality was greatest at the extremes of the life span, with infants and the elderly most affected by the combined exhaustion, dehydration, exposure to the elements, and infections such as malaria.

After fleeing Laos, Hmong people spent several months to a few decades in the refugee camps of Thailand. Refugee camp life also involved resumption of some, and loss of other, traditions. The Hmong could plant and tend gardens, build houses of a familiar style, reorganize into various clan groups, and reciprocate with one another in traditional ways. Women's roles could continue in ancient ways, i.e.: giving birth, tending small children, cooking, cleaning the house, hauling water, making and mending clothes. On the contrary, men lost several major roles: those of farmer, hunter, warrior, village chief. A few men could function in recently acquired roles of teacher or health care worker.

This initial "inundation" provided learning experiences that could be achieved in other cross-cultural settings. These experiences included acquisition of a new language, the need to learn–through observation and participation in the culture–the unspoken values and beliefs of the people, and the ability to live productively and even happily in another people's society. By the same token, several unique features of my particular "inundation" occurred as a matter of happenstance, related to war, subsequent relocations within Laos, and later flight from Laos to the United States. These events could not have been predicted, much less influenced. I was swept along by these events, and they have strongly influenced my personal life, professional activities, and research since that time. Basically, they had to do with being closely involved with a people caught in changes and conflict above and beyond their control. (It was relatively easy to identify with their plight, as my maternal grandparents, with whom I spent much time when young, had likewise been forced unwillingly from Ireland by economic, political, and cultural upheaval.) These unanticipated circumstances led to my interests in culture change, in differences among ethnic groups who live in close proximity to one another, in refugees and other victimized people, and in veterans of combat.

Refugee Studies in the United States, 1976 to the Present

The first phase of my work with and for the Hmong proceeded over a decade, 1965-1975, primary in Laos. The next phase in my work with the Hmong began more than two decades ago in the United States and still continues today. This phase brought interesting and unexpected opportunities, as well as challenges. Due to their defeat in the struggle against the North Vietnamese (a loss that I shared in various respects), the Hmong began relocating to the United States as refugees in 1976. This crisis provided me with an opportunity to both serve and study the Hmong in yet another context. However, on this occasion they were a foreign refugee group trying to adapt to my culture—the opposite of the earlier decade. This serendipitous circumstance permitted me to observe those aspects of their Asian-bound culture and experience that facilitated their adaptation to the United States, as well as those that impeded their adaptation. By virtue of my clinical role, I was also able to study psychosocial problems that some of them experienced in the Unites States, as well as some of the past and current bio-psychosocial factors contributing to those problems.

Within hours of the communist regime taking control of Laos in 1975, the Hmong began to flee. After a year or longer in Thailand refugee camps, they relocated to the United States (as well as to several other countries, including China, Thailand, France, and Canada). Initially distributed evenly throughout the United States, by 1980 they had begun to relocate in several focal areas (e.g., California, Montana, Wisconsin, Minnesota, Rhode Island) in order to be closer to relatives. These relocations out of the Annamite Mountains, and indeed out of Asia itself to various parts of the United States again forced unfamiliar circumstances on the Hmong:

- Unfamiliar climates, often involving extremely cold weather;
- Unfamiliar housing structures;
- At least initially, distance from relatives;
- In the initial years, food that was unfamiliar;
- A new *lingua franca*, English.

Following relocation to the United States, Hmong women were able to continue initially in familiar roles. During the early years in the United States, however, Hmong men faced further dramatic changes, such as:

- Absence of employment for those who were illiterate or barely literate, and who knew only farming or soldiering—this affected most of the men;
- Loss of status, from being the "masters of the mountains" or the "high Laotians" as ethnic Lao people labeled them—the predominant ethnic majority in the mountains—to being among the smallest, poorest, and weakest groups in the United States;

- Limited ability to pursue those vocations and avocations that conveyed status in Laos (e.g., hunter, horse racer, bull fighter, warrior, military leader, village chief, iron smith).

Virtually from the beginning, my interactions with the Hmong in the United States involved continued social or "field" interactions, as well as work in a clinical context. Whereas my earlier role in the 1960s was that of a generalist physician-surgeon, by 1970 it was that of a psychiatrist (following psychiatric residency during 1967-1970).

Experience with Other Ethnic Groups in Laos and the United States

During the three years that I lived in Laos during the decade 1965-75, my work also involved other ethnic groups besides the Hmong. These groups included:

- Ethnic Lao people;
- Other ethnic minorities indigenous to Laos (e.g., Khamu, Iu Mien or Yao, Akha, Laven Dyahun, Tai Dam, Lu–tribal peoples living in the mountains);
- Expatriate Asians from China, India, Pakistan, Thailand, Vietnam, Cambodia, Burma;
- Expatriate Caucasians from Europe, Australia, and the United States.

Familiarity with these other ethnic groups in Asia contributed significantly to my work with Hmong people, providing a background against which to observe remarkable differences and unexpected as well as expected similarities. These various observations led to numerous studies, undertaken in an effort to document both similarities and differences, as well as to consider possible explanations for these observations.

During the period 1971 to 1996, approximately another year was spent in other countries of Asia besides Laos (e.g., Thailand, Malaysia, Hong Kong, Singapore, Indonesia, Burma, Philippines, India, and Cambodia). These trips (about twenty-five of them) were undertaken primarily under the auspices of the World Health Organization, with a few trips funded by the United States Agency for International Development, the Special Action Office of the President for Drug Abuse Prevention, and a Norwegian aid group. These efforts produced publications on methodology, alcoholism and drug addiction, cultural psychiatry, and psychiatric epidemiology.

From 1967 to the present time, several studies were undertaken among American Indian people of the north central region of the

United States (Westermeyer, 1978; Westermeyer, 1980; Westermeyer and Peake, 1983, Westermeyer, 1989d). These peoples bore many similarities to the Hmong as a tribal ethnic minority (e.g., strong commitment to family, continued reliance on an oral rather than written tradition, an animistic worldview), along with many differences, including historical ones. Experience with both American Indians and Hmong provided an opportunity to observe the adaptation of North American tribal groups to a complex multiethnic nation-state.

The notion that familiarity with these other ethnic groups would enhance work in understanding the Hmong refugee experience was not an overarching thought at the time that the work was initiated. Rather, it has become apparent in retrospect that work with other ethnic groups served as a basis for understanding both Hmong-specific aspects of their refugee experience, as well as more general aspects of the Hmong as Asian refugees like other Asian refugees, or an American minority like other American minorities. At times, the hypotheses so derived were virtually self-evident. At other times, the hypotheses were more uncertain, with little concrete data or general principles to support them. The findings were often unexpected and sometimes counter-intuitive.

Clinical Experience with Hmong Refugees in the United States

In 1977 Hmong collaborators and I initiated a community-based study to examine mental and social adjustment of the first hundred Hmong refugees in Minnesota. In preparation for that study, a meeting with members of the Hmong community was held at the University of Minnesota to discuss the study, to let them inquire about matters of interest to them from such a study, and to address their concerns. Much to our surprise, virtually the entire Hmong community in Minnesota (along with their children) came to that meeting. The research coordinator (Tou Fu Vang, a Hmong leader) and I recommended that they establish an association. A steering committee of volunteers began that day and led to an association that continues to exist (initially the Minnesota Hmong Association and later the Minnesota Lao Family Association). Through that association, the Hmong asked that a clinic be established to address their problems "of the heart and the mind." A weekly clinic began and continued over the next twelve years. Several hundred Hmong and then hundreds of other refugees were assessed and received care in this clinic, which eventually opened three days per week.

Several reports have evolved from this clinic, and further reports are in progress. One series of articles focused on general matters of diagnosis across cultural boundaries (Westermeyer, 1987), including work with interpreters (Westermeyer, 1990) and with refugees who had been wounded, tortured, or otherwise traumatized (Westermeyer, 1985; Westermeyer and Wahmanholm, 1989). Through this clinic, an epidemic of opium smoking in the United States was first identified (Westermeyer, Lyfoung, and Neider, 1989). *Folie a Deux* or "psychosis of two," an unusual form of psychopathology first recognized in France during the 1800s, was identified. Literature reports indicated that it was infrequent and primarily a paranoid psychosis (or type of Delusional Disorder). We found it to be frequent among the Hmong, to be associated with symptoms of Major Depressive Disorder in many cases, and to respond often to antidepressant medication rather than requiring antipsychotic medication as frequently occurs in such cases (Westermeyer, 1988b, Westermeyer, Lyfoung, Wahmanholm, and Westermeyer, 1989). A few reports described the clinical problems encountered among refugee children and adolescents (Williams and Westermeyer, 1984; Westermeyer and Wahmanholm, 1996). This clinical experience resulted in three books, one formulated primarily for those planning resettlement and mental health services for refugees and prepared with co-author Williams (Williams and Westermeyer, 1986), a second oriented for clinicians, especially psychiatrists (Westermeyer, 1989), and a third primarily for those concerned with public mental health issues and migration (Westermeyer, 1989).

Advantages of Clinical Research across Cultures

Research in clinical settings offers certain potential advantages for psychiatry generally, and for refugee mental health in particular. Regarding the Hmong, our salient findings included:

- The early and unexpected interest of the Hmong community in having mental health services available;
- The acceptance of mental health services by large numbers of Hmong refugees (over six hundred Hmong received psychiatric care over twelve years in the clinic that they requested);
- The need to develop special methods of assessment and care, including work with interpreters, psychotherapy approaches consistent with Hmong world view, and special considerations regarding pharmacotherapy;
- The considerable overlap of psychiatric diagnosis among the Hmong and indigenous Americans (e.g., major depression and the various anxiety disorders were most common, with smaller numbers of virtually all possible psychiatric diagnoses);

- Increased numbers of particular disorders that Hmong share with other refugees (i.e., Post-Traumatic Stress Disorder, organic brain syndromes from combat trauma, torture while incarcerated, epidemic infectious disease in refugee camps, and malnutrition during incarceration and flight);
- Increased rates of certain disorders among the Hmong as compared to other refugee groups (i.e., opium addiction, Shared Delusional Disorder or *Folie a Deux*);
- Special psychosocial issues involving refugees, such as "unaccompanied children" arriving without parents or families, delayed or missed grieving, high rates of rape in certain groups, the "alexithymia" phenomenon, grieving the loss of the former country and culture, new and unexpected intergenerational problems, special adjustment problems during periods of life change (e.g., marriage, parenthood, retirement, death of a parent or spouse), unfamiliar laws and methods of solving interpersonal discord, distrust of their own culture and of the receiving culture in some cases.

Disadvantages of Clinical Research across Cultures

Disadvantages may accrue from examining mental health and social problems only in clinical settings. Examples are as follows:

- Clinicians encounter problems only when they reach crisis proportions and surface to clinical recognizance.
- The biological, psychological, and social progenitors of the clinical problem may not be apparent once the person has reached a clinical setting. Or clinicians may identify a characteristic in refugee patients that seems "atypical" and possibly etiologic, but may simply be a common characteristic within that ethnic group or among refugees in general. Such misidentification can lead to diagnostic errors and therapeutic misadventures that fail to benefit the patient or his/her family.
- Once a problem has reached clinical recognizance, it often requires considerable time, effort, and expense to resolve, and it may not resolve completely. Thus, considerable time may be devoted, with relatively narrow or limited data to show for the time expended.
- More "minor" but common problems may not reach clinical settings but these problems can result in major life crisis and maladaptation, such as school drop-out, marriage failure,

violence, incarceration, unemployment, chronic unhappiness, and other psychosocial maladjustment. Although these problems may be "minor" from the clinician's psychopathological perspective, they are not necessarily minor from the perspective of the person possessing the problem or from the perspective of societal agencies that must help in coping with these personal and social failures.

Clinical and Community (or "Field") Investigation

Background

Soon after Hmong people began arriving from Laos in the United States, old friends and colleagues from Laos began to contact me. This led to visits back and forth, including staying in one another's homes. Advice and instrumental assistance was provided along with information about jobs, means of re-establishing one's occupational credentials in the United States, and so forth. These informal, but frequent contacts provided "field" knowledge and first-hand experience with the problems and advantages, successes and failures of Hmong refugees in the United States. Since they had been friends, acquaintances, and/or coworkers in Laos, it furnished an opportunity to observe the same individual coping with life in two highly different circumstances.

Rationale

Combined clinical and community (or "field") investigations can lead to useful information. For reasons listed above, clinical studies alone are limited in their capacity to shed light on general social or psychological phenomena. Likewise, field studies of clinical phenomena can be limited, due to the expense and time required to obtain clinical data of large numbers of people. Survey work may lead to findings with minimal or no important clinical implications. It is difficult to show that any health problem has been prevented through conducting only field studies. Without combined field-clinical studies, one does not know whether conditions being "treated" are merely self-limited problems that might resolve with time alone. Symptom checklists and clinical rating scales especially require a combined field-clinical approach in order to demonstrate their utility as clinical and epidemiological instruments.

The Sample

In order to generalize the findings of a study to a larger group, one must be able to specify the characteristics of the sample. In the study

to be described below, the subjects consisted of all Hmong aged fifteen or over living in Minnesota in 1997. (The age fifteen was used
because, within Hmong tradition, young people assumed adult
responsibilities and married around that age.) These first arriving
Hmong were all refugees whose community-of-residence in the
United States had been chosen for them by the U.S. government.
Although there had been some minor in-and-out migration from/to
Minnesota with adjacent areas of Wisconsin and Iowa, for practical
purposes, the subjects were a randomly distributed group. Since the
U.S. Department of State had distributed the refugees as small
nuclear families, with perhaps a grandparent or solitary aunt/uncle,
no one family group was inordinately represented in the sample.
The refugees were mostly young, in their twenties and thirties. During subsequent follow-up studies one and a half years later (phase
one), and then six to seven years after that (phase two), another two
subjects (both older widowed women) were identified as being in the
community at the time that the original study group was selected.
Thus, the original group comprised 102 people, but data were not
obtained on more than 100 at any time.

This sample size was deemed adequate for the original purpose of
the study, which was to identify broad issues of social adjustment and
mental health. In addition, we had plans from the beginning to follow this group over time in order to assess their outcomes. Finances
to support the study was a limiting factor, especially during the first
two phases of data collection. The third phase of data collection
(about ten years after leaving Laos) was well funded and permitted
extensive follow-up and data collection.

It would seem relatively straight-forward to obtain demographic
information from these Hmong subjects. And indeed, it was so for
items such as gender, marital status, and residence. However, some
apparently simple items could be quite complex. One of these was
age, since there were no birth certificates in "Hmong country" in
Laos, and the Hmong did not traditionally note birth dates nor celebrate birthdays. Further, many Hmong had furnished the United
States authorities with erroneous ages for a variety of reasons (e.g., to
be young enough to qualify for education, to be old enough to qualify for Social Security retirement). Thus, we had to expend considerable time ascertaining the year of birth. Nonetheless, it was feasible
to identify birth dates by year, since people recounted time, not by
year, but by significant events that could be traced, such as an
unusual tornado, a large battle, the death of the Laotian king.

Demographic information was obtained for two times periods: (1)
at the time of flight from Laos and (2) the current time in the United

States. These data included years of education, occupation, village-versus-town residence, size of household, etc., in Laos and in the United States. We compared both sets of demographic variables with current and subsequent social functioning, as well as with rating scales (Westermeyer, 1983; Westermeyer, Vang, and Neider, 1983b). One of our early studies was to assess differences between refugees who sought psychiatric care, as compared to those who did not do so (Westermeyer, 1983c; Westermeyer, Vang, and Neider, 1983a and 1983b).

Developing a Structured Interview

At the time of the first data collection two years out of Laos and the third data collection ten years after leaving Laos, we conducted structured interviews. The interview at time-one required about an hour; the interview at time-three required three to four hours. Items in the scheduled interview, which were based on the goals of the project and the hypotheses to be tested, originated from three sources: (1) the Hmong community (as represented by their association), (2) Hmong co-investigators (especially T.F. Vang, G. Lyfoung, M. Bouafuely, G. Vang), and (3) my interests and intuitions regarding potentially important factors.

In devising these items for the scheduled interview, we emphasized observations and questions that would produce reliable data (i.e., could be replicated by others in subsequent studies). Observations consisted of the subject's dress, grooming, and (at time-three) facility with English. Questions that could be answered factually (rather than impressionistically) were stressed, such as material possessions or months of employment in the last five years (at time-three). We also inquired regarding items that we knew were highly subjective, such as health condition, marital problems, satisfaction with living in the United States, and interest in returning to Laos. For these latter questions, we were careful to ask open ended questions, with the expectation that we would have to develop a coding system to transform these "qualitative" data to data that could be analyzed quantitatively.

Parenthetically, I believed that some of the Hmong-initiated questions in the time-one and time-three interviews would not lead to useful or practical information. Most of these items subsequently proved to occur very infrequently, to predict nothing, or to be associated with virtually nothing. However, even these items produced responses that were of interest to the Hmong in learning about their own people and their life-way in the United States. Unexpectedly from my point of view, some of these items did produce significant information. For example, my Hmong colleagues wanted a question regarding subjects' interest in returning to Laos. We discovered ten years after leaving Laos that more men than women wanted to return to Laos–although the men were considerably more accultur-ated to the United States. Many men missed their traditional roles and freedoms, whereas many women liked not having to collect fire-wood, haul water, or have children every year. I had thought that acculturation and the wish to remain in the United States would be associated with each other, but I was wrong.

Coding Responses to Open-ended Inquiry

Despite the subjective nature of the open-ended questions, it was fea-sible to code responses so as to permit quantitative analysis and sta-tistical testing. Since we permitted as many responses as the subject wished to make, the number of responses usually exceeded the num-ber of subjects. Codification was a lengthy process, consisting of the following: listing all possible responses along with the number of sub-jects providing the response; examining whether certain responses could be grouped together into more generic categories; and keeping track of the number of subjects associated with a particular response so that statistical analysis could be conducted. For example, too few subjects in a category would not support statistical comparisons. Like-wise, too many subjects in a category would not enable statistical comparisons. A "miscellaneous" category was sometimes necessary. For some items involving considerable supposition, many subjects replied "I don't know."

Translating Rating Scales

Beginning with our first data collection in 1977, we employed two symptom checklists of self-rating scales derived from scales already in use: the 90-item Symptom Checklist (the unrevised SCL-90) (Derogatis, Lipman, and Covi, 1973; Boleloucky and Horvath, 1974; Derogatis, Rickels, and Rock, 1976) and the Zung Depression Scale (Zung, 1965; Zung, 1971; Zung, 1973). We chose two scales for sev-eral reasons. First, I was familiar with them from my earlier work with Dr. Schiele. Second, these checklists had been widely used around the world, so that a considerable literature existed regarding them. Third, the symptom items in these scales were well based in universal somatic, psychological, and interpersonal experience, so that they had been fairly easily translated out of their original Eng-lish into many languages, including Asian languages. Perhaps the fact that they were developed in part by researcher-clinicians, who had immigrant backgrounds and were interested in cross-cultural aspects of psychiatric phenomenology, aided in producing symptom items that were relatively culture-fair.[3] And fourth, they had been widely applied in both clinical and community populations.

In translating these scales, we followed the methods largely worked out by Brislin and Butcher. First, one highly fluent Hmong man did the original translation (he had attended senior year of high school and five years of college in the United States, and had lived in the United States for an additional two years at the time of conducting the translation). In addition, Hmong was his first language, and he had lived among the Hmong in Laos for over two decades. Four Hmong, two men and two women, all fluent in English, conducted the back-translation. At that point, the Hmong translators and I met on several occasions to resolve differences and to construct items that would be the semantic as well as clinical equivalent of the original English wording. Since the items largely reflected physiological, psychological, interpersonal, and behavioral constructs familiar to the Hmong, this process went smoothly. My own limited familiarity with the Hmong language and communication was also useful (since many French and Lao terms had entered the Hmong working vocabulary and we sought to avoid these when possible). Careful work at this level was critical in facilitating the ease with which subsequent steps were accomplished. Qualitative knowledge regarding the language and culture were thus key in developing this instrument that would allow us to collect quantitative data. Examples of issues that required discussion and careful problem solving were as follows:

- Our original translator had used Hmong terms that assumed that the subject was a male; we had to redesign items so that both men and women could answer them.
- The English version regarding sexuality does not qualify whether or nor the subject is single, married, or sexually active. A literal translation could be insulting, especially to single Hmong women who could conclude that the questionnaire assumed that they were sexually active—a highly taboo behavior for single Hmong women when they were residing in Asia.
- In Hmong, a single term was equated with two English words: "pain" and "sick."

Next we conducted a pilot study involving Hmong subjects from diverse educational and occupational backgrounds, young and old, men and women. These subjects were asked to complete the test and to comment on any difficulties understanding or rating the item. This led to a few minor revisions so as to clarify items for the rater.

Once we had well-translated instruments that performed well on pilot tests, the restandardizing and renorming tasks required less intimate knowledge about the Hmong language and cultural views. However, it did require access to a community or non-clinical sample so that we could see how the instruments "performed" (i.e., the distribution of scores per item, the relatively frequency of endorsed items relative to each other, the patterns of scores that evolved). This was accomplished in the community study of one hundred Hmong, described above. Second, we needed access to Hmong psychiatric patients so that we could describe the differences of Hmong "normals" and Hmong "psychiatric patients" on the tests. Over the subsequent twelve years, we assessed several hundred Hmong patients using the rating scales. In a few instances, qualitative cultural knowledge helped to explain the results. For example, "normal" Hmong endorsed a "compulsivity" item having to do with checking doors and locks more frequently than did the patients. For the majority of Hmong, the use of locked doors was a new experience that required much trial and error. Rather than being an automatic behavior, as with most Americans, the Hmong had to remind themselves to lock their doors. They often worried that they had left their homes or cars without locking them. Those with psychiatric disorders were less bothered by the need to check doors and locks.

The translated Zung Depression Scale did not provide much additional information over and beyond the translated Depression Subscale of the SCL-90. However, use of both instruments served several research goals. First, we found that the scoring convention imposed on the subject did not change the results. Greater symptom levels on the SCL-90 are scored to the right on all 90 items, whereas greater symptom levels on the Zung may be scored to the right or left depending on the item. Second, the two scores were very highly correlated with one another, indicating that the subjects were scoring on a central experience even though the items differed from one another (with some overlap). Although the translated SCL-90 Depression Subscale performed well in our studies, the Zung is a "gold standard" test for self-rated depressive symptoms. Since we wanted to conduct studies of depressed Hmong patients, use of the longer Zung test lent greater reliability to those studies.

Psychiatric Rating Scales

At time-three, ten years after the Hmong had left Laos, I conducted a one and a half to two and a half hour psychiatric assessment. Those subjects reporting numerous symptoms required more time, as these symptoms required assessment regarding their duration and severity. This involved both open-ended inquiry regarding health, social functioning, and psychological well-being, as well as a number of specific questions (e.g., sleep disturbance, appetite, orientation to time and place). After completing this interview, several psychiatrist-rated scales were completed. These included the following: MiniMental State Exam (Folstein, Folstein, and McHugh, 1975); Global Assessment Scale; Hamilton Depression Scale (Hamilton, 1969); Hamilton Anxiety Scale (Hamilton, 1959); Brief Psychiatric Rating Scale (Overall and Gorham, 1960); Inpatient Multidimensional Psychiatric Scale (Lorr, Klett, McNair, and Lasky, 1963); and Nurses Observation Scale for Inpatient Evaluation.

These clinician-rated scales provided several advantages. First, we observed that the self-rated Zung was as effective as the psychiatrist-rated Hamilton in separating Hmong with Major Depressive Disorder from "normals." However, the psychiatrist-rated Hamilton distinguished clinical severity better than did the self-rated Zung, especially in the more severe psychotic ranges. Second, scales such as the MiniMental State Exam cannot be easily self-administered since some items involve examiner observation of the subject's performance. Third, these tests scanned various forms of psychopathology rather than simply replicating each other (e.g., anxiety symptoms, depressive symptoms, memory problems, cognitive abilities, social function). Some of these tests relied heavily on the clinician's eliciting and evaluating symptoms in the patient (e.g., the two Hamilton tests). Others relied heavily on responses to specific queries and on observation (e.g., MiniMental State Exam, Brief Psychiatric Rating Scale).

Developing Our Own Rating Scales

We wished to assess the extent to which the one hundred Hmong had persisted in their traditional ways ten years after leaving Laos. To accomplish this, we identified various behavioral items that could be decreased or abandoned in the United States (e.g., speaking Hmong, eating Hmong food, participating in Hmong rituals/ceremonies). To supply an adequate number of items for quantitative analysis, but not extend the interview needlessly, we settled on ten items, most of which could be answered along a spectrum rather than "yes or no." Likewise, we wanted to assess acculturation to the United States. To accomplish this, we identified items that could be avoided in the United States, but which could be indices of cultural adaptation, involving new behaviors that were not typical or even possible for the Hmong in Laos (e.g., using the banking system, using mass media). Various other scales were developed using particular items in the interview and/or rating scales (e.g., religious belief and practice, English language competence). Those Hmong with greater acculturation also reported and manifested better mental health (Westermeyer, Neider, and Vang, 1984).

Using data collected at time-one, we were able to identify those early factors associated with English language competence at time-three (Westermeyer and Her, 1996). Improved social adjustment was strongly associated with better English competence. Thus, the capacity to identify early on those not likely to become fluent in English may provide refugee planners and resettlement agencies with useful information. (This would need to be studied prospectively to see whether specific English language training might enhance social adjustment to the United States, since those who learn English better may also make better psychosocial adjustments regardless of language acquisition.)

Analyzing Translated Rating Scales and Associated Findings

We conducted various analyses to assess the reliability and validity of the translated scales, as well as the application of psychiatric scales among the one hundred Hmong in the community. For example, one of our early analyses compared social adjustment (e.g., marital status, employment) with self-rated symptoms. Those making a more successful social adjustment to the United States also reported few psychiatric symptoms (Westermeyer, Neider, and Callies, 1989). We have done some item analysis with various scales and subscales (Westermeyer, Schaberg, and Nugent, 1995); however, we are still engaged in this lengthy process. In a study of validity, Hmong psychiatric patients with Major Depressive Disorder were found to have significantly higher scores prior to treatment as compared with Hmong "normals." Following treatment, their depressive symptoms scores were lower for some months to a few years, but then they drifted up again over the subsequent several years (Westermeyer, 1986; Westermeyer, 1988b).

Based on psychiatric interviews of the one hundred refugees in the community at time-three, approximately one-fourth of them were found to have a current psychiatric disorder. This rate was higher than point prevalence studies of United States residents, but not notably different from lifetime prevalence rates (Westermeyer, 1988a). Psychiatric status was highly correlated with certain SCL-90 subscales, the Zung Depression Scale, and certain psychiatrist-rated scales. Of interest, these diagnostic assessments were made while blind to the SCL-90 and Zung scales.

We also conducted a few studies to assess the validity of the self-rated scales for depressive symptoms (Westermeyer, 1986; Westermeyer, 1988b). One of these involved an analysis of the Zung Depression Scale and the Depression Subscale of the SCL-90, comparing those Hmong in the sample of one hundred who were not treated for Major Depression Disorder (MDD) and those who subsequently were treated for MDD between time-one and time-two. Those who were subsequently treated for MDD had significantly higher scores on the Zung and the SCL-90 Depression Subscale (along with several other subscales) at time-one. Of additional interest, those who received treatment during the interim had normal or even slightly lower Zung and SCL-Depression scores at time-two, suggesting that treatment had been effective. At time-three (when none of the one hundred subjects had received psychiatric treatment for MDD in recent years), the Zung and SCL-90 Depression scores were again somewhat elevated among those who had a previous MDD. Hmong patients in our clinic who had MDD also had elevated scales as described above.

Among these one hundred Hmong refugees, welfare status and mental health symptoms differed with duration of time on welfare. During the early months on welfare, anxiety and depressive symptoms were high. After Hmong had been on welfare for three years or longer, such symptoms ameliorated to a considerable extent. However, those on welfare became increasingly isolated from mainstream American society and from interactions with other Hmong refugees (Westermeyer, Callies, and Neider, 1990).

The somatic expression of psychosocial distress (termed somatization) has long been described among refugees and victims of trauma. In our survey of the one hundred Hmong, we were able to demonstrate the correlates of somatization (Westermeyer, Bouafuely, and Neider, 1989). Of interest, we found somatization to be more common among our refugee patients with less education, and especially common among the Hmong mountaineers as compared to Lao, Cambodian, and Vietnamese lowlanders.

During the first few years in the United States, self-rated depressive symptoms of the refugee participants abated remarkably, along with some other symptoms (Westermeyer, Vang, and Neider, 1984). Initially, symptoms tended to be higher among men and employed women; several years later this finding was reversed, so that women who had remained at home reported the highest symptom levels (Westermeyer, Bouafuely, and Vang, 1984). Some types of symptoms more associated with character than stress or loss tended to change relatively little when reassessed at times one, two, and three. One example was paranoid symptoms, which were relatively high in a small number of subjects, borderline in a large minority of cases, and normal or nil in about half of the one hundred Hmong refugees. Of interest, the number of subjects with paranoid symptoms in the high or borderline range was considerably greater than one would find in a group of non-refugee Americans. A measure of validity for these paranoid symptoms in the refugee community was the high rate of paranoid disorders that occurred over several years even in this small group of one hundred Hmong (Westermeyer, 1989).

Commentary

Over the last thirty-two years of my research with Hmong people and communities, the initial stages of primarily qualitative work evolved gradually into a balance of qualitative and quantitative work. It would have been simpler to collect qualitative data only, and leave it at that. In order to obtain quantitative data, we had to go through all of the steps that are required for careful qualitative work. Since qualitative data often depends upon idiosyncratic observations and participation in the life of a people, it can be impossible to replicate a qualitative study. Since such work cannot be shown to be either accurate or inaccurate, it remains open to each individual's interpretation. As such, it comprises a poor foundation for developing policies, programs, and procedures.

Quantitative work unsupported by careful qualitative work can likewise be misleading. At times quantitative data can be easily collected, especially if not preceded by careful qualitative work or not involving translation. For example, had we accepted our Hmong subjects' ages at face value, rather than methodically to ascertain their year of birth, the actual ages of our one hundred Hmong subjects would have differed from their actual ages to a considerable extent. In addition, qualitative work often involves hunches or curiosity that must be pursued in qualitative, open-ended, or "pilot study" format before quantitative instruments can be devised. For example, useful data resulted from information that Hmong collaborators themselves wanted to know (e.g., interest in returning to Laos), whereas these had escaped my attention as a non-Hmong and a non-refugee (despite my lengthy experience with Hmong people and with refugees over three decades).

Quantitative work should involve careful preparation, explicit descriptions of sample and method, and an open acknowledgment of the process, with all of its imperfections and potential foibles. Quantitative work can even be limiting or misleading if begun too early in a project. Intuition is less likely if doing quantitative work only; it usually (although not invariably) requires qualitative work as well.

In sum, this approach argues for both qualitative and quantitative work, each supporting and informing the other. This is not the easiest approach, but it produces insightful and reliable work. It requires either learning more than research modality, or the collaboration of qualitative and quantitative researchers on the same project. Neither of these alternatives is easy: learning more than one research method is time-consuming and difficult, but then so is finding two or more researchers from different fields to collaborate on a single project.

A related issue consists of investigation in clinical settings versus those in non-clinical, community settings. For many research topics, research in only one of these settings is adequate. For example, working on the best methods of treating Major Depressive Disorder can occur solely in a clinical setting. Conversely, the optimal means for learning English-as-a-Second-Language should not occur in a clinical settings. However, many problems relative to mental health and social adjustment can be best addressed in both settings, again with data from each setting informing the other.

A logistical problem with these recommendations is that training programs, governmental institutes funding extramural research, private foundations, and even university policies do not lend themselves to these recommendations. Research training and funding for clinicians is less and less available. Non-clinicians seeking do conduct research in clinical settings get in the way of "lean and mean" operations conduced by HMOs, for-profit organizations, and managed care systems. National priorities are veering away from subspecialized training of clinicians, effectively undermining the research training programs and structures that promulgate the combined clinician-investigator. Efforts are underway on a national level to withdraw public funding for cross-training in more than one clinical discipline.

Combined qualitative-quantitative research and coordinated clinical-community research largely fall to the province of the individual, rather than the department, institution, or agency. During my own career, I have been most fortunate in finding a variety of funding opportunities depending on their needs and my interests. These have included three National Institutes (of Drug Abuse, Alcohol Abuse and Alcoholism, and Mental Health), other governmental agencies (e.g., U.S. Agency for International Development, Special Action Office of the President for Drug Abuse Prevention), various foundations (e.g., Laureate Foundation, Minnesota Medical Foundation), and international bodies (especially the World Health Organization). I have also been fortunate in having departmental chiefs and other supervisors who have supported, or at least not opposed my work. Hopefully, adequate research funding and academic leaders will permit future clinician-investigators the same opportunities.

Notes

1. Acknowledgment: David Johnson, M.D., M.P.H., Assistant Professor of Psychiatry, for providing valuable critique in the preparation of this manuscript.
2. The term "Laotian" refers to all the people of Laos, whereas the ethnic term "Lao" refers to the valley-dwelling people who comprised about half of the people in the country.
3. The term "culture-fair" is employed to convey the notion that the test-maker has attempted to construct, reform, or restandardize the test so that the target group for the test is not at a disadvantage because of cultural factors.

References

Bernatzik, H. A. (1970). *Akha and Miao.* New Haven: Human Relations Area Files.

Boleloucky, Z. and Horvath, M. (1974). SCL-90 Rating Scale: First experience with the Czech version in healthy male scientific workers. *Activ. Nerv. Sup., 16*:115-116.

Butcher, J. N. and Garcia, R. (1978). Cross-national application of psychological tests. *Personnel Guidance, 56*:472-475.

Butcher, J. N. and Pancheri, P. (1976). *Handbook of Cross-National MMPI Research.* Minneapolis, MN: University of Minnesota Press.

Butcher, J. N. and Spielberger, C. D. (1985). Current developments in MMPI use: An international perspective. In Burcher, J. N. and Spielberger, C. D. (Eds.), *Advances in Personality Assessment, Vol. 4.* Hillsdale, NJ: Lawrence Erlbaum Press.

Derogatis, L. R., Lipman, R. S., and Covi, L. (1973). The SCL-90: An outpatient psychiatric rating scale. *Psychopharmacology Bulletin, 9*:13-28.

Derogatis, L. R., Rickels, K., and Rock, A. F. (1976). The SCL-90 and the MMPI: A step in the validation of a new self-report scale. *British Journal of Psychiatry, 128*:280-289.

Folstein, M. F., Folstein, E. S., and McHugh, P.R. (1975). "Mini-Mental State": A practical method for grading the cognitive state of patients for the clinician. *Journal of Psychiatric Research, 12*:189-198.

Geddes, W. R. (1976). *Migrants of the mountains: The cultural ecology of the Blue Miao of Thailand.* Oxford: Clarendon Press.

Hamilton, M. (1959). The assessment of anxiety states by ratings. *British Journal of Medical Psychology, 32*:50-55.

Hamilton, M. (1969). Standardized assessment and recording of depressive symptoms. *Psychiatria, Neurologia, and Neurochirurgia, 72*:201-205.

Leighton, A. H. (1981). Culture and psychiatry. *Canadian Journal of Psychiatry, 26*:522-529.

Lemoine, J. (1972). *Un Village Hmong Vert du Haut Laos.* Paris: Centre National de la Recherche Scientifique.

Lorr, M., Klett, C. J., McNair, D. M, and Lasky, J. J. (1963). *Inpatient Multidimensional Psychiatric Scale.* Palo Alto, CA: Consulting Psychologists Press.

Overall, J. and Gorham, D. (1960). The Brief Psychiatric Rating Scale. *Psychological Reports, 10*:799-812.

Poggie, J., DeWalt, B., and Dressler, W. (1992). *Anthropological research: Process and application.* New York: State University of New York, pp. 15-132.

Westermeyer, J. (1971). Use of alcohol and opium by the Meo of Laos. *American Journal Psychiatry, 127*:1019-1023.

Westermeyer, J. (1978). Sex roles at the Indian-Majority interface in Minnesota. *International Journal of Social Psychiatry, 24*:189-194.

Westermeyer, J. (1980). Sex ratio among opium addicts in Asia: Influences of drug availability and sampling method. *Drug Alcohol Dependence, 6*: 131-136.

Westermeyer, J. (1983). Refugees who do and do not seek psychiatric care: An analysis of premigratory and postmigratory characteristics. *Journal of Nervous and Mental Disease, 171*:86-91.

Westermeyer, J. (1985). Psychiatric diagnosis across cultural boundaries. *American Journal of Psychiatry, 142*:798-805.

Westermeyer, J. (1986). Two self rating scales for depression among Hmong refugees: Assessment in clinical and nonclinical samples. *Journal of Psychiatric Research, 20*:103-113.

Westermeyer, J. (1987). Clinical considerations in cross-cultural diagnosis. *Hospital and Community Psychiatry, 38*:160-165.

Westermeyer, J. (1988a). DSM-III psychiatric disorders among Hmong refugees in the United States: a point prevalence study. *American Journal of Psychiatry, 145*:197-202.

Westermeyer, J. (1988b). A matched pairs study of depression among Hmong refugees with particular reference to predisposing factors and treatment outcome. *Social Psychiatry and Psychiatric Epidemiology, 23*:64-71.

Westermeyer, J. (1989a). *Mental health for refugees and other migrants: Social and preventative approaches.* Springfield, IL: Charles Thomas.

Westermeyer, J. (1989b). Paranoid symptoms and disorders among 100 Hmong refugees: a longitudinal study. *Acta Psychiatria Scandanavica, 80*:47-59.

Westermeyer, J. (1989c). *The psychiatric care of migrants: A clinical guide.* Washington, D.C.: American Psychiatry Press, Inc.

Westermeyer, J. (1989d). Research of stigmatized conditions: Dilemma for the sociocultural psychiatrist. *American Indian and Alaska Native Mental Health Research, 2*:41-45.

Westermeyer, J. (1990). Working with an interpreter in psychiatric assessment and treatment. *Journal of Nervous and Mental Disease, 178*:745-9.

Westermeyer, J. (1992). The sociocultural environment in the genesis and amelioration of opium dependence. In: Poggie, J., DeWalt, B., and Dressler, W. (Eds.), *Anthropological research: Process and application.* New York: State University of New York Press, pp. 15-132.

Westermeyer, J. (1997). Substance use disorders among young minority refugees: Common themes in a clinical sample. *Substance Use and Misuse, 32*:1979-1984.

Westermeyer, J., Bouafuely, M., and Neider, J. (1989). Somatization among refugees: An epidemiological study. *Psychosomatics, 30*:34-43.

Westermeyer, J., Bouafuely, M., and Vang, T. F. (1984). Hmong refugees in Minnesota: Sex roles and mental health. *Medical Anthropology, 8*: 229-245.

Westermeyer, J., Callies, A., and Neider, J. (1990). Welfare status and psychosocial adjustment among 100 Hmong refugees. *Journal of Nervous and Mental Disease, 178*:300-6.

Westermeyer, J. and Chitasombat, P. (1996). Ethnicity and the course of opiate addiction: American versus Hmong in Minnesota. *American Journal of Addictions, 5*:231-240.

Westermeyer, J. and Her, C. (1996). Predictors of English fluency among Hmong refugees in Minnesota: A longitudinal study. *Journal Nervous Mental Disease, 2*:125-132.

Westermeyer, J., Lyfoung, T., and Neider, J. (1989). An epidemic of opium dependence among Asian refugees in the U.S.: Characteristics and causes. *British Journal of Addiction, 84*:785-789.

Westermeyer, J., Lyfoung, T., Wahmanholm, K., and Westermeyer, M. (1989). Delusions of fatal contagion among refugee patients: Some usual and unusual aspects. *Psychosomatics, 30*:374-381.

Westermeyer, J., Neider, J., and Callies A. (1989). Psychosocial adjustment of Hmong refugees during their first decade in the United States: A longitudinal study. *Journal of Nervous and Mental Disease, 177*:132-139.

Westermeyer, J., Neider, J., and Vang, T. F. (1984). Acculturation and mental health: A study of Hmong refugees at 1.5 and 3.5 years postmigration. *Social Science Medicine, 18*:87-93.

Westermeyer, J. and Peake, E. (1983). A ten-year follow-up of alcoholic Native Americans in Minnesota. *American Journal Psychiatry, 140*:189-194.

Westermeyer, J., Schaberg, L., and Nugent, S. (1995). Anxiety symptoms in Hmong refugees 1.5 years after migration. *Journal of Nervous and Mental Disease, 183*:342-344.

Westermeyer, J., Vang, T. F., and Neider, J. (1983a). A comparison of refugees using and not using a psychiatric service: An analysis of DSM-III criteria and self-rating scales in cross-cultural context. *Journal of Operational Psychiatry, 14*:36-41.

Westermeyer, Vang, T. F., and Neider, J. (1983b). Migration and mental health: Association of pre- and post-migration factors with self-rating scales. *Journal of Nervous and Mental Disease, 171*:92-96.

Westermeyer, J., Vang, T. F., and Neider, J. (1984). Symptom change over time among Hmong refugees: Psychiatric patients versus nonpatients. *Psychopathology, 17*:168-77.

Westermeyer, J. and Wahmanholm, K. (1989). Assessing the victimized psychiatric patient: Special issues regarding violence, combat, terror, and refuge-seeking. *Hospital and Community Psychiatry, 3*:245-249.

Westermeyer, J. and Wahmanholm, K. (1996). Refugee children. In *Children in war and communal violence: A mental health handbook.* New Haven, CT: Yale University Press.

Williams, C. and Westermeyer, J. (1984). Psychiatric problems among adolescent Southeast Asian refugees: A descriptive study. *Journal of Nervous and Mental Disease, 171*:79-85.

Williams, C. and Westermeyer, J. (1986). *Refugee mental health in resettlement countries.* New York: Hemisphere.

Zung, W. W. K. (1973). A cross-cultural survey of symptoms in depression. *American Journal of Psychiatry, 126*:116-121.

Zung, W. W. K. (1971). Depression in the normal adult population. *Psychosomatics, 12*:164-167.

Zung, W. W. K. (1965). A self-rating depression scale. *Archives of General Psychiatry, 12*:63-70.

Conclusions and Implications for Future Research

Frederick L. Ahearn, Jr.

The purpose of this volume has been the exploration of the psychological dimension of the refugee experience with a special interest in how this has been studied in the past and how research findings have added to our understanding of this problem and influenced policy and program planning and implementation in this area. There has been much debate in the refugee field about how to define the emotional problems that refugees face, what concepts to employ in order to understand and measure these reactions, and what methodological strategies should be used in this enterprise. In this volume, investigators with much experience in studying the problem of psychosocial wellness have addressed each of these issues from varying perspectives and approaches.

Not long ago, the mental health aspect of forced migration was not considered important by many. It was assumed that the critical issues were limited to safety and physical health, and that all refugees either adjusted to their experience without problems or encountered problems that resulted were ephemeral or short-lasting. However, in recent years, mental health has gained recognition as a prominent factor for refugees, and financial support for programs of psychological intervention with refugees are commonplace. Petevi (1996) states that "the necessity to respond to mental health needs of refugees is being recognized and becoming an integral part of humanitarian relief work." Harrell- Bond (1986) noted that we probably underestimate the degree of psychological suffering experienced by refugees and displaced persons from violence and war.

Some claim that the mental health needs of refugees are massive. For example, it has been noted that more than a million Bosnian refugees and displaced persons suffer from Post-Traumatic Stress Disorder (PTSD) and that their problems will continue for a generation or more (Agger, Vuh, and Mimica, 1995). Responding to what he considered an exaggerated boast, Summerfield (1998) noted that "trauma work in humanitarian operations is rooted in the way that medicine and psychology have displaced religion in western culture ..."

It is well documented that refugees and displaced persons may suffer greatly before, during, and/or after the forced migratory event(s) as their losses and traumas accumulate. Being forcibly displaced is a traumatic experience that may produce great stress, loss, and depression. We know that this uprooting is often accompanied by violence as some refugees witness death of loved ones, or are tortured, raped, or wounded themselves. Moreover, studies have shown that stress may accumulate over time, that is in the immediate aftermath of migration as well as in the day-to-day situations of being a refugee. However, in all cases, we should keep in mind that refugees are "normal" individuals who have had an "extraordinary" experience and their behaviors could be considered quite appropriate given the circumstances.

There is, however, considerable debate as to: 1) the nature of these psychological difficulties; 2) how they might be studied; and, 3) what interventions at what time period facilitate and foster wellness and adjustment. It is our position that careful research can inform this debate by verifying mental health behaviors, symptoms, and needs, evaluating interventions programmed to assist them, and supporting the utilization of research findings for policy, planning, and implementation of psychological assistance for refugees.

The contributors to this book highlight a number of cautions. First, practitioners and researchers who assist or study traumatized refugees must have a sensitivity to the culture and context of the population. Local norms, traditions, and practices influence what is considered to be psychosocial health and illness in the studied population, and those definitions that may vary greatly from Western notions, standards, and interventions. Knowledge of local interpretations and approaches to health and illness is essential for the researcher. In addition, if Western measures are to be used, then cross-cultural validation of measures and mental health interventions and how these link with local norms and customs are necessary (Petevi, 1996).

A related issue is language which is the window to understanding. It is imperative for researchers to master the local language and avoid depending greatly on translators. When relying on translation, many additional complexities arise because of nuances of word meanings vary and differ from culture to culture, and even within cultures given class, gender, age, etc. These complications require careful consideration in the design and process of a research project.

The emphasis of this volume has been on the strengths perspective acknowledging that most refugees are able to manage well enough in the aftermath of their experience. Existing literature confirms that the human being is adaptable and resilient as most do not exhibit long-term consequences of forced migration. Available investigations link resiliency to personality factors, ability to cope well, self-esteem, and the availability and use of social supports. Psychological outcome are determined by a combination of risk and protective factors, especially those located in the family and in the community (Hicks, LaLonde, and Pepler, 1993). In speaking of children, a Save the Children document advises that "[h]elping war-effected children to build on their own strengths and resilience, in collaboration with trusted care-givers, is, we believe, a more effective and appropriate strategy" (Save the Children, 1996). Key questions for researchers are how or why many refugees survive their experience with little long-term effects, and what are the elements that are associated with wellness and resilience.

There is another side of the strengths and resiliency perspective. Refugees do not consider themselves mental health patients and they consider any mental health label or diagnosis as a stigma. Researcher and psychosocial workers have been cautioned not to "medicalize" the problems of refugees (Stubbs and Soroya, 1996; Bracken, Geller, and Summerfield, 1995).

In this volume, the authors have presented a range of quantitative and qualitative approaches in their study of refugee mental health, noting the strengths and limitations of each. There is support for employing both methods as a means of formulating research questions and hypotheses, using the voices and stories of refugees to illustrate data, and verifying or triangulating findings. Both practitioners and students who have an interest in working with or studying the psychosocial elements of the refugee experience can benefit from a background in qualitative methods (participant observation, keeping diaries, use of life histories, case scenarios, focus groups, and other ethnographic methods) as well as quantitative methods (statistics, measurement construction, sampling, etc.).

Future Research Agenda

In studying the psychosocial concerns of refugees or evaluating the effectiveness of program interventions, both qualitative and quantitative investigators may wish to focus on the following concerns that are enumerated below.

1. Long-Term Effects: There are very few examples of studies of the long-term adjustment of refugees as most existing studies are short-term comparisons that have little relevance or applicability to other situations. Longitudinal investigations and/or long-term case studies would contribute to our understanding of how and why refugees survive their experiences.

2. Community Focus: The preponderance of existing research in refugee mental health examines the individual, his/her reactions, and interventions useful at this level. As a person's support system is a crucial factor in psychosocial adjustment, the family and community should also become the foci for investigation. The social and cultural system of the refugees, the supports of extended family, employment, religion, and spirituality, and governmental and non-governmental services and benefits are areas for understanding the protective factors of a refugee's wellness.

3. Prevention as well as Remediation: The factors that promote and/or prevent a refugee's trauma and stress are probably those that also will heal quickly the wounds of forced migration. Obviously, the ultimate preventive measure in most cases is the absence of war or conflict, or the rapid settlement of such disruptions. But when hostilities result in migration, researchers could evaluate the early elements that seem to be associated with health, such as increased safety and protection, re-establishment of trust, ability to make decisions that controls one's life, participation, self-identity and esteem.

4. Evaluation of Psychosocial Programs and Interventions: Governmental and non-governmental organizations have a responsibility to measure their outcomes in order to assess effectiveness of their programmatic strategies and also to be accountable to their funders and the refugees themselves. Program evaluations, follow-up case histories, process assessments, organizational case analyses, and studies of interventions within the context of the local culture would add greatly to our understanding of what services are and are not beneficial.

5. Replication of Studies: In order to test the reliability and improve the usefulness of studies, it is necessary to replicate these under similar and different conditions. If measures are utilized to assess psychosocial factors, they must be reliable in the culture in which they are utilized. By replication, we can confirm certain findings, increase our knowledge base, and plan with greater certainty psychosocial interventions for individuals, families, and communities of refugees.

A lot of progress has been noted in the study of refugee mental health, but many needs remain. Improved, competent, and sound research, both qualitative and quantitative, will inform the development of refugee policy and programming. It is hoped that the practitioner, administrator, researcher, and student alike will accept the challenge to strengthen their knowledge and skills in qualitative and quantitative methods and techniques so that they may advance the understanding of refugee behavior, and the planning, implementation, and evaluation of culturally sensitive and appropriate intervention programs.

References

Agger, I., Vuk, S., and Mimica, J. (1995). *Theory and practice of psychosocial projects under war conditions in Bosnia-Herzogovenia and Croatia.* Zagreb: ECHO/ECTF.

Bracken, P. J., Geller, J. E., and Summerfield, D. (1995). Psychological responses to war and atrocities: The limitations of current concepts. *Social Science and Medicine, 40:* 8: 1073-1082.

Harrell-Bond, B. (1986). *Imposing aid. Emergency assistance to refugees.* Oxford: Oxford University Press.

Hicks, R., LaLonde, R. N., and Pepler, D. (1993). Psychosocial considerations in the mental health of immigrant and refugee children. *Canadian Journal of Mental Health, 12:* 2: 71-87.

Petevi, M. (1996). Forced displacement: Refugee trauma, protection and assistance. In Danieli, Y., Rodley, N., and Weisaeth, L.. (Eds.), *International responses to traumatic stress.* New York: Baywood Publishing Company.

Save the Children (1996). Promoting psychosocial well-being among children affected by armed conflict and displacement. *Working Paper No. 1.* Westport, CT: Save the Children.

Stubbs, P. and Soroya, B. (1996). War trauma, psycho-social projects and social development in Croatia. *Medicine, Conflict and Survival, 12:* 303-314.

Summerfield, D. A. (1998). "Trauma" and the experience of war: A reply. *The Lancet, 351:* 1580-1581.

Contributors

Alastair Ager is Director of the Centre for International Health Studies and Professor of Applied Psychology at Queen Margaret College, Edinburgh, and a Research Associate of the Refugee Studies Programme, University of Oxford. He has over fifty publications spanning the fields of disability, community integration, and refugee studies. His work in the latter area has included research studies of the experience of Mozambican refugees in Malawi and, more recently, analysis of the social integration of refugees in Scotland. Dr. Ager is a member of the Editorial Board of the *Journal of Refugee Studies* and editor of the recent volume: *Refugees: Perspectives on the Experience of Forced Migration* (London: Cassell). He is a regular contributor to the education programme at the Refugee Studies Programme, University of Oxford, with whom he is collaborating on the development of a multimedia training course for humanitarian assistance workers on "Psychosocial Responses to the Refugee Experience." He has worked with a number of agencies involved in refugee assistance, including UNHCR, MSF-Holland and Oxfam, with field experience across Southern Africa, South Asia, and Eastern Europe.

Frederick L. Ahearn, Jr. is Professor and former Dean of the School of Social Service at the Catholic University of America, Washington, D.C. Affiliated with the Refugee Studies Programme at the University of Oxford since 1996, he is currently a tutor in their Summer Programme, an occasional reviewer for the *Journal of Refugee Studies,* and is a member of the editorial boards of *Social Work, Social Thought,* and *Revista de Trabajo Social* (Chile). Dr. Ahearn, who has done extensive research on forced migration in Nicaragua, is co-author of *Refugee Children: Theory, Research, and Practice* and *Handbook of Mental Health Care of Disaster Victims* both published by the Johns Hopkins University Press.

Morton Beiser is the David Crombie Professor of Cultural Pluralism
and Health at the Centre for Addiction and Mental Health (Clarke
Division) and the University of Toronto Department of Psychiatry.
He also heads Culture, Community, and Health Studies, an academic
program of research and training focusing on immigrant and refugee
resettlement, the health of First Nations people, cultural influences on
the expression of illness, and developing models of health care appropriate for a multicultural society. Dr. Beiser is also the Director of the
Centre of Excellence for Research on Immigration and Settlement
(CERIS), a center operating under the auspices of Ryerson Poly-
technic University, the University of Toronto, York University, the
Ontario Council of Agencies Serving Immigrants (OCASI), the
Social Planning Council of Metro Toronto, and the United Way. Dr.
Beiser is Principal Investigator of several longitudinal studies, including the Refugee Resettlement Project, a decade-long investigation of
the resettlement and mental health of Southeast Asian refugees in
Canada; the Refugee Youth Project, a study of the children of Southeast Asian refugees; the Flower of Two Soils, focusing on emotional
and cognitive development among First Nations as well as non-native
children; and the Markers and Predictors of Psychosis, a study of the
course of first-episode psychosis. In 1986, Canada Health and Welfare, together with the Secretary of State-Multiculturalism, appointed
Dr. Beiser to chair the Canadian Task Force on Mental Health Issues
Affecting Immigrants and Refugees. He was principal author of the
Task Force report, issued in 1988, and entitled *After the Door Has Been
Opened.* He is the author of more than 125 publications including a
forthcoming book, *Strangers at the Gate* and the recipient of numerous
awards including a Canada Health National Health Scientist Award,
the Tanenbaum Award for research in schizophrenia, a Josiah Macy
Foundation faculty scholar award, and a Rockefeller Foundation res-
ident scholar award.

Didier Bertrand received his Ph.D. in cross-cultural psychology in
1992 at Toulouse le Mirail University, France. He did his field
research in Southeast Asian refugee camps about identity crisis and
later studied inter-ethnic relations and spiritual healing of boat men
living on the Perfume River in Hue, Vietnam. Dr. Bertrand lived
three years in Cambodia where he taught in the Department of Psychology of the Royal University of Phnom Penh and conducted
research on the role of psychology in a developing country, especially on the topics of therapeutic possessions and mediums and the
healing techniques of monks. He is now a Research Fellow at the
Refugee Studies Programme, University of Oxford, where he is

doing a comparative study of ethnicity in the politics of mental health and of Vietnamese refugee community associations in France and the United Kingdom.

Marita Eastmond is Associate Professor at the department of Social Anthropology at Göteborg University, Sweden. Her research interest is mainly in social and cultural processes of exile communities in responding to violence, displacement and exile. Her ethnographic work includes refugees of the Chile who reside in the United States and Bosnian Muslim refugees in Sweden.

Dr. Ilene Hyman is a Research Scientist in the Culture, Community and Health Studies Program (CCHS) of the Centre for Addiction and Mental Health (Clarke Division) and an Assistant Professor in the Department of Public Health Sciences, Faculty of Medicine, University of Toronto. Dr. Hyman has been the recipient of Doctoral and Post-Doctoral Fellowships from the National Health Research and Development Program of Health Canada. Dr. Hyman's doctoral and post-doctoral research focused on acculturation, addressing methodological issues as well as exploring the mechanisms through which acculturation impacts on health status and health behaviors. Dr. Hyman's current research projects include a longitudinal investigation of the mental health and adaptation of Southeast Asian refugees and their children in Canada, the analysis of national data on the health status and behaviors of new and long-term Canadian immigrants, the analysis of national data on the effect of poverty on the health and development of new Canadian children, a study of pathways and barriers to mental health care for Ethiopians in Toronto, and a study of barriers to cancer screening for Chinese and Vietnamese women in Toronto. Prior to her appointment in CCHS in January 1994, Dr. Hyman conducted over ten years of health and social sciences research with ethnocultural communities in Canada and in several North and West African countries.

Maryanne Loughry has occupied the Arupe Tutorship at the Refugee Studies Programme, University of Oxford since 1996. A native of Australia, she has had extensive experience working on forced migration issues in Vietnam, the Philippines, Hong Kong, Gaza, Palestine, and Africa. She is currently on leave from the University of Adelaide, Australia, where she is a lecturer and doctoral candidate in psychology.

Dr. Colin MacMullin is a child psychologist and Senior Lecturer in Special Education at the Flinders University of South Australia. He teaches courses in counseling and educational consultation, and conducts research into the social and emotional difficulties experienced by children in Australia and in the Middle East. Dr. MacMullin presently devotes part of his time each year teaching courses in the Gaza Strip, the West Bank, and in various locations in Southeast Asia.

Nguyen Xuan Nghia is a lecturer in general sociology, social research, and rural sociology at the Ho Chi Minh Open University and also in the College of Social and Human Sciences at the Ho Chi Minh National University. He has a Diplome d'Etudes Approfondies from the Institut d'Estudes Economiques et Sociales de Paris where he is now a doctoral candidate.

Samuel Noh is an Associate Professor in the Department of Psychiatry, University of Toronto, and Senior Research Scientist at the Centre for Addiction and Mental Health (Clarke Division). Following his undergraduate and graduate training in sociology, he studied epidemiology under the supervision of R. Jay Turner at the University of Western Ontario in Canada. Dr. Noh's scholarly work focuses on theoretical and methodological issues relevant to social stressors and the stress processes through which experienced stress is manifested as either physical or mental pathology. Most recently, Dr. Noh's work has shifted to concentrate on studying the stress process among racial or ethnic minorities including new immigrants and refugees. His current research projects include a cross-cultural study of the stress process in adolescents, a study comparing adolescents and youth of Asian immigrant families, Southeast Asian refugee families and Canadian-born parents, and a multi-ethnic community study that addresses issues of racism and mental health, development and delivery of culturally-sensitive, mental health services, psychological resilience of immigrant children and children of immigrants, and the long-term effects of the childhood experience of war trauma. His original and collaborative works appear in well recognized journals including *Journal of Health and Social Behavior, Journal of Nervous and Mental Disease, Psychological Assessment, Social Science and Medicine, Journal of Marriage and the Family,* and *Cross-cultural Research.*

Patricia A. Omidian is a medical anthropologist, currently an independent consultant working in Pakistan with local populations and with Afghan refugees. Her research has focused on family conflict and life-course issues in an Afghan refugee community in Northern California. She has been working with this community since 1985 and is particularly interested in the formulation and (re)production of identity by Middle Eastern and Central Asian immigrants and refugees. The work has included issues of aging, youth and gangs, religion as the focus of identity, ethnicity and forced migration with the Afghan refugee population in the United States and Pakistan. Her book *Aging and Family in an Afghan Refugee Community: Traditions and Transitions* focuses on the refugee population in Northern California.

Miriam Potocky-Tripodi, a native of the Czech Republic, is Associate Professor and Acting Doctoral Program Coordinator in the School of Social Work, Florida International University, Miami, Florida. Her major area of scholarship is refugee resettlement in the United States, on which she has published numerous articles. Dr. Potocky-Tripodi has also written on research methodology. She is founding co-editor of *The Journal of Social Work Research and Evaluation* and she is a board member of the Society for Social Work and Research.

Raija-Leena Punamäki is a psychologist who currently works as a senior researcher at the University of Helsinki, Department of Psychology. Her research has focused on mental health and child development in conditions of political violence with a special emphasis on the therapeutic process, resiliency and coping, cognitive abilities and attitudes, and symbolic processes such as dreaming, playing, and drawing. Dr. Punamäki has participated in projects in primary care and refugee administration, and is a founding member of Finnish Psychologist for Social Responsibility. In addition, she is a member of the Advisory Board of the Gaza Community Mental Health Programme, Gaza, Palestine.

Nhi Vu has recently completed a Master's Degree in Education in the Department of Human Development and Applied Psychology at the Ontario Institute of Studies in Education, University of Toronto. Between 1993 and 1996, she was employed as a research assistant for the Refugee Youth Project (RYP) of the Centre for Addiction and Mental Health (Clarke Division), and the University of Toronto's Department of Psychiatry. Ms. Vu was the principal interviewer for the in-depth assessments and focus groups with Southeast Asian refugee youth and she continues to be involved with many project activities on a contractual basis. Ms. Vu intends to pursue doctoral studies in education. She is particularly interested in the relationship between child development and the cultural, institutional, and historical contexts within which it occurs.

244 | Contributors

Joseph Westermeyer started his professional career as a family physician in St. Paul, Minnesota. Part-time graduate study in anthropology heightened his interest regarding the interface between culture and health care. This led to his doing a two-year stint with the Public Health Division of the Agency for International Development (AID) in Laos during the period 1965-1967. During the 1960s and early 1970s, Dr. Westermeyer completed training in psychiatry, anthropology, and public health/epidemiology. The work that he began in Laos in 1965 continued with various projects in Asia over a twenty year period. Serendipitously, his work with Asian refugees in the United States expanded as refugees from Laos, Vietnam, and Cambodia arrived in Minnesota. Over time, the methods that he employed reflected the types of challenges that his projects required, reflecting his broad training and experience in medicine, psychiatry, anthropology, and public health.

Index

A

Acculturation, 185, 222
    and school adjustment, 183
    assessment of, 225-226
    definition of, 14-15
    intergenerational conflicts and, 187, 189-190
    Scale, 11
    stress and, 8, 10
Action research, 119-120
Adaptation, 10, 12, 30, 133,137-138, 147, 214, 225
    of refugee children, 9
    process of, 50
    psychological, xv-xvi
Addiction, 209-210, 215
    alcohol abuse, 179, 181, 191, 203, 215
    Centre for Addictions and Mental Health, 180
    drug abuse, 159, 179, 191, 203, 215
    National Institutes of Drug Abuse, Alcohol Abuse, and Alcoholism, 229
    opium use, 209-210, 215, 218
Adjustment, xvi, 12, 25, 30, 32, 39,42, 51, 60, 103-104, 111, 113-114, 154, 178, 182, 208, 220, 226, 229, 235, 237
    children's, 110
    health, 103
    measurement of, 11, 26, 31, 156
    psychological, 107, 109
    school, 177, 183
    social supports and, 9
    trauma and, 107, 110, 114

Afghan Health Education Project, 42, 44, 48, 53-54
Afghanistan/Afghani, v, 39-66
    gangs, 42, 47
Africa/Africans, xiii, 120
Alienation, 9
    Scale, 11
American Psychiatric Association, 9
Anxiety disorders, xv, 8, 14, 120, 122, 170, 217, 227
    and loss, 6
    and stress, 173-174
    and trauma, 160
    measures of, 11, 14, 162, 170, 225
Assessment, 90, 217
    clinical, 75, 224
    measures of, 10-11
    needs, 62
    program, 24
    Quality of Life, 35
Asylum, 6, 95, 153-154
Autobiographical method, 88-102
    analysis of content, 88, 95-97
    empathy, 90, 92-94, 100
    exploration of, 88
    position of the researcher, 90-92
    setting for, 89

B

Behavior, 4, 10, 12-13, 18, 42-43, 50, 155, 173, 224, 238
    aggressive, 156, 168-170, 172
    delinquent, 156, 170-172
    emotional, 3, 6, 60, 118
    measure of, 25-26, 156-157
    physical, 3, 6